Reeves & Mortimer

'Conceptually they are ahead of the bunch. That's what makes them the most important comics of their generation.'
Matt Lucas

Reeves & Mortimer

Bruce Dessau

ORION

First published in 1998 by
Orion Media
an imprint of Orion Books Ltd
Orion House
5 Upper St Martin's Lane, London WC2H 9EA

A CIP catalogue record for this book
is available from the British Library

ISBN 0–75281–781–7

Typeset by Deltatype Ltd, Birkenhead, Merseyside

Printed and bound in Great Britain by
Butler & Tanner Ltd, Frome and London

Contents

Acknowledgements

In recent years comedy has been widely documented in the media and Vic Reeves and Bob Mortimer have had more than their fair share of coverage. Nothing, however, has come close to cracking the secret of their success, which has its roots in the early Eighties. There is always a 'secret history' to any story, and to get to Vic and Bob's I have gone directly to the people who were there in their early days. I also had the good fortune to see the *Big Night Out* at the Goldsmiths Tavern in the pre-TV era myself. It was already a phenomenon in south London, despite no press coverage whatsoever. Vic's fame was purely word-of-mouth at the time – one of the few interesting cultural events of the Eighties to happen without any hype. With so many television channels searching for the next big thing, it is unlikely that anyone will ever emerge like this again.

While nothing can beat first-hand experience, if only I had known that a decade on I would be writing a book about those days, I might have laughed a little less and jotted down a lot more, but in retrospect I think I got the balance right. My main memory is of seeing a type of comedy which connected perfectly with my generation and my philosophy. I had enjoyed comedy before and I have enjoyed comedy since, but there has never been anything like Reeves and Mortimer.

Inevitably my thanks go primarily to Jim Moir and Bob Mortimer, who kindly gave up their time to be interviewed specifically for the book and remained as enigmatic as ever.

I would also like to thank the following (in no particular order) for kindly giving me their time. With some it was minutes, with others it was hours. It is an indication of how fondly those early days are remembered that once people started talking it would have taken much more than George Dawes bellowing 'Shut it!' to stop them: Mark Lamarr, Ulrika Jonsson, Charlie Higson, Paul Whitehouse, Simon Day, Jonathan Ross, Alan Marke, Peter Orton, Mark Mylod, Mark Robson,

vii

Seamus Cassidy, Jools Holland, Alan King, William Wilding, Dorian Crook, Graham Smith, Malcolm Hardee, Karen Koren, Tom Fawcett, Wendy Acres, Joan Newton, Bill Whittingham, Keith Bridgewood, Simon Hoolihan, John Whiston, David Housham, John Irvine, Jack Dent, Adam Ross, Matt Lucas, Sally Adams, Cath Lanham, Steve Grant, Elaine Paterson, Jon Ronson, Peter Paphides, Lee Davies, Ben Caudell, Rachael House, Jo David, Rachel Howard, Carl Glover, Andy Grumbridge, John Tackley, Louise Russell, Catherine Greenwood, Simon Palmer, Steve Beresford, Andy Darling, Haydn Williams, John Turner, Frankie Jack, Morwenna Banks, Mike Wattam, Peter Brooke Turner, Stevo Zivanovic, Rhys Thomas, Philip Ilson, Gordon Gapper, Jo Gapper, David Liddiment, Gill Whyte, Glenn Tilbrook, Tim Grace-MacDonald, Brett Turnbull, MacKenzie Crook, Steve Brody, David Walliams, Annalisa Barreto, Valerie at Helicon, Jill Tulip and Andy Rossiter. Plus Abby and Greg of Nettleton Road and Iain Muirhead and stalwart companion Mark Wilson who found the Chelsea boots. Also to Paul Morley and Kevin Hewitt, whose *Omnibus* documentary pointed me in a multitude of directions. And, of course, those I've forgotten to mention, others who spoke off the record and a very strange chap who now lives in Italy.

My thanks also go to Chiggy and Mel at PBJ Management, to my agent Lisa Eveleigh, to the Virgin Megastore in Oxford Street for filling in the gaps in my video collection, and to Cutting It Fine, who helped out with the newspaper research. And to my colleagues at *Time Out*, who will now have to put up with me on a full-time basis again.

Chapter One

Darlington Alien

There is no such thing as an average Reeves and Mortimer show. The fact is still true now, but it was even more true ten years ago. By 1988 Vic and Bob's weekly Thursday evening *Big Night Out* at the Goldsmiths Tavern in New Cross had become a ritual for south Londoners with a well-defined sense of the absurd. Start the evening with *Top of the Pops* (it has never been the same since it moved to Fridays), go out for a few drinks, then head for the side door of the Goldsmiths Tavern and weave your way through the pub regulars into the small back room. And wait.

You had to get there promptly to get a seat. The room was a sea of Eighties fashion choices. For men it was usually flat-top haircuts and denim; for women jumble-sale dresses held sway. Many were open-minded students from nearby Goldsmiths' College or the Laban Dance Centre next door. Heavy smoking helped to create a fog of expectation that meant that devoted fans often refused to leave their seats. Nip to the bar for a bottled Pils and you could lose pole position.

Eventually something happens. From the cramped booth at the back sound-man John Irvine puts the intro cassette on. Snippets of the Sex Pistols, some classical music, maybe some Gregorian chants and invariably some early Seventies heavy metal play in quick succession. Something monumental is about to happen. Vic Reeves, suited, booted, his hair greased back – he claims with whale blubber – walks on from a discreet side door. He is holding a small puppet of Elvis Presley. It has, for no apparent reason, boxing gloves on.

What followed would be up to three hours of sheer madness. Even when it wasn't brilliant it was startlingly different from the post-Ben Elton right-on humour that dominated many clubs. Even Vic's northern accent made him stand out. There was something about the lilt of his pronouncements as he stood behind his lectern with a scruffy sheaf of notes that made you want to listen. His voice – and his distinctive dress sense – were just as riveting as his view of the world. Each week the show would be different. It was just like our own private TV series, an astonishing feat on the live circuit where other acts did the same twenty minutes every week.

Certain elements would soon become favourites. Novelty Island, introduced by the old Pathé News theme 'The March of Time', in which Vic's mates dressed up in weird costumes and stood in a paddock, or Bob Mortimer as The Man with the Stick. No one really cared what he had on the end of the stick, of course, it was simply the daftness and difference of it all that appealed. And, of course the use of ritualistic catchphrases, which harked back as much to childhood pantomime as it did to music hall.

There were some ideas that never really caught on. The vegetables were probably a bit of a mistake. One week Vic attempted ventriloquism through cabbages in a fish tank, disappearing offstage and letting them do the talking. Another time he attempted to make a hat-cum-cassette-holder out of a hollowed-out cauliflower. The shrink-wrapped celebrity turds given out as prizes in the talent competition went down better.

Other ideas needed a bit of honing. The rambling group known as Tinker's Rucksack consisted of about half a dozen men in blatantly false beards singing about the summer of 1975 while holding tankards. It might have worked if only there had been room for them all on the tiny, cramped stage.

But the audience all knew that, whatever the quality of the material, Vic was something special. The show was already a piece of comedy history. Was he a former farmer? Was he an avant-garde artist? Who cared? After the comedy there was a disco. Sometimes a football appeared and an indoor football match ensued. At one o'clock in the morning people left. Often confused, always delighted. All we know was that Vic Reeves seemed to be able to combine Sixties suits, Seventies rock and Eighties post-modernism and concoct something completely original. The only question was whether others would get the joke. Or was it a south London thing? The next decade would provide the answer.

*   *   *   *

If you want to begin to understand Reeves and Mortimer, you have to start in the north-east of England. Start in Leeds and follow the A1. Until you hit Darlington. That was what the Moir family did in 1964. It was a relatively short journey, but one that would have a dramatic impact on Neill and Audrey Moir's son. Then again, he exhibited early signs of verbal ingenuity even before the move at the age of five.

'My mother always tells me that when I was tiny we used to go shopping at Littlewoods in Leeds and I used to call it Bigwoods and I used to think that was absolutely hilarious.'

James Roderick Moir was born in St James's Hospital in Leeds on 24 January 1959 the same date as both his father and grandfather. By 1964, a period of unimagined affluence was about to descend upon Swinging Britain. At least that was the way it seemed if you lived off the King's Road. If you lived 250 miles further north things took a little longer to have an impact. In the towns just south of Newcastle, dominated by heavy industry, boutiques for men would have been viewed with at least suspicion. Even if you didn't go down the mines or into the mills, any self-respecting man would end up in a factory, striking a blow for the dignity of labour. Nine hundred and ninety-four, nine hundred and ninety-five ... don't let the bastards grind yer down. Nearly thirty years on, Jim would name *Saturday Night Sunday Morning* as his favourite film in the *Big Night In* spin-off book. It was clearly an era and lifestyle that left its mark on him. The arts, it seemed, were for soft southerners or those sensitive sorts from Yorkshire, Alan Bennett and David Hockney.

On the surface Darlington was just another northern post-industrial town, but there was something distinctly strange about the area. Leeds had a brashness and a confidence. It strutted like a big city. Darlington had quakers and Lewis Carroll. It meandered around a bit. The author of *Alice's Adventures in Wonderland* was brought up in Croft, just over the

3

River Skerne. The city had an unsettling quality, too. In the centre, its Wynds and Yards were medieval alleys and lanes which linked the main shopping streets. A century earlier Carroll had wandered down Post House Wynd; by the late 1970s, Rod Moir, a smart young boy with a ruddy complexion, scarpered over the same cobbles, chased by his early critics who did not take to his drainpipe trousers.

Home to the Moirs was a tidy little semi-detached house, built between the wars. Theirs was a tight-knit family; his mother Audrey, his father Neill, a linotype operator on the *Northern Echo*, and his sister Lois, who was three years younger than Jim. Today he is known as Jim off-duty, but as a youngster he was actually known as Rod to avoid confusion, because his father's first name was also Jim – though he used his middle name of Neill.

A friend who grew up in nearby Stockton at the same time as Jim does not remember Darlington as a particularly appealing place: 'If you didn't live there, there wouldn't be much point in going there.' At an early age Jim too had ambivalent feelings about the town. There wasn't a lot to do, but there was always the countryside a quick cycle ride away. By his early teens he would regularly escape. Perhaps escape, along with re-invention, was in the blood. There was a rumour that a distant ancestor had once been a top butler, but had been involved in a scandal above stairs. To keep the matter quiet he was given £400 and a one-way ticket to Canada, but instead he went to live in Leeds, moving constantly to avoid detection. Once Jim tried to escape too fast and, showing off, came off his bike, grazing his hands, knees and face. When he was about thirteen, he and a friend went out cycling. It soon got dark and they found themselves lost and without any lights on their bikes. They were about fifteen miles from home, and instead of panicking they did what any teenage boys would do and viewed the whole thing as a big adventure. But it ended disastrously. Jim's friend hurtled down a hill, crashed and broke his leg. Jim was laughing so much that he also lost balance, went flying over his handlebars and ripped open his face.

It was a typical incident in a childhood punctuated by daredevil stunts. In September 1993 he told the *Daily Mail* that he used to terrify his mother by climbing to the top of pine trees and hanging precariously from the branches. Later in life he developed a fear of heights which seemed to over-compensate for this adolescent rashness.

On his first trip to America he had a nasty turn in New York: 'I was up the Empire State Building and I froze. I was about twenty feet from the edge and I had to pin myself back against the wall to stop myself from jumping.'

Like most small boys, Jim was fascinated by natural history. He would spend hours in a world of his own, searching for pond life in the back garden. 'When I was little I had a crew cut and was drawn to water,' he told *Today* in 1991. 'I had a jam jar which contained great diving things. Newts and all that lot.' In the *Mail on Sunday* Jim looked back on his formative years. 'I was always constantly laughing as a child – a wild baby always scurrying off somewhere. I think I got it off my mum. It's quite mad.'

The Moir household seemed to be constantly filled with laughter. Without anyone trying, even the most mundane events turned into a comic interlude. One day, for instance, his father arrived home in a new car. It was a three-wheeler and Jim thought you had to get in through the window, much to the amusement of his family. He and his sister used to have great fun painting funny faces on each other. Lois gave Jim an extra set of eyes. Jim painted a second mouth on to Lois. There was a lot of good-humoured mucking about. His father was rather partial to silly walks long before John Cleese did them and would regale Jim and Lois with amusing stories about his own childhood. Once his grandfather had taken him to the pub and then absent-mindedly returned home for dinner, leaving the young James senior behind.

At times it seemed like a very old-fashioned family, one that made its own entertainment. Jim's dad was the definitive 'handy-man' father of the DIY age. He liked nothing better than to make furniture for Jim and Lois. Small chairs and tables would appear in their rooms when they weren't expecting them. He once even made him a surfboard out of a plank of wood with a diamond shape cut into the middle of it, which Jim used on the coast at Redcar and Seaton Carew. His father's unusual working hours meant he was able to spend more time with his young children during the day than many parents. He loved his children and indulged them whenever he could. Jim recalls being taken by his father with Lois to see Walt Disney's *Snow White and the Seven Dwarves*. Jim and Lois loved it; their father was less impressed. 'My sister and me were so small we stood up behind the chairs. My dad snored right through it.'

All of this had a powerful effect on Jim Moir. One part of him embraced his family, another part felt suffocated and needed to break free. He could be both an introvert and an extrovert. One minute he might be drawing by the fire while *Coronation Street* was on, the next he might be doing impressions at the window to impress the neighbours. At a very early age he was interested in appearances and music, two things which still fascinate him: 'I'd watch *Top of the Pops* and think, "Mick Jagger looks good, I'll dress up like that."' A lot of friends thought they mustn't if they wanted to look hard. 'I used to stand at my bedroom window doing Mick Jagger impersonations. And Cilla Black.'

At his junior school Jim Moir was a popular child. He recalls having two girlfriends at the same time, Maureen Coxon and Pauline Robertson. Already he had revealed a prodigious artistic talent and sound business sense. He used to do their drawings for them so that they got good marks, and in return they would follow him under the table when he dropped his pencil. Looking back on those hormonally charged days, however, Jim betrays an innocence that was unusually endearing in an age when most boys couldn't wait to get their hands on the opposite sex: 'My first proper girlfriend packed me in after three weeks because I wouldn't interfere with her.'

Although he was bright and clearly artistic, Jim never showed a great deal of conventional academic ability, and at the age of eleven went to Eastbourne College, the local comprehensive school. It was a tough, large school on the east side of Darlington. Rodney, as Jim was known by the teachers, was actually one of the posher children. Many were from rough council estates or council houses. Jim's family owned their own home.

When he started, the school had just changed from a secondary modern to a comprehensive. Wendy Acres taught Jim English in the first year and remembers that 'he was rather keen on being the class clown. When I saw him on television all I could see was young Rodney at the back of the class. He was a bit of a reluctant worker at first, but he did knuckle down for his exams. He was underachieving, a clever boy, but he treated school like a social occasion. He was bright, but reluctant to put pen to paper. What he did do was good, but always on the short side: if he thought he could get away with a page he wouldn't write two.'

He was one of those attractive children who tend to be mischievous rather than disruptive. While others might throw things and shout, he took a more subtle, subversive route. He once got everyone to sigh in biology class when the teacher was writing on the blackboard. Every time he turned round the noise would stop. It was annoying for the teacher, very funny for the class.

Yet by the time he was in his mid-teens he had calmed down. While others misbehaved, he could be studious when the mood took him. Joan Benson taught Jim science just before he left and remembers him quite differently from the English teacher: 'There were other boys that played the fool, but he wasn't like that.'

The only lesson he really enjoyed was art, but this was only because he had the chance to draw aeroplanes. 'At school I used to do really dull technical drawings of aeroplanes. I used to make kits as well – hundreds of them – and I'd paint all the men's faces and give them paisley shirts.' Once Jim's obsession with model Second World War aeroplanes nearly ended in disaster. He used some gunpowder and nearly burnt his house down by causing a fire while trying to recreate a *Luftwaffe* raid.

He was always happier larking about outside the classroom. He used to have great fun walking into sweet-shops and asking for penny chews in a puerile high-pitched voice. The shopkeepers would get annoyed and Jim looked forward to being an adult when he could put on stupid voices and shopkeepers wouldn't be able to throw him out. He was the kind of child who couldn't wait to be grown-up – only so that he could behave in the same irresponsible fashion and nobody would be able to tell him off.

It seems that the family was such a self-contained unit that it didn't need any input from the outside world, but this was the Sixties and there was no way for a child not to be influenced by the media. In fact it is quite unusual that the television had not become essential viewing for Jim Moir until the arrival of *Monty Python's Flying Circus* in 1969. It was the first time Jim had come across something funnier than his own family. It was a revelation. He later recalled falling off the sofa and laughing so much he was sick. *Monty Python* seemed to provide a link between his own distinctive sense of humour and the outside world.

There was only one thing that excited Jim Moir more than *Monty Python*, and that was music. In the late Sixties he was taken by the extraordinary axe antics of Jimi Hendrix. He told the *People* how he had nearly worn out his record of 'Voodoo Chile' and simultaneously exhausted his father's patience. One day his father snapped. 'My dad got so sick of hearing it. He said, "Anybody can play the guitar like that." I remember thinking, when I grow up I'm going to buy a guitar, give it to you and say, "Right, get on with it."'

Fortunately his mother was more tolerant and indulged her son's unusual tastes; she was more than happy to run up a pair of velvet hipsters for him and bought records for him when she went shopping. Another of Jim's favourite bands was The Who. In 1971 they released the single 'Let's See Action', a dynamic little ditty which confirmed that The Who were definitive hard rockers with a pop sensibility. The band, with its twin-pronged front-line of gritty Roger Daltrey and arty Pete Townshend appealed to Jim. There was something of the foppish mod about him, but one who would talk his way out of a fight rather than get involved. He even had a pair of precious Hush Puppies; to some they were the preserve of out-of touch schoolteachers, to others they were the epitome of style. At an early age he seemed to grasp the elementary rules of 'cool' and would change his image almost on a weekly basis.

Jim's mother Audrey doted on her son, often to his embarrassment. At fourteen he was your typical Seventies teenager, a long-haired ginger urchin in school uniform and obligatory loose-fitting tie. His mother tried to smarten him up by combing his hair in the mornings, but Jim would always ruffle it up the moment she was out of sight.

It is convenient for a biographer to be able to point to a pivotal childhood incident and say that was the reason for the way the person is today, but it is hard to do it with Jim Moir. Five million schoolchildren must have memorized *Monty Python* when it was first broadcast. How many of them are still funny? Jim Moir somehow managed to harness a normal childhood and turn it upside down, with the result that he now has a unique take on life. It is almost as if his nondescript upbringing allowed him the freedom to be different. Perhaps his greatest stroke of fortune was his academic anonymity, which meant that his skills, verbal and visual, were never recognized by the conventional education system, enabling him to keep a low profile. He wasn't the victim of bullying, which might have forced him to develop a traditional sense of humour as a hard carapace against a brutal world. He wasn't head boy, singled out as a future Civil Service high flyer, destined for dull success. He was just an ordinary lad in an ordinary northern school. But an ordinary lad who discovered that he had an extraordinary gift which could make him the centre of attention.

In 1993 he told the *Daily Mail*: 'I was always one of those children who was desperately trying to make people laugh or do something they shouldn't.' Not the noisiest, but always at back of the class with the wild bunch. He was bored with school, but devoured history and natural history books, something which his parents found difficult to understand. When Jim was interested in something, he would really throw himself into it, but there seemed to be little in the syllabus that appealed to him. Owing to a reorganization of the educational system in Darlington in the early Seventies known as the Peter Plan, none of the schools except the Roman Catholic one had a sixth form, which meant that whatever he did, he was going to move on. His parents hoped he might become something respectable like a teacher, something white collar, but when Jim left school at sixteen with no qualifications there was little chance of that.

At the time there was only really one career option. The factory. It would take five years but it would be a passport to a lifetime of steady employment – or so it had always seemed. When Jim Moir left school, the one thing he knew was that he wanted to escape from the factory. For a while he even considered joining the Navy, and then he realized what he really wanted to do. Like Pete Townshend, what he really wanted was to go to art school. His father didn't approve: 'Do you know any artists who are making a living out of painting?' Jim didn't, and the subject was closed. Art school just didn't seem a realistic option.

As a schoolboy Jim had had a part-time job at weekends on a farm, which gave him plenty of opportunities to lark about. 'I used to castrate pigs. I had to slit their testicles and pull out the tender bits to stop them going mad and killing each other. We'd ride on the pigs' backs until we fell off and then climb on to the sileage.' He used to earn £2.50 for the day, which he promptly went out and spent on loon pants.

'I was swilling out a hundred pigs and forty cattle. I had to change

9

clothes after work and take frequent showers, but still stank to high heaven. They wouldn't let me on the bus so I had to cycle home on an old bike after every shift.' Chastened by the experience but still drawn inexorably towards the countryside, he became a cabbage farmer, which was hardly an improvement: 'It was red hot around Darlington that summer of 1976. The cabbages started to go off and rot. They smelled worse than the pigs – and so did I.'

Eventually the lure of the manure wore off and he changed direction. Having exhausted various other options, he finally succumbed to factory work. He signed on for a five-year apprenticeship at SAB Brake Regulators in nearby Newton Aycliffe and trained to become an inspector. 'I had to do scientific tests on torque and tension. On the factory floor they would make three thousand parts for a jet engine. I had to take one into a room and if it was no good tell them to start again. I used to go round in a white lab coat.'

When the work was plentiful many men over the age of sixty-five would return to the factory, just for something to do, and they would stay there until they dropped. Sometimes Jim felt strange having to tell these men who had worked there for over forty years that they had to scrap their work. 'I had bright orange hair, and there would be these old blokes who had been there for sixty years and I had to tell them to stop and do it again.'

In its own way Jim's job offered prospects; he was even chosen as Apprentice of the Year, but in the same way that at school he would try to get away with a shorter essay, so he would try to make the work more painless. During tea-breaks he would pick up tabloid newspapers and systematically deface the pictures. It was a juvenile pastime, but drawing small black Hitler moustaches on celebrities helped him keep his sanity. He would then change the names around, so that instead of saying 'Joanna Lumley receives an award', it would say 'Hitler receives an award.'

Another way of perking up the day was to mock anyone who had a strange habit. If he saw someone standing at their machinery in an usual way he and his friends would surround them and ritualistically chant, 'Stance, stance, stance.' If all else failed to keep him amused, he would crawl into crates that had sawdust in them and go to sleep.

The factory was a bizarre environment, and Jim came across some people who had developed even stranger ways of livening up their days:

'The biggest collection of perverts that I've ever met are people that worked in factories. One bloke I used to work with had a very large penis and every day he was working on his milling machine and he would get his oily rag out, lower the bed of the milling machine and put his knob on the rag. The tea woman would come round and offer the tea to him and pretend she hadn't seen it and then say "Good lord, put it away" – and it would just be laying there. Every day this happened. She loved it and he loved it. That was the sort of behaviour that went on.'

Jim recalls how his potential career as an aeronautical engineer came off the rails because it got in the way of his youthful drinking sprees: 'I was a mechanical inspector and was expected to get up really early, looking bright and chirpy and ready for a hard day's work. It was vital for you to be on the ball. I had to quit because that meant I couldn't give boozing in the evening the time I wanted to.' Jim's way of relaxing was music and alcohol. As a teenager he constantly wanted to be in bands and learnt to play the guitar. He once coaxed a potential girlfriend back to his room and proceeded to play her Hendrix riffs on the guitar for two hours when any normal adolescent could have essayed a more direct seduction technique. Jimi Hendrix was one of his few constant loyalties. Jim's tastes were broad and his heroes used to change with the wind. There were pop groups like Roxy Music, formed by the north-east's Bryan Ferry, then Slade and T Rex. But in the early Seventies his real interest was in hard rock. Free, led by Paul Rodgers, could do no wrong, but given his name, it was aptly Rod Stewart who became his icon: 'I used to try and look like Rod Stewart. He had no lips at all. I had the perfect haircut and I got the scarf.' His allegiances were fickle, but he would always go that little bit further than his mates; at times he would furiously back-comb his copper-coloured mop, making it frizzy in a feeble attempt to resemble Paul Kossoff, the guitarist from Free.

Jim's under-age drinking was done at the city centre's Green Dragon pub. While still at school he fell in with an older crowd and, to fit in with them, started to grow his hair longer than ever and wear an Afghan coat that one contemporary says made him look like a criminal. Through his older friends Jim was even able to become the bass player in a local band called Trout, a progressive outfit fond of strange rhythms and stops and starts.

There was one aspect of his job at SAB Brake Regulators, however, which brightened up the week. He used to spend one day a week studying at Darlington Technical College. It was while there that he met a group of mates who would help him get his life back on course.

John Irvine, Geoffrey Dent, Rob Colbrook and Graham Bristow were all doing their A-levels at the nearby sixth form college and Jim got to know them one by one. John Irvine was one of the first to hit it off with Jim: 'He was working in a factory, but he preferred to hang around in our common room.'

Geoffrey 'Jack' Dent recalls how he first met Jim in the autumn of 1975. 'We had all just left different schools and were able to grow our hair long and wear jeans at college. I was into Genesis, King Crimson, and the rest of us used to meet up on Saturday mornings in the town centre, and there was this guy who was completely weird. That was Jim. He had long hair, a big great coat, a Jimi Hendrix badge, and smelt of Patchouli oil. He seemed like the biggest hippy there had ever been and looked like he lived in a dustbin. I was surprised to find that his parents were fairly middle-class and came from the same kind of home as me.'

As the quintet became a virtual surrogate family – known as the Fashionable Five – they also acquired nicknames. Jim was Chin or Roddy, Jack was Jiffy Jackson, John was Doccy, Graham was Herman, Rob was Cot. The group had two particular interests – music and jokes. With their membership cards and secret salutes they were able to extend their adolescence well into their late teens. Pranks were very popular, and the more pointless they were, the more they enjoyed them. Jim once pretended to have a brass hand; another time all five of them followed a man through Darlington in single file for half a mile. It seemed to give no one except for the five of them any pleasure, but that was what was most important. If their humour appeared to be different from the rest of humanity in Darlington, that was probably because Jim had little interest in television at the time, apart from the obvious programmes: 'It was mainly *Monty Python* and Spike Milligan. I hadn't seen Morecambe and Wise then. I never watched much telly anyway. I used to spend most of my time listening to the radio, climbing trees and pretending I was a space alien. And hanging around on street corners eating chips. And drinking cider and having fags.'

At weekends when money was at its tightest, however, the gang would gather at Jim's house and watch the black and white movies on BBC2. They became particularly excited when an old British comedy was on. *The Titfield Thunderbolt*, about a group of villagers who take over a tiny branch line was a favourite, as was anything starring Will Hay or Terry Thomas as a cad. *Tawny Pipit*, another quaint film, this time about two birds nesting in a villiage during war-time and disrupting life there was another popular one. Jim's mum would offer biscuits around and cheap fun would be had by all.

Whenever there was money around, it would frequently be spent on music-related activities. For a while the quintet followed pomp rock band The Enid around. Jim, in particular was excited when they actually managed to speak to the band. After one gig at the Coatham Bowl in Redcar he even got a hint of what being a celebrity must be like. The band weren't that successful but had invested in a glamorous old Rolls-Royce. Jim was unable to get home, and they gave him a lift back to their place and let him sleep on their floor. It certainly beat pig farming.

Over the next few years the group were to have countless adventures and scrapes, usually related to music events that they went to. Gradually the Fashionable Five discovered punk, but in the same way that the Swinging Sixties took their time to travel up the A1, so punk rock took the scenic route north. By the middle of 1977, however, it was a big influence. The Sex Pistols even played a secret gig at Middlesbrough's Rock Garden under the name of Acne Rabble. John Irvine and Jack Dent were the first of the bunch to take the plunge and cut their hair. Jim seemed more reluctant. He always stuck out as the particularly weird member of the gang; he wasn't even into football that much, and when the others went out for a kickabout he would often stay in his room, taping music off the radio. In fact he was never much of a fan of sport. When he used to play rugby at Eastbourne College his speciality tactic was 'an odd stare' which looked a bit vague and wrongfooted people. He claimed that he set out not so much to make people laugh as to 'freak them out a bit'. When he went shopping with his mother he would stare strangely. 'I'd think to myself that nobody knew I was actually an alien.'

Darlington did not have that many big punk gigs, but it was a simple train ride away from Newcastle, and the group used to go to the City Hall to see big bands and the University's Canteen to see up-and-coming outfits. On 22 December 1977 they went up to Newcastle to see the Ramones. The American band had been one of the seminal forces of the punk movement and still had a strong, passionate following. Many of the audience members copied the band's outfits of jeans, Converse All Stars trainers and leather biker jackets. Some of the Fashionable Five had even started dressing like this. But Jim had yet to commit himself, as Jack Dent recalls. 'It was my sister's birthday and on the way to the gig me and Graham took the plunge and had a haircut. Not short by today's standards, but not long either. Then we got there and Rod [aka Jim] turned up looking like Sid James in a car coat.' He sat down and for the whole of the gig was the only one seated in City Hall, while everyone else was pogoing and jumping around. 'He went along, but the punk thing hadn't taken hold of him yet. It was seeing the Clash in early 1978 that he got into it and got his hair cut.' Rod had obviously registered the Ramones' jackets; he would eventually appear in his own leather jacket, but with a distinctive twist. Instead of saying 'The Adverts' or 'The Buzzcocks' on the back, his had 'Debussy' spelt out in silver studs.

The Fashionable Five liked to express their individuality by dressing the same as each other, but differently from everybody else. For a period they used to all wear yellow jumpers and white trousers, loosely modelling themselves on the quirky American band Devo. Sticking together, they would often cause quite a stir at concerts, and they had the most fun when they could combine gigs with practical jokes. One night, as Jack Dent remembers, they went together to see Generation X at the Canteen in Newcastle: 'We were sitting on a bench in a corridor between the dressing-room and the stage when the band walked past. Billy Idol, the singer, clocked us and did a double take. About six months later Generation X came back, and I must admit we engineered it a bit to be in exactly the same place in exactly the same clothes. Billy Idol walked past again and did this incredible double take. We must have looked odd the first time, let alone the second.'

Although Jim was supposed to be working and the others were supposed to be studying, they found plenty of time to travel too. Jack and Jim went hitching a lot and got to the Isle of Wight, where they found the only dope dealer on the island, and in summer 1978 went to the Glastonbury Festival. There they met up with another Darlington mate, Ian 'Wally' Wallis. The music was great, but they pitched their tent next to hippy veterans Gong – and then, as Jack recalls, they found out why that was the only space left: 'We couldn't sleep because of all the noise. They seemed to have about forty kids.'

By now Jim was getting the hang of the punk look and as well as his leather jacket wore a pair of baggy pants with a cigarette packet stuck to the back. When the Fashionable Five started wearing punk gear they became virtual outcasts in Darlington. With his striking bright orange hair Jim was a particular target. 'We were the only five people in town with straight jeans. I used to get chased down the street and called a poof.' Darlington was the kind of town that didn't tolerate difference, and Jim was always different. 'I had the first centre-parting at school and that caused a lot of grief. I was called Hairy Mary because I had long hair. Everything I did seemed to attract raised eyebrows.'

Inevitably, like teenagers everywhere, they formed their own band, but it could hardly be described as punk. Rob Colbrook was into Kraut rock bands like Faust; John Irvine was into experimental stuff. Irvine remembers the gigs as shambolic affairs. 'The first one was at a youth club on Skerne Park, the roughest local council estate in Darlington, supporting a band who became Major Accident. There were twenty-odd kids spitting at us and we made an absolute noise. There was this other band in Darlington who used to do cover versions and they were our enemies. They chased us all the way down Post House Wynd one night.

'At the gigs we did around Darlington, the best bits were always Jim's vocals between the music,' continues Irvine, 'which was inspired by industrial bands like Throbbing Gristle and Cabaret Voltaire.' The other thing that set the group apart was their selection of names, which seemed to change on an almost weekly basis. 'Bobby and Jackie Charlton's Eerie Mansion was one,' says Irvine. 'Jackie Milburn's Terrible Scar,' says Jack Dent. 63 Colliers was another moniker. Jim clearly had a hand in the names, but they were a team effort. Everyone shared the same fundamentally daft sense of humour.

As well as providing free-form vocals Jim was also playing bass and saxophone. He bought a fretless bass in Newcastle and had an improvisational jazz style, which didn't necessarily sit comfortably with the other members' influences. Onstage, Jim's humour started to emerge. Jack Dent can recall that Jim had a distinctive way with words even then, although they all found the same things funny: 'He had the same voice and mannerisms then as he has now. He used to do the high voice like Davey Stott, which I think was based on someone who worked in the factory, back then. We used to go on about Slender Lorises and there was a dress shop in Darlington called Slendos, which we used to think was fantastic. We all loved playing about with words.' The Situationists, the French political/philosophical movement that Malcolm McLaren claimed inspired him to construct the Sex Pistols, call this verbal activity '*détourner*'. To Jim and his mates it was just a case of having a laugh and relieving boredom.

Jim created a secret world with his friends. The mundane backdrop to his life seemed to help his imagination to run riot. It was the best method of escape. He was also busy doing drawings and cartoon strips, mainly for his and their amusement. Jack Dent saw him come up with one called Gavin the Fashionable Bear, 'about a bear who joined a rock band called Whitey White', in 1976.

This group of teenagers cultivated their own linguistic sense of humour. They didn't realize it, but they were all contributing to Jim's future career. Unlike, say, the Pythons or the Footlights alumni, they had no aspirations, academic or otherwise. The others were only doing A-levels to avoid going to work, in a factory. Jim never used to feel intellectually inferior in their company, but he did sometimes feel the need to joke about his work, justifying his choice of training: 'It's as good as an A-level, an apprenticeship, and probably better.' Behind the jokes, however, he was looking for a way to escape even further.

Chapter Two

Five Go to London

By 1979 Darlington was proving to be too small a world for the Fashionable Five and they decided to head south. Graham Bristow had joined the Civil Service and secured a transfer to Trafalgar House in Central London. He also managed to get clerical jobs for Jim, John, Jack and Rob at the Department of Health and Social Security – 'in the medicines division, controlling doctors and limb-fitters'. That March they all moved to 67 Arodene Road, in Brixton. Jim remembers it as 'the bleak midwinter', but worse was yet to come. James Callaghan's Labour government was becoming increasingly beleaguered and destined for electoral defeat. There was a strange sense of gloom and foreboding in the air. Something had to give.

The initial momentum of punk rock may have subsided, but London still seemed like the place where things happened. County Durham left a lot to be desired where celebrity was concerned. Darlington's roll-call of showbiz alumni began and ended with sitcom star Wendy Craig. The capital had been a pop-cultural magnet for anyone with a keen interest in looking good. Someone with a distinctive style would be tolerated there. For a young provincial with broad horizons, sooner or later there was no other option. At least he wouldn't get chased down the street for wearing drainpipe trousers.

But coming to London was the simple part of the equation for Jim Moir. Deciding on what he should do once he was there was rather more difficult. Ideally, it was going to be something in the arts, most probably music. Something that would make him famous. And in the back of his mind there was always the possibility of art college in a city where it wasn't considered 'poofy'. But first of all he had to get some bearings.

Within two days of moving to Brixton, the quintet had found the Moonlight Club at the Railway Tavern in West Hampstead. It was on the other side of London, but its adverts boasted a list of the kind of bands they wanted to see: indie bands specializing in a do-it-yourself ethic such as the Raincoats and the Swell Maps.

Eventually they found some entertainment closer to home. 'Jim has always been a bit starstruck and we used to meet in the Ship in Wardour Street, near where the old Marquee used to be. He would get very excited at seeing people like Lemmy from Motorhead,' says Jack Dent. In fact they soon found some entertainment even nearer to their house. The George Canning on Effra Road just around the corner had live music on a regular basis, though most of it was rubbish, and less than a mile away there was the Half Moon in Herne Hill. At the time Jim loved going out drinking before going to gigs, and if the band was awful it didn't really matter. In fact it even made them think that they could do better, and the quintet started rehearsing again.

One Sunday night they went down to the Half Moon to see a new Irish band called U2. Jim, Graham and Jack had been doing a lot of drinking that day and started to take the piss out of the band, as Jack remembers: 'They were in all this shiny new leather and we thought, "Fucking hell, this is shit." I think Graham even spat at them a few times because they were trying to look like punks. At throwing-out time Graham and I were in the toilets about ten urinals apart still laughing, when this bloke came and stood in the middle and thought we were laughing at him. When we got outside he was waiting with his mates to give us a thrashing. Jim was off like a whippet. He's a good runner when it comes to fighting.'

Money was not a huge problem. The quintet had all got jobs and if you kept your head down you could do the minimum of work and the maximum of drinking. As John Irvine says, 'None of us were into careers, it was all a big adventure.' Jack shies away from inevitable comparisons with *The Young Ones*; besides, the BBC2 sitcom hadn't even been made at the time – 'It wasn't being lived to any plan, me and Jim used to share a room because it was a three-bedroomed house and John and Graham could be moody' — but the similarity is there. Jim's dirty socks would gradually form a large pile in the corner of the bedroom. There were advantages to communal living, though. Between them they seemed to have every record that came out and there was always music on in the house. As their confidence grew, the quintet started to really enjoy themselves on the party front. Huge tubs of henna were purchased and they all followed Jim's example and dyed their hair.

After the stultifying conservatism of Darlington, Jim found himself in such a new environment that he didn't need to reinvent himself, he simply had to absorb his surroundings. It was a steep learning curve but one he handled with ease. As newcomers to London, the group threw themselves into the social scene with an almost religious zeal. Jack Dent got himself a fashionably baggy suit and used to go clubbing at Le Beat Route, where Spandau Ballet and Boy George — when he was still George O'Dowd — used to hang out. In the same way that it took a while for Jim to commit himself to punk, he wasn't much interested at the time in new romantics. One night, though, the Fashionable Five thought they had really arrived when Boy George turned up at the house with his friend Marilyn, who was dressed as Bo Peep. George, in line with his later remark about preferring tea to sex, went up to their kitchen in the attic and made himself a cuppa.

It was an exceedingly happy time. The Fashionable Five seemed to have struck lucky in London. In fact they seemed to have a knack of meeting the right people wherever they went. At a party at the Notting Hill Carnival Jim met Phillip Salon, one of Boy George's mentors. Jim had a habit of hooking up with stars and would-be stars and making useful contacts long before it was called networking. In Darlington they had attracted a young acolyte, Alan Davidson. He had now gone off to the University of East Anglia. Jim and the others used to go up there for parties and stay for long weekends. There they met Alan's new friend Charles Higson, who was known as Switch. He was in a cult college band called the Higsons, who would later catch the tail-end of the Two Tone movement and have a couple of modest hits.

While in London, the group reactivated their own experimental band and took their gigs a little more seriously. Again the name would change on a regular basis, but two of the more stable banners were Dig Me I'm Django and They Called It Rum. It often seemed like a closed all-male shop, but for a while a woman, Jocelyn Rossiter, played flute with them.

As Dig Me I'm Django they did a gig supporting a band called Dry Romance at the Middlesbrough Empire on 5 October 1980, admission 50p, and got a review in a fanzine, *Jesus Idiot* which was the peak of their career. By now Jim was starting to draw attention to himself more than ever onstage. The review was critical, but ultimately positive. The anonymous writer said initially that 'they seem to be very image conscious'. By this time they were a nine-piece band – not surprisingly things were free-form in the extreme. The writer picked Jim out, saying that 'the sax player looks like a frog when he blows out his cheeks'. He was confused by their held-up signs, which said things like 'Fin' and 'Pal', but was finally impressed: 'The sax player and clarinet player walk among the audience and dance. This is hilarious. I observe some of the crowd blocking their ears ... The Pop Group at their noisiest, these nutters never let up. On the whole it was loud and fun.' 'People would walk up and have a look and then walk away,' remembers Irvine of the audience response to the signs.

Dig Me I'm Django persevered and even sent out press releases to the music papers, surreptitiously xeroxed at work by Jack, who was still a civil servant. In retrospect the group's biography reads like a rough draft of an opening sketch on *The Smell of Reeves and Mortimer*: 'Venice, 1760. Casanova lies dying in a gondola, the victim of a vicious attack by a flute wielding debutante ...' Elsewhere it talked about the Portuguese revolution, the Gobi Desert, Egypt 832 BC and suggested that Irish writers Joyce and Becket (sic) were 'noted for their contribution to Polish acrobatics and the invention of the non-stick pan'. In the line-up, Jim was known as 'Hespond Van Chin'. It was very funny, but you wouldn't necessarily know it was about an aspiring pop group.

Jim's behaviour was becoming more distinctive all the time, but apart from a few brief public glimpses onstage it would still be for the benefit of his mates. One day he created an American character called Jim Bell. They would be wandering around London together and he would assume the persona of this big, deep-voiced American tourist. At other times, for no apparent reason, says Jack, he would 'pretend to be an old fellow who couldn't walk very well'. The music was a strange activity for them, straddling ambition and having a laugh. They did actually produce music for sale — albeit to a select coterie. Jim made a tape, entitled 'International Cod', which he advertised in the *New Musical Express*. John Irvine thinks Jim sold eight copies to people in Europe. 'It was a healthy rivalry. I once did a concert in our living-room. The audience was Jim and the other people that lived there.'

Eventually the Civil Service job ran its course. Jim resorted to the one qualification that he had on paper. The former Apprentice of the Year landed a job as an inspector at an aircraft parts factory in Croydon. It was an odd place, and he made some odd friends; one, Crested Mick, was a six-foot, animal-rights-supporting punk with a large mohican who joined the band.

A responsible job in a factory and a lifestyle of full-on partying didn't mix, however. The hours were long and there wasn't much time to unwind. Eventually he had had enough and in 1981 left for a job behind the counter at Our Price Records in Charing Cross Road. It may seem strange now, but at the time, compared with the engineering world, this seemed a short step away from an appearance on *Top of the Pops*. Our Price had an impressive stock and many of the staff members were in bands. Others had close connections with bands. Spandau Ballet often used to pop into the shop and hang around in the basement. While other staff members scoffed at their kilts and fringes, Jim was quietly impressed.

Jim enjoyed certain aspects of the job but not others. At the end of the day it was just another way of earning beer money. It could get tedious but he managed to find ways of amusing himself. One prank was a more sophisticated version of his old Hitler renaming game: 'We used to get posters out of Police albums and write "Sting" on them. Then when people bought them we used to say, "You're really lucky — you've got the personally autographed copy."'

The new job coincided with a move from Brixton. After a couple of years, the five had decided they were paying too much in rent and one day Graham said he had seen an ad in the *London Evening Standard* saying that hard-to-let flats were available in Bermondsey. With lengthy homeless lists and a growing student population, various inner-city councils had decided it would give accommodation to the needy if they queued up all night. The gang tried out this option and in February 1981 ended up in a hard-to-let council flat on the Silwood Estate. They soon found out why the flat was hard to let. Having come to a city to escape persecution, it seemed to have followed him: 'It was a shit-hole. As soon as we got in there, eggs were thrown at the door. People used to shout, "Get out, northern bastards."' There were countless burglaries, and after Jim left, heroin began to appear on the estate and there was a serious drug problem among the children. The way John Irvine remembers it, they were being picked on not for their northern accents but simply because they were not ex-dockers. Within six months Jim had had enough. While the others stuck it out, he started looking for somewhere else to live. The only good thing about moving from Brixton was that they got out just in time. It was an indictation of how apolitical this bunch of young hedonists were that a few weeks after leaving they were driving home through Brixton in the middle of the night in Graham's old Morris Oxford when the wheels started bumping up and down. They got out to have a look and saw that the road was covered in broken bricks. John Irvine then looked over at the houses and noticed gangs of people cowering in doorways. The Brixton riots had started, but had passed the Fashionable Five by.

At Our Price Jim heard that the store manager, Tom Fawcett, was in a band. The Native Hipsters were hardly stars, but they had had a cult single, 'There Goes Concorde Again', which John Peel had played to death. Jim soon sought out and became friendly with his colleague and suggested that they do some recording together. Fawcett recalls thinking Jim's nickname was odd but apt. 'I thought he was called Chin because he was always growing different types of facial hair, goatees and things. He was still slightly new romanticish, but slightly coming out of it.' For Fawcett, though, one thing has always been consistent with Jim: 'His sense of humour has always been the same, but his appearance used to change from minute to minute. His hair would be red, then orange, then black. He was already quite a character. People would stop him in the street and ask him what he had come as. He was always ahead of style and probably still is.'

Tom and Jim ended up spending countless evenings recording music in Tom's cramped living-room. 'We used to spend days and days and days making all sorts of strange music, just the two of us. There was a brief craze for albums only available on cassette and we did two, one called *Epic* and one called *Shepherd's Galore*,' recalls Fawcett.

The recording sessions started off as fun, but things soon became more serious. Gigs were set up, initially as a duo under the name of

Fawcett and Moir. One show, at the 101 Club in Clapham on 17 June 1981, was actually part of an embryonic comedy night, although at the time Jim had expressed little interest in becoming a comedian. The advert for the evening even included a line which could have come straight out of a *Big Night Out*: 'Prize for the Best Presented Cucumber'. The duo went on and did their music, oblivious to the fact that they were surrounded by aspiring variety acts.

William Wilding, who promoted the Clapham show, was given a tape made by Jim and Tom as a gift, continuing the wordplay/farming theme that was destined to become familiar, entitled 'Never Challenge a Goat/The Goat is Challenged'. The eclectic nature of the styles on the mainly instrumental tape suggest that Jim hadn't yet sifted through the jumble of his mind and found his true voice, but there is no mistaking the Darlington twang in his Bonzo Dog Doodah Band-influenced intro: 'Moir here, Fawcett's partner. Make yourself at home and listen with both ears. Listen to that drumming. Mmmm. That's mean. Listen how it grows faster and faster.'

The following forty minutes are a bit of a musical rollercoaster, taking in tribal drumming, free jazz, tape loops, electronic rhythms and general clattering about as if someone was doing some DIY next door, culminating in a fairy story read by a child. The music sounds as if it was recorded under the influence of something stronger than tea. It is not without merit, but on this basis Fawcett and Moir were hardly about to take the charts by storm.

Things went quite well, well enough in fact, for Jim and Tom to decide to form a full band, which they called Design for Living, inspired partly by the Noël Coward play and partly by an interior design-based *Sunday Times* supplement which had the same name. This confused some fans because the band called Warsaw, who later became Joy Division, had released a record entitled 'Ideal for Living'.

What with spending so much time recording on Tom's four-track recorder and generally jamming, combined with the fact that he was unhappy on the Silwood Estate and he had not yet found anywhere else to live, Jim inevitably ended up staying with Tom and his wife Julia. The arrangement had its advantages. Their flat was also exceedingly well situated for the centre of London. It was just south of the river above a café on the corner of Lower Marsh, the location of a regular street market, a stone's throw from Waterloo Station. Tom's wife tended to feed Jim: 'If she didn't, he didn't seem to eat.' Both Jim and Tom left Our Price and the music became more important. They weren't just artists, they ran their own label, which they called Boy Smells: 'When *The Smell of Reeves and Mortimer* came along I wondered if there was a thread there,' muses Fawcett. But as soon as things started to happen professionally the friendship began to suffer. A high point was supporting the supremely naff A Flock of Seagulls at the Moonlight Club in West Hampstead: 'Half-way through the set I asked Jim to get up and do one of his poems, which he used to write under the name of Jim Bell the Shepherd. They were mostly about sheep. The poetry seemed to go down really well and gave him the confidence to do more verbal things onstage.' The content reflected his appearance, which had changed again. Marooned in the city, Jim seemed to be looking for his rural roots. Offstage he liked to wear brogues and tweed suits and 'walk around south London as if he was looking for his flock'.

Musically, Design for Living was 'pretty loose and jazzy and interested in making a lot of noise', says Fawcett. Pigbag, The Pop Group, Rip Rig and Panic and African rhythms were big influences, but Fawcett recalls that at the time Jim used to idolize people like Mark E. Smith of the Fall, Captain Beefheart and Frank Zappa – 'and Ozzy Osbourne. He always was partial to a good bit of British heavy metal.' Jim started to call himself JR Moir; it sounded enigmatic and also like the power-crazed soap magnate played by Larry Hagman in *Dallas*. 'We were like Captain Beefheart without the discipline to shut ourselves away for six months to rehearse.'

In fact things started to go downhill after about six gigs in 1983, culminating in a disaster at Wapping following another image change. 'We played one of the very first warehouse parties,' says Fawcett. 'I sang and played trombone, Jim played bass and sax and we had a drummer and a flautist. We were dressed as Polish peasants, in big black workmen's boots with no laces, a selection of interesting trousers, quite baggy and tied at the waist with a piece of string. Plus miners' hats and collarless shirts, very romanticized images of north European miners.' The exotic image didn't prevent fate and arguments ensuing: 'But it was the beginning of the end of our musical collaborations. It all got a bit messy that night.'

The clash of personalities meant that Jim left the band, which continued without him. His friendship with Tom and his wife survived, to the extent that he went on holiday with them, but once again things had a nasty habit of not turning out as expected, according to Tom: 'One Easter everybody seemed to be going away on holiday. Jim seemed quite upset that he was the only one not going anywhere. We were renting a narrow boat to travel around the canals in the Midlands, and we took him with us on the understanding that he would have to sleep on the floor. Somehow, though, after one night it was us that ended up on the floor.' Jim seemed to have a way of turning awkward situations to his own advantage.

Jim flitted from band to band. He was never in any of them long enough for real success to be a possibility. It was the same with accommodation. For a while he lived in ramshackle New Cross housing cooperatives at 41 Billington Road and then at 8 Nettleton Road with some of the people who formed Test Department, the bleak avant-garde industrial outfit that beat out rhythms on society's metal detritus. Test Department became fashionable and moderately successful, and in the late Eighties Jim said he was once a member. He once told Jonathan Ross this story, but the television presenter had his doubts: 'He said he liked these experimental noise bands that used to appear at the ICA. He said he was in Test Department, but he is a fantastically elaborate storyteller, which can be embarrassing. Sometimes if you confront him you expect him to buckle but he doesn't.' In fact, according to John Irvine, there is some truth in Jim's claim. 'He did one gig with them at a Goldsmiths' College band contest. It was one of their first gigs, when they were a conventional band and he played bass.'

About a year later he supported Test Department at the Fridge in Brixton, dressed, Irvine recalls, 'in an assemblage of cardboard boxes decorated with photos of footballers. He was screeching into the microphone while all the time dropping potatoes out of the bottom of the boxes. I was doing the music and he was shouting over the top. It was an earlier version of what he became successful with, but back then it probably hadn't occurred to him to be a comedian.'

Jim's unlikely Test Department connection virtually deserves a chapter in its own right. It came about mainly through his friendship with Brett Turnbull, a Zimbabwean who had relocated to south London. Turnbull first met Jim at a gig at Camberwell School of Art where Jim was playing saxaphone in the support band just after Design For Living had split up. Like may people, Brett was struck by Jim's appearance: 'He was sporting a long dyed red fringe and a beret. Brett found that they both had similar artistic aspirations. 'He was always beavering away,' remembers Turnbull. 'If he wasn't doing collages with pictures he was making tapes of weird noises. This was in the pre-sampling days, so he had to do it with two cassette decks back to back. The other thing he noticed about Jim was his distinctive northern accent that he made absolutely no attempt to conceal. 'He used to recite strange poetry and sounded like a northern Captain Beefheart.' They started hanging out together and had various money-making schemes which came to nothing, such as running second-hand clothes stalls in the Portobello Road and Deptford market. They also attempted to sell old records, but only ended up building their own collection of Sixties soundtrack albums and kitsch Europop.

Jim and Brett also did a lot of performance art together. 'We were always dressing up and making super 8 films. Whenever we got a dole cheque we'd go to the post office and cash it and buy more film,' remembers Turnbull. One of their earliest projects was *Return Of The Killer Elvises*. They gathered all their mates together, got them all to wear suits and gave them xeroxed pictures of Elvis Presley to stick over their faces. Jim and Brett then filmed them walking through New Cross. Another time they filmed dummies being chucked into the Thames and had to disappear quickly when people began to notice what they were doing. In another short film called *The Hip Priest* after the song by The Fall, Jim played 'a blind preacher like the one in *Wiseblood*, who was also a DJ. He enjoyed dressing up in the mad clothes and putting on the large hat.'

Eventually they started making music together and formed a trio, Fantantiddlyspan, or, for convenience, just Fantan. Turnbull describes the music as 'The Righteous Brothers meets The Human League.' Around the same time though, Turnbull became involved in the nascent Test Department line-up, and when the line-up was unsettled Jim and Brett ended up in both bands. 'It was crazy,' recalls Turnbull, 'because one week Test Department were supporting us, and a couple of weeks later Test Department were on the cover of the *New Musical Express*. Turnbull threw in his lot with Test Department, realizing that Fantan could never be serious contenders with Jim in the line-up:

'Fantan wasn't supposed to be comic, but with Jim in the band it inevitably was. There was one song that only had one line in it. 'Baby I love you' — by the end of the number the audience was often in hysterics.'

By now the Fashionable Five had begun to disperse and put down roots elsewhere. Gradually they had moved from Brixton to south-east London, the area around Goldsmiths' College in New Cross that had a plentiful supply of less threatening council flats and a plentiful supply of tolerant, liberal and adventurous art students, which meant that eggs were more likely to be thrown at canvases than at Jim's door. One day Jim contacted Tom to tell him that he had found a student house through Lewisham Council. 'He called to say that he had a house but it was too big. He wanted the upstairs and we could have the downstairs. So we moved in, but it didn't really work out.' The result was a volatile cocktail of newly-weds and party animals.

Jim was still unsettled, but his new area seemed to be inspirational. Whereas Brixton meant a long haul into the centre of London for a night out, this new area seemed to have a life of its own. Living a little bit further out, people were prepared to make their own entertainment, and as a result there seemed to be a thriving local social scene. The recently rebuilt Albany Empire had bands on, pubs frequently had live shows and, inevitably, there was an endless round of student parties to gatecrash.

This was an odd hybrid of a district. Look one way and you had Blackheath village, the Hampstead of the south, full of Georgian architecture and greenery. Look the other way and you had the over-urbanized squalor of Deptford and New Cross. As local comedian and entrepreneur Malcolm Hardee says, 'On one side they wouldn't have heard of Eddie Izzard, on the other they wouldn't have heard of Jim Davidson.' One side was straight out of Beau Brummel, the other straight out of Hogarth.

It was also an area with a huge amount of history, another of Jim's passions. There was the *Cutty Sark* near by, the Greenwich Meridian and the Observatory. Not to mention a fine selection of pubs. There was also an alluring punk rock connection. One of the definitive new wave bands Squeeze had been formed by a group of lads who had grown up around here. During the punk boom, they had been produced by former Velvet Underground linchpin John Cale, briefly but seductively linking gritty south London with Andy Warhol's Exploding Plastic Inevitable Happenings in New York a decade earlier.

There had even been a local record label, ironically titled Deptford Fun City, run by Mark Perry, who, as the editor of the fanzine *Sniffin' Glue*, had been a prime mover during punk's heyday. His fanzine famously showed the fingering for the three basic chords and advised ordinary fans to promptly go out and form a band. Danny Baker, who would later re-emerge in the Eighties older and wiser, got his first journalistic break on *Sniffin' Glue*. For Jim, though, the contradictions of the area were an echo of his own internal contradictions. He knew he could make people laugh and he wanted to be the centre of attention, but he also had a desire to be taken seriously as an artist. 'He was looking for his own thing, but he wasn't quite sure what it was. He knew he had the ability to make people laugh but he also wanted to be thought of as a serious artist,' says Tom Fawcett.

With no job and not many prospects, Jim applied to Goldsmiths' College to study art. He didn't get a place, but he was undeterred and used their studio space and equipment anyway. By now he already had a distinctive style of his own, but he still wanted to fill in the historical details: 'I wanted to learn, you can't learn enough of that sort of stuff. I wanted to go to art school in Darlington, but peer pressure there meant that you went out to work. College was too poofy and you needed the money.'

If his oil paintings were not yet attracting attention, his appearance certainly was. Following his departure from Design for Living, Jim seemed to be in demand on the south London music scene. His instrumental skills were limited, but his appearance and charisma singled him out as someone worth having on your team.

Tom had looked on as Jim became involved in two shortlived outfits, Fantandiddlyspan and Hot Murder, which John Irvine played in. 'There were people within the scene that we were part of that definitely saw him as something that they wanted to acquire. They definitely saw something, which was not necessarily musical, more entertainment, so he got tempted into a couple of things by people whose talent wasn't anywhere near the level of his,' remembers Tom Fawcett. Things were very mutable in those days and line-ups and styles changed on a frequent basis. Often the same members cropped up in different bands. One week Jim's band would have an American lead singer, one week there was a cover version of the rock and roll standard 'Johnny Remember Me'. The image was equally fluid, involving kilts, grungey cardigans and anything else picked up at local jumble sales that looked out of the ordinary. Jim's own looks oscillated wildly: he resembled a proto-crusty for a while, with his shoes barely held together by string. Another time he might turn up as a tweedy country squire. Dressing up and altering everything about himself seemed to be half the fun, but he was also trying to find a persona that felt right. His hair was still changing colour and he played saxophone or bass guitar, but given the opportunity he would sing too. Despite the fact that it was all very haphazard, Tom Fawcett could see that Jim wanted to be a star, he just needed the right vehicle for his unique gift: 'He was burningly, explosively, destructively ambitious.'

His bands subsequently took the punk rock disposability ethic to its logical conclusion, as Jim later told Q magazine. 'We had the attitude that we wouldn't have any songs or rehearse, but just make a terrible row. In Hot Murder we had a proper song called 'Banzai Gasleak', which was about a gas leak that invaded the BBC and they had to call off all their shows; and there was one about Jackie Charlton when he was doing that TV show where every week he used to kill a different animal. One week he'd shoot pigeons, and the next week he shot a stag, and then he did fish. The entire British animal population he shot, so we did a song about that. That was quite good.'

Comedian Mark Lamarr, on the other hand, has heard some of Jim's early work. While he agrees that the music was certainly free-form in the purest sense, he isn't quite as impressed with it as Jim is: 'He is genuinely proud of his efforts, but by all conventional musical standards they were shit.' Lamarr says that Fantantiddlyspan sounded a little like the Walker Brothers: 'If I listen to it now I think I may vomit.'

Lamarr was once sent a tape of one of Jim's earlier recordings: 'Someone sent me a tape of Jim's band when they were a goth band and Jim said, "Nah nah, they were good", but they were atrocious. They did this song called "Fantasia" – I've never heard anything so bad, it was just loads of drumming for ages, then every few minutes you'd have three people going "Fantasia" and they were shocking, but Jim was going "Oh yeah, I remember that gig, it went really well", there are no chinks in his armour at all.'

Having been turned down by his local art college, Jim applied to do a foundation course at Sir John Cass College in Whitechapel. This time he had more luck and started a one-year part-time course there in September 1983. It wasn't all it was cracked up to be. The highlight seemed to be making light bulbs out of wax: 'I didn't think I was getting taught anything and preferred to do my own thing. I thought there must be more to life than this.' At Sir John Cass Jim met Dorian Crook, a former air traffic controller with film-making ambitions. They hit it off quite quickly in the bar when Jim, by this time sporting Sixties-style suits and long dyed black hair, revealed his extensive knowledge of German war planes: 'He knew all about one unusual one called the Blohm and Voss, which had the cabin on one side and the engine on the other,' recalls Crook. 'He specifically knew it, which was surprising in an art school environment. He was an arty person but was interested in other things too and he was not afraid to admit to knowing about things that weren't fashionable. I was very impressed.' Jim and Dorian became friends and used to go on shopping expeditions, looking for unusual clothes. Dorian found Jim inspirational in and out of college: 'He taught me about three-button suits, and he was also very confident about his art. He had enormous self-belief. He had quite a convincing manner and would be very enthusiastic about things. I don't think not getting into Goldsmiths' had done him much harm.'

Crook came to south London and moved into a flat with Jim's friend from Darlington, Alan Davidson. With more time on his hands Jim was painting prolifically, but still fairly itinerant, and during one move there was a mishap in Crook's car: 'I remember driving down Peckham High Street with these oil paintings in the back of my car and one of them fell out on to the road. I think it was of him dressed as the Pope, or maybe one of Elvis Presley. We had to get out and pick it up off the kerb.'

The social life continued to be focused around Deptford. Various permutations of the remaining Fashionable Five members and their London friends would go out to whatever gigs were on locally. The type of music didn't seem to matter, although it helped if the band was trendy.

One week Jim went to see Working Week at the Albany, leading lights of the latest British jazz revival; the next week it was Test

Department, the industrial outfit he had briefly played with. By the mid-Eighties they were creating a stir in the media, and Jim may have thought he had missed the boat. At their gig at the Albany Empire the centre of the auditorium was filled with a huge drum and the noise they created – it could hardly be called music – could have woken the dead. Jim even started dressing the part, donning distressed denim and his favourite 'Debussy' biker jacket. It wasn't exactly mainstream, but it was spectacular, whereas Jim's bands never quite gelled.

Jim's distinctive looks and regular appearances in the college bar had already helped him to make a name for himself in the area. Contemporaries recall how the Fashionable Five used to behave as if they were the hippest people in New Cross because of their tenuous connection with the new romantic scene. Jim was already widely known among the students and had a girlfriend, Lucie Russell, who was involved in the Students' Union. He was so frequently seen at gigs that some people even thought that he had been elected as social secretary.

Having left college Jim was constantly broke and eventually found a job, this time in the art world. The Garden Gallery was a small independent gallery just off the New Cross Road at 26 Monson Road. There was not much culture in this particular area, unless one included Millwall football ground on nearby Cold Blow Lane. Jim's rooms were covered with examples of his art, and now seemed to be the best time to start to sell some. The money would be handy and the public showing might help him get some wider exposure for his art as well. It was also quite a handy contact to have because Jim and John's band were able to rehearse in the basement.

Gordon Gapper, who ran the Garden Gallery with his wife Jo, had come across Jim's work in a local free newspaper, *The Telegraph*. They decided to take Jim on as a gallery assistant and he set about persuading them to let him have an exhibition. Although Gordon knew Jim was talented, it was only when he went to his house that he realized he had enough work for an exhibition. When Test Department had started to take up all of his time, Brett Turnbull had given Jim his old paints and Jim had certainly been busy with them. 'His work had a definite style,' remembers Gapper. 'He was technically very capable and could mimic any style. He would have been a great forger.' He was certainly a better painter than a curator. He used sit on a chair with wheels on the legs and he kept rolling over other people's work

Gordon helped Jim apply for a £150 grant from Lewisham Council so that Jim could put together an exhibition. In the autumn of 1985 the gallery mounted Jim's show. The pictures were priced at around £30 each and they quickly sold out. Lucie's friends bought a lot, Glenn Tilbrook's wife bought some. The exhibition was a success, even though Gordon and Jo thought the subject matter was rather strange. 'It all seemed to be based around large, overweight pigs,' says Jo Gapper. 'But there was no theme to it, except that everything he did had a twist. It was very bizarre, very *Monty Pythony*. There was one picture based on *Thunderbirds*, but it wasn't what you would have expected. The poster for the exhibition was a reclining figure, but just when you thought it was going to be a man, Jim drew a Medusa's head on it and added a brick dropping out the sky.'

In the early Eighties the comedy scene had undergone a similar revolution to that of the music scene in the wake of punk rock. Soho's Comedy Store played host to a succession of young humourists who believed they could be funny and become stars without slogging their way through endless summer seasons at Butlins in the hope that they might one day get a spot on *Opportunity Knocks*. Rik Mayall, Adrian Edmondson, Nigel Planer, Peter Richardson, Alexei Sayle, Dawn French and Jennifer Saunders had knocked down some barriers, and with the help of Channel 4, which had been launched in 1982 with a remit to provide an alternative to the other TV networks, were becoming youth icons. The BBC had soon wanted a piece of the success and while Channel 4 had signed up the Comic Strip to make short films for them, BBC2 notched up a significant cult hit with *The Young Ones*.

Tom Fawcett recalls an early attempt at humour from Jim in 1984 which didn't bode very well. 'I remember one night there was a cabaret event at Goldsmiths' Union and he said, "Come down, I'm going to do something." It was the first time he had done anything to do with stand-up, and unfortunately we polished off a bottle of whiskey between us and by the time he went on with his acoustic guitar he had decided that the audience was so stupid all he had to do was get on stage and say "pig". That's what he did repeatedly, and people didn't like it very much.'

In the same way that his bands had perversely changed names to preserve their anonymity, Jim opted for a different *nom de guerre* when he entered the world of comedy at the Parrot Café at the Goldsmiths

Tavern on the New Cross Road in December 1985. Among other candidates for names, he briefly toyed with the idea of reviving Jim Bell the poet. On another occasion John Irvine recalls him calling himself Mr Mystery and reading poems wearing a false beard and wig, trying to look like Alan Ginsberg. As 1985 was turning into 1986, Jim Moir was about to turn into Vic Reeves.

The music, however, seemed to be going nowhere, and eventually Jim decided to get some personal exposure by becoming more of an entrepreneur. In 1986 he started running a club night at Winstons, a wine bar in Deptford, on the corner of Armada Street and McMillan Street, a backwater between the Thames and Jim's latest flat with John Irvine on the Crossfields Estate. It was in a decidedly rough part of town. The Japanese owners used to keep a baseball bat behind the bar for when things got out of hand. As Jim told the *Mail* in 1991: 'It was the sort of place where regulars came in with car aerials so they could whip people they did not like.' It was a small, unattractive, poky venue, but it seemed a reasonable enough place to start a Seventies disco.

Even making the most of the effective Greenwich grapevine, Winstons wasn't a great success. Friends loyally turned up, but it was too far off the beaten track to attract a substantial following. Jim tried various esoteric concepts to try to make it work, but each one seemed more *outré* and inaccessible than the last. When Seventies kitsch failed, he tried a classical music disco. He even tried a Gregorian chants night. The budget wouldn't stretch to live music. Eventually the only option left was a newfangled concept called a comedy night.

Fawcett and Moir started to lose touch, but one day in 1986 Tom had a message that Jim was setting up a club: 'He wanted my help with the music, but I didn't have his phone number because he had moved so many times. I couldn't track him down, and he probably thought, "You bastard, you can't even be bothered to phone back." Pretty soon after that it started to take off. I still kick myself that I couldn't phone him back.'

Jim Moir had always been able to make people laugh, and suddenly the opportunity to do it on a more professional basis would come about, almost by accident. Jim, now working on his own and oblivious to the live comedy boom, could not afford to book any acts for Winstons. In fact, when it came down to it, he didn't even know where to go to book acts if he could raise the money. Some people auditioned, but he knew enough to know that they were awful. The only solution was to perform himself. Jim had no idea what the current trends in comedy were. He knew *Python* and Milligan and *The Young Ones*, but, luckily for him, the militant political humour of Ben Elton was a mystery to him. He had no alternative but to invent his own comedy persona. It came as a surprise to Dorian Crook: 'It did seem a bit of a shift. We didn't have much knowledge of comedy, and it seemed like a bit of a gamble the first time he did it.'

To John Irvine, however, it didn't seem like a shift at all. 'Jim's music always was comedy. If you listen to the old tapes it was just a daft backing track and him improvising with words. He is very good when let loose and on a roll. He used to do a spiel in the form of character on top of a lot of noise, and his early comedy gigs were really that. Stuff would splurge out of him which you couldn't believe.' Irvine thinks that is one of the things that people who see Vic Reeves only on television miss: 'Directors and producers agreed it was scripted to the detriment of Jim.'

Don't ever ask comedians if they've ever had a bad gig. They all have. I recently put this question to *Jonathan Creek* star Alan Davies and he sarcastically replied: 'No, I've been a comic genius ever since I first set foot onstage.' Jim Moir is atypically candid about his early comedy efforts. Vic Reeves Variety Palladium started at Winstons in June 1986. 'I was shit,' he recalls. 'Through an entire lack of pride I didn't give a fuck about what people thought, but they seemed to like it. I was only going to do one night, so I thought up the name of Vic Reeves.' Some of his friends, who had always found it easy to laugh at Jim in the bar, had mixed feelings about new stand-up comic Vic Reeves. But, once again, he had certainly made an effort. He handed out home-made cut-out masks of Sylvester Stallone to members of the audience to wear while he was preparing the next section of his act. He tried to balance a carrot on the end of a stick.

Things were fairly primitive at this stage. But Jim managed to carry it off simply because he really didn't care. People paid their pound to get in, and it was up to them to take it or leave it. Most of them left it, and there was violence too. Someone threw a chair. Jim threw it back. This was not so much an early review, more a consequence of mixing alcohol and Deptford's colourful population. He may not have been too pleased with the first show, but Jim was quietly determined, and ended up doing six weeks at Winstons, despite more violence. One night there was a siege at the venue, and Jim, John Irvine and their friends could not get out until the police intervened.

The humour didn't seem to fit into any easy category. Was it music hall? Was it alternative? What the hell was it all about? Tommy Cooper had appeared at Deptford's Albany Empire in 1984 and his one-liners seemed to be an influence. Tom Fawcett, who had seen Jim mature during his London years, saw the strong connection with Jim's artistic side: 'He wasn't inspired by the Comedy Store, he was much more arthouse. I think he wanted ultimately to be taken seriously. I always thought he saw the thing in a Warholian sense, with happenings, nights that involved everything.' At the Parrot Café, dancers from the Laban Centre and art students could attempt anything from ironic country and western to surrealist poetry. At times it had seemed as if Jim was the only person at the Parrot Café who wasn't an art student. He always seemed slightly apart from everyone else there, doing his turn and then heading to the bar on his own or simply leaving. Warholian music hall seemed to be Jim's destiny. As Fawcett concludes, 'He couldn't get away from the fact that ultimately he was always funny.'

One of the few people in the tiny audience at Winstons that August who did appreciate the madness onstage was Glenn Tilbrook, the singer/songwriter of local band Squeeze. Tilbrook was there to celebrate his birthday with another local resident, the band's pianist Jools Holland. Jim Moir had always been on the fringes of the celebrity world. He was about to start the long march to the centre. Holland was particularly impressed with the way Jim got everyone to hum the theme from *Star Trek*, while Tilbrook got onstage and played a cardboard keyboard and mimed to 'Tie A Yellow Ribbon Round The Old Oak Tree'.

As with everything else Jim had ever done, there seemed to be a great sense of occasion whenever he mounted his own comedy shows. He would spend endless days preparing props and gadgets in his kitchen, and the show would be the highlight of his week. He dubbed himself 'the north-east's top light entertainer' and while there seemed to be an irony to the title, it also seemed to fit him perfectly. Though of course, when one thought about it, it was hard to think of a current star who was clearly from the north-east. Television comedy was dominated by cockneys, Mancunians and Liverpudlians. Unless they featured James Bolam, TV sitcoms seemed to give the north-east a wide berth.

This was one of the factors that helped Jim to attract an audience. The distinctive accent drew in fellow exiles. They also identified with what Jim calls the typical north-eastern sense of humour – 'taking something very trivial and taking it very seriously'. People from Darlington had such a soft, concerned accent that southerners often couldn't tell whether they were sending you up when they asked, for instance, how you were. Combining the accent with smart bright suits and his newly slicked back hair, Jim Moir straddled a thin line between ironic future icon and colour-blind travelling carpet salesman.

Winstons wasn't popular just because of Jim's appearances there, recalls Crook: 'People could go there for a late-night drink, which kind of worked against having decent comedy on. Apart from the staff and Jim and his mates, the rest of the audience was south London boozers wondering what the hell was going on while Jim balanced carrots on a stick or somebody played a Moog organ made out of cardboard.'

Concentrating full-time on his shows, Jim went on to the Enterprise Allowance scheme, even opening a bank account in the name of Vic Reeves, so that he could pay his mates their wages when they did spots. Marijne van der Vlugt, who later fronted the band Salad, did a duet with Dorian Crook, impersonating Peters and Lee. Salad's guitarist Paul Kennedy who had been in Hot Murder also had a bash at comedy. No one took things very seriously, and as a result everyone had a lot of fun. If you got chatting to Jim in the pub and you seemed funny, the following week you could get up onstage.

The Allowance Scheme was the Tory government's latest ploy to keep the unemployment figures down. Instead of claiming benefit, young entrepreneurs could apply to this scheme, which meant that they came off the dole queue, received forty pounds a week and didn't have to forgo any of this if they earned money through their nascent business ventures. In other words, it meant that people who had previously been signing on and working at the same time could now do the same thing legitimately – in turn the government would appear to be getting people back into employment as the number of dole-claimants went down.

Eventually the residency at Winstons came to an end. Vic had not been an overnight sensation, but Jim decided that it had enough promise to be worth sticking at. If nothing else, the shows were a fun-packed creative variant on just sitting round a pub table with his mates, attempting to be funny. As John Irvine puts it: 'It became a competition to see who could come up with the daftest ideas.' Jim contacted the Goldsmiths Tavern at 316 New Cross Road, where he had done his early gigs, and booked Thursday evenings for a show which he christened the *Big Night Out*.

Over a decade on, the main thing Jim Moir remembers about the shows at the Goldsmiths Tavern is that they were 'very Hogarthian'. Images of sawdust, vagabonds and Gin Alley spring to mind, and while the scene wasn't quite as debauched as that, there was definitely something earthy about those shows: 'It was a great night out, instead of just sitting in the pub. The funny thing is I saw a video of a bit of the show recently and the thing that strikes you is that no one in the audience is fucking watching it.'

It was at the Goldsmiths Tavern that I first saw Vic Reeves. Jim is right that it was a great night out. There was a genuine feeling that what one was about to witness was like nothing on the comedy circuit or on television at the time. There was a genuine thrill of being in on something very special. It wasn't just the fact that Vic performed a whole show, where most comedians did a twenty-minute spot. It wasn't the fact that he did a different set every week, where others were endlessly dragging the same routine around the country. The humour of Vic Reeves seemed to tap into a demographic that had been weened on a diet of television and punk rock. In fact the comparison that comes up when speaking to others who were there is that seeing the live *Big Night Out* was like seeing the Sex Pistols before they signed their recording contract.

The references seemed to be instinctively right. And when they weren't, they were just plain odd. At one point there was a fish tank with two cabbages on the stage. During the evening Vic would leave, ostensibly to sort something out backstage, and with the aid of hidden microphones and speakers, the cabbages would start talking. In a similar vein he produced a paper plate on which the Beatles sat in miniature. When he lifted a handkerchief that was covering them, a Lennon and McCartney song emerged from the venue's speakers. One of the weirdest acts was Jim himself as Dr Heinz Mindpeeler, a man who could 'peel back your mind' and read it with the aid of his 'all-seeing egg'.

While the Goldsmiths Tavern had seemed like a good venue at the time, problems soon emerged. The pub had a late drinks licence for the Thursday night show. While the devotees would arrive early to be sure of a seat, as the bell for last orders rang in the main bar, the pub's clientele would also decide to pay an extra £1.50 for the chance of an extra couple of late-night pints.

What these new arrivals didn't expect was the sight of a man at a lectern, togged up in dandy ruffs, conducting a bizarre parody of a light entertainment show. Other elements were hardly likely to reassure the casual observer. There was the cardigan-wearing, pipe-smoking Brooke Turner, the transatlantic man whose theme tune was 'Easy Listening Man'. There was another character dressed in cricket whites who would wander on to the stage and then wander off again. Alan King, a local friend from Middlesbrough, would come on, having been introduced as Jean-Michel Jarre, and would produce two torches and a miner's helmet, in a feeble attempt at replicating the French keyboard wizard's light show. Another time he came on as Dr King and his Flying Mallets, swinging a string around his head and crying, 'Look at him go. Hey Kes! Look at him go.' King could be as funny as Jim, but wasn't as ambitious. He was once asked to write topical jokes for Terry Wogan and produced one-liners about the jungle. When the director asked him why, he said, 'I thought you said tropical jokes.'

By this stage the original Fashionable Five had begun to disperse. John helped out with tapes, but Graham had gone back to Darlington, Rob was at college and Jack was in the process of returning to the north. Jim's activities in south London meant that he now had a new network of friends to help him out. Dorian Crook became a regular performer during this run. Jim needed someone to go onstage and fill in during a costume change. They had the idea of the Toff, a stand-up comedian who was posh and drunk. Crook had a fairly regal bearing anyway – he just had to add a glass of brandy and a purple nose. The first time he went on he was planning to do some jokes, but Jim came back and said 'Fuck off, toff.' It was one of those lines that caught on very quickly. The audience would promptly shout it whenever Crook appeared in character, and he never got to tell any jokes. It was something of a mixed blessing for Crook. On the one hand it meant that he didn't ever have to prepare any material; on the other hand, the expletive nature of his passive catchphrase meant that his integral part of the live show could not be transferred on to television, and he missed out on his big break.

At this stage, though, no one seriously believed that this different kind of comedy could ever transfer to television anyway. Cath Lanham, who met Jim at the Parrot Café, recalls him telling her that his parents were still waiting for him to get a proper job. 'He did talk about TV, and said that if he ever had a show he would like his first guest to be Jack Hargreaves, the presenter of *Out of Town*. He seemed more interested in farm animals than showbusiness.'

Chapter Three

Big Nights Out With Bob

Bob Mortimer first saw Jim Moir in action at the first night at the Goldsmiths Tavern. He was more interested in contemporary comedy than Jim – although he had never considered performing – but only got round to going to see him after he had split up with his girlfriend and was virtually dragged along by Alan King, who he had been at school with in Middlesbrough. When Bob had gone off to university and then qualified as a solicitor they had drifted apart, but now, both based in south London, they renewed their friendship. Bob was feeling particularly low. He had been homeless for a while and had ended up living in a hostel in north Peckham. In the room next door a disturbed tenant used to hoard hand grenades. One night a suspicious fire virtually gutted the building. It all felt a bit like being a student again, only worse, and what made it even more depressing was that he was approaching thirty.

There were still only about twelve people in the audience when Bob first saw Jim's act in autumn 1986, but he was hooked. He was particularly impressed by Jim's Tappy Lappy, the northern tap dancer wearing a Bryan Ferry mask and wooden planks on his feet and dancing to easy-listening music. Jim's rendition of 'Fly me to the Moon' added to the magic. The joke had come about because the Parrot Café had once featured a tap dancer, but the stage was so low that no one could see their feet. With planks as shoes, no one could miss them this time round. 'Tappy Lappy' was a northern phrase meaning carefree and the *Big Night Out* was about as carefree as comedy got.

The Bryan Ferry connection may not have been completely coincidental. Ferry was also from the north-east: he was a miner's son, and, like Jim, had a fondness for the fine arts. Ferry had been fortunate enough to go to art school in Newcastle. He had also been taught by Mark Lancaster, who had worked with Andy Warhol on his Marilyn Monroe pictures. Ferry was a link between the New York pop art scene and the north-east of England. Reeves' early shows had that touch of Warhol about them too: the Goldsmiths Tavern performances were more like happenings at Warhol's Factory than the usual worthy line-up of Thatcher-baiters one had become accustomed to on London's alternative cabaret circuit. And, funnily, Nick De Ville, who designed Roxy Music's record sleeves, taught at Goldsmiths' College.

The similarities didn't end there. It is even possible to trace a through-line from Ferry's music to the comedy of Vic Reeves. Simon Frith and Howard Horne, writing in the book *Art into Pop*, pointed to the way Ferry had incorporated references to popular culture in his lyrics: he used 'throwaway clichés and amusing phrases that you found in magazines or used in everyday speech – stylistic justapositions'. The title of Roxy Music's first single, meanwhile, 'Virginia Plain', had been the name of a brand of cigarettes. Vic Reeves also had a habit of dropping brand names into his work, though in his case it was more likely to be Spiller's Dog Food.

Bob and Jim quickly became good friends as they found they had a lot in common with each other. Middlesbrough, Bob's home town, was about twelve miles away from Darlington; both had somehow found themselves in south London. Bob was born, at home in Tollesby Road, Robert Renwick Mortimer on 23 May 1959, making him just four months younger than Jim. They were both passsionate about music. The only significant difference seemed to be Bob's unbending faith in Middlesbrough FC, whereas Jim had steered clear of soccer for most of his life; when his school mates had been playing football, he had been making tapes of Anne Nightingale's radio show in his bedroom.

But there were clear differences in personality. Bob seemed more open and friendly, whereas Jim could be diffident and obscure. But this, again, would be to judge things by superficial appearances. In the same way that there has been an in-joke in recent years that Bob is the funny one and Jim is the straight man, so there is a case to be made for Bob being the weird one and Jim being the conventional one. If Jim has a vivid imagination, Bob, at times, seemed to live in a complete fantasy world, concocting stories for the sheer hell of it.

Bob's family background was very different from Jim's. Bob was the youngest of four brothers, and his father Charles, at times a sales rep for a paper company and later a biscuit saleman, died in a car crash when he was less than ten. Apart from those quite crucial differences, however, their upbringing seems remarkably similar. In fact there are periods when their youthful activities seem to converge so narrowly that one begins to wonder if they are actually two different people.

Like Jim, Bob's family was close. With his mother Eunice back at work and bringing them up on her own, times were tough, but not that tough. One year she had told her sons that they wouldn't be getting a Christmas present because money was tight. On Christmas day she unveiled a snooker table, which was a brilliant surprise because they had resigned themselves to not getting anything. It was a supportive, sharing household that, having coped with the trauma of a death, could now cope with any hardship.

Like Jim, Bob also grew up with a keen interest in Second World War aeroplanes. He can remember going to the cinema to see *The Battle of Britain* and overhearing someone else pretending they knew about Messerschmitts when they clearly did not. And they both claim to have had awkward moments with early girfriends. Jim had played too much Hendrix to his, while Bob didn't know what to do with his first girlfriend Briony Richardson. He says he lay like a board on top of her for five minutes 'and then went home'. And of course they had *Monty Python* in common. For most schoolchildren of their age, Thursday nights on BBC2 were something of a ritual, as was reciting the previous night's highlights in the playground the following morning. In this respect, of course, Jim and Bob were no different from a million other adolescents.

Keith Bridgewood met Bob at Acklam School when they were thirteen. They were seated next to each other and have been best friends ever since. Keith, who is now a sculptor, doesn't recall any defining moment that told him Bob had a future in comedy. 'We just had a laugh and we have done ever since. He probably became a comedian because he didn't like getting up in the morning and preparing for his court cases.'

Keith thinks that without Jim, Bob might well still be pursuing a career in law: 'He was a good solicitor and he still enjoys it. Given half a chance he will still talk about the law and suing people.' What is most notable about Bob is that he comes from a family of high achievers. Two brothers were also solicitors and another brother was a printer and ended up owning the printing company.

Bill Whittingham taught Bob in the sixth form. He remembers him as funny, but very much a team player. 'It was never a case of "Let's sit back and admire Bob's brilliant repartee."' The subjects Whittingham taught Bob – then known as Robert – were government politics and sociology, which were quite new subjects at the time. He also did history and left with three A-levels. The school was very different from Jim's Eastbourne College; while the latter had changed from a secondary modern to a comprehensive in the early Seventies, this had made the transition to comprehensive from grammar school. The sixth form college, now part of Middlesbrough College, was an eighteenth-century manor house in its own grounds, and there was a gentle, relaxed air to the place. It was only a brisk twenty-minute walk to Middlesbrough's Ayresome Park ground, and Bob and his friends would all be regular supporters at a time when soccer violence was a regular weekly occurrence. Bob always went to see Middlesbrough play. 'We'd look in the papers to see how many arrests there had been as well as the results,' says Keith. Bob was a fanatical fan. At one local derby against Sunderland there were about seventy arrests and Bob and Keith were lucky not to get involved. Keith remembers him being proud of starting off some rhythmic clapping that spread throughout the stadium.

Bob was a keen footballer at school and even had trials for the Middlesbrough boys' team. Keith recalls that he 'looked like a good footballer, he was stocky and looked like a little sprinter. He could run fast and take people on. He did have a very good slide tackle, where he would slide in and hook away the ball. He could be tough too – if he didn't get the ball he took them out.' Bob himself claims that Peter Beardsley stole his technique for lying down on the ball so that his unsuspecting opponent would trip over him.

Bob made his academic mark very quickly: 'He was very good at political analysis,' says Bill Whittingham. 'Within a very short time he could understand ideas; he cut through things like a knife through butter and he was a hard and conscientious worker. But he could be pretty inscrutable too and didn't let on about his ambitions.' He could also be a joker; if not the ringleader certainly one of the mischief-makers. One famous complex stunt involved a group of boys hiding a tape recorder above a classroom's polystyrene tiles. They turned the tape on before the class began, and as the lesson went on a buzzing sound got louder and louder, but no one could quite work out where it was coming from. Suddenly there would be some shouting on the tape. According to Bill Whittingham it contained some 'unacademic words'. According to Bob, a voice on the tape cried: 'Cunt, fuck off, get off you cunt'. It was a remarkably sophisticated piece of humour backed up by some earthy coarseness. (It was even used again in the second series of *Shooting Stars*. A fly could be heard buzzing in the studio, but instead of swearing erupting, Mark Lamarr swallowed it.) Some of the elaborate stunts were definitely Bob's ideas. Keith recalls that when they were in the sixth form they set up a lunchtime origami class, putting up notices advertising it. 'All these young kids came along and we handed out some paper, but we didn't have a clue what to do ourselves. We just took turns to fold it and didn't have the slightest idea what we were making. It was all very funny.'

Another joke was so weird that to this day Bill Whittingham doesn't understand it: 'I walked into a classroom one morning for the government politics class and Robert and another boy were perched on top of a wardrobe, about five foot high, just rocking gently. I've got no idea why they wanted to get up there.' Bob's own elementary explanation seems the most sound: 'We just used to do whatever came into our heads for a laugh.'

From very early on Bob was clearly a deep and original thinker in both his work and his play. Keith Bridgewood remembers that one of their teachers always had a soft spot for Bob: 'One day she asked him to do a talk on something. He went to the blackboard and spoke about this rock festival that he had been to. He drew a sketch on the blackboard, showing where the stage was, where the campsite was, where the food was. And when he came back and sat down I said, "I didn't know you went to a festival," and he said, "I didn't." Telling stories was part of his make-up. He used to tell stories about how he used to live out in the country in a big house and how he used to come in to school on a special bus. But that's what being a kid is – don't pull it out of proportion.'

Yet in adult life Bob still retains this facility for fiction. Keith's friend Sally Adams recalls travelling up to Middlesbrough in the car with Bob: 'Whenever we pulled up he would look across at people in cars next to us and come up with complete stories about the people in the cars. He just had this ability to make things up and sound convincing.' As funny as he was though, the idea of Bob performing seemed strange to her: 'Later on he told me about the comedy club and said he helped out. I thought he meant that he swept up.' Onstage this facility can be a remarkable gift, allowing him, like Jim, to come up with convincing nonsense off-the-cuff. The world they created onstage was very much a fantasy world with the slimmest of toeholds on reality. It may well have also helped him in his legal profession, where confidence with words and economy with the truth can be vital. But it makes one wonder about some of the stories he has told about himself. Did he really inscribe 'Boro Boot Boys' on the side of Barclays Bank in Middlesbrough town centre? Sometimes it appears that this role-playing has led to the onstage character of Bob bleeding into the real-life Bob every bit as much as Jim has become Vic.

In the mid-Seventies Bob also got into hard rock in a serious way and while Jim was trying to model himself on Paul Kossoff of Free, Bob wanted to be Andy Fraser, the band's bass player who was from Middlesbrough. 'I tried desperately to look like Andy Fraser out of Free. I know it sounds stupid, but I bought the jumper he wore on *Free at Last*. He had big lips. Free were very big in the north-east,' remembers Bob. 'They always used to kick off their tours there and they had a residency near by.'

At one point he had a fashionable Afghan coat. Or at least he almost did. 'It was actually me mam's, but it looked a bit like an Afghan. I still got a kicking once when I was wearing it.'

'He was more a hippy than a skinhead,' explains Keith in reference to the rival youth factions in Middlesbrough at the time, 'though he used to change nearly every week.' In the mid-Seventies Bob grew his hair long and had a centre-parting. 'A well-groomed Andy Fraser look,' says Keith. With Keith and another friend on drums, Peter Harriman, who is now 'in fruit machines', Bob formed a band, Dog

Dirt, which used to thrash its way through some heavy rock covers. Later, when the punk influence filtered through, they used to do 'songs about breaking rules, rhyming things like Mars and scars', remembers Keith. He looks back fondly on their brief musical career together: 'Bob had good timing and played bass and sang. We'd play anywhere, people's gardens, church halls.' At first Bob and Keith had musical differences. Bob's tastes were always defiantly British, where Keith was a bit of a yankophile: 'He preferred Free and Rod Stewart, whereas I liked Santana, Chicago and Crosby, Stills and Nash.' During the school holidays Bob and Keith would hang around together. Every summer they would go off for weekends to Keswick in the Lake District. One of Bob's older brothers would drive them there and then they would set up their tent. Money was always tight and to fund their expeditions they got part-time work whenever possible. They could usually be sure of some casual work at Head Wrightsons, the steel foundry in nearby Thornaby. In the mid-Seventies Bob and Keith would take any work going, however menial. One summer they had to clean the dust off the lights so that the crane could move along smoothly. The work was tedious, but Bob and Keith put up with it by making sure they had a good laugh. One year they were taken on as painters and had great fun painting the pipe that led to the furnace bright yellow. It could be seen from outside the factory and on their way home from work they would sight it and, as a private joke, chime, 'There's our yellow pipe.' On another occasion Bob, Keith and another chum had to paint the floor of the boiler room. Having reached the door they suddenly realized they had missed a patch in the middle. As Bob was the smallest the other two decided to use him as a giant human paintbrush. They lifted him up by the corners of his boiler suit, got him to dip his brush in the paint and then held him over the remaining bare patch. It was a wholly impractical way of completing the task but it passed the time.

Bob worked as a dustman too, and they did painting and decorating, anything to make money. Like Jim, Bob also found himself working with animals at one point. A job in a chicken factory meant cleaning out the discarded guts, but when the time came for Bob to push the innards towards a huge hole in the middle of the floor his nerve failed him – he climbed out of a window and ran all the way home without stopping. In 1977 Bob went to study law at Sussex University; Keith went to Reading, but they used to meet up to go to gigs. 'He liked the Jam and was very keen on the Tom Robinson band when they had a hit with "2–4–6–8 Motorway", but he never wore the punk gear,' Keith recalls. 'Punk was the time when I left home so I really could indulge myself and behave like a twat. I wore a suedehead outfit for a laugh,' chuckles Bob. 'The bottom line was to attract girls.'

At Sussex Bob really got into the punk scene: 'That was really what I did all the time. I saw the Slits and the Clash and for some reason I kept seeing the Vibrators. But there always seemed to be a lot of violence. I saw Madness in the Cellar bar in Brighton, and there were about twenty skinheads, big lads, headbutting the fuck out of each other.'

While they were studying apart, Bob and Keith would regularly meet up in London at weekends to get the day return to Middlesbrough to see their team when they were playing at home. It was on those long journeys that Keith saw that Bob was developing an ever more oblique way of amusing himself. 'We would come back on the night train and we would pass the time by getting into the luggage racks. Once the train stopped between stations and we decided to climb out and get on the roof.' Keith points out another juvenile pastime which Bob spookily shared with Jim. Both seemed to be developing an identical sense of humour born out of a cocktail of boredom and booze. 'On the way to the match we would each buy a paper and then spend the time drawing Hitler moustaches on everyone and swap people's names in stories for "Hitler". At the end of the trip we would swap papers and have a good laugh at what we had done.'

After graduating, Bob went back to Middlesbrough. He then started to move around the country, studying welfare law in Leicester before starting to work and completing his qualifications in Wythenshawe, Manchester. By all accounts Bob was a very good solicitor. He was also extremely committed. Welfare law was the least lucrative form of litigation. He had studied extremely hard to qualify and most of the work he did was relatively poorly paid. It could also make him more than a little obsessive. Often after a hard day's work he would go to the pub to unwind and it would take a few pints before he could stop talking about his job. In the mid-Eighties he started to work for Philcox Gray at 92 Camberwell Road. Invariably he spent his days in Camberwell Magistrates Court just around the corner. He says he had a good acquittal rate, getting seventy per cent of his fifteen hundred cases off. But by the time he met Jim maybe he was ready for a change of direction. There was some talk that he was a little jaded with his job, which may have been to do with the fact that he felt that many of the people he got off were 'probably guilty'. If he was that good a speaker, maybe he could put it to another use on the stage.

By the mid-Eighties Bob had hooked up with Stevo Zivanovic, a wiry, charismatic Londoner. They ended up sharing a council flat behind Southwark Town Hall. It was a cramped one-bedroom flat, but with a bit of creativity the duo made it cosy. The main problem was that the bathroom was only accessible via the bedroom. This created difficulties when Bob had women staying in his room and Stevo needed the toilet in the night. One day, however, Bob had an idea. He suggested that they build a hatch to link the lavatory to the lounge. Together they hacked out the bricks, put a frame up and added a small door halfway up the wall: 'We wanted to hang a picture of a toilet on the front of it, so that when guests came round we could say we were just off to the toilet, lift the picture up and disappear, but we never got round to that,' laughs Stevo. Nevertheless, the hatch was a huge success and a talking point at parties. Bob would be sitting on the toilet and Stevo could poke his head through to say hello or pass him a cup of tea.

Stevo lived in the flat rent-free and in return tried to encourage Bob to look after himself, but it was hard going. 'All he would eat was black pudding and sausages and he used to have seventeen sugars in his tea. He could always tell if you had put in eighteen or sixteen spoonfulls.'

Bob always got on extremely well with Stevo and they could always be very funny together. But there was something different between Jim and Bob. As well as having the same set of cultural references they had the same sort of voice: 'I didn't have this wonderful Middlesbrough-Darlington accent,' observed Stevo. 'There was a certain surrealism to it. That was why they were so funny.' The Jim and Bob alliance was soon noticed by their drinking-mates. Fred Aylward, another member of the ensemble who came to prominence with the intellectually challenged, silent-as-Harpo Marx assistant Les, is reputed to have said to Jim: 'Eric, you've met your Ernie.'

It was quite an apposite observation. Many people would make the comparison in the ensuing years, and maybe the duo did seem to be unwittingly fulfilling a wish of the comedy duo. In their 1981 autobiography *Morecambe and Wise: There's No Answer to That* the veterans talked frankly about growing old. The workload was as heavy as ever, but they didn't want to retire. Ernie had a solution: 'It would be marvellous if we could find two fellows who are about twenty-one and look exactly like Eric and me, and then send them out on tour.' Ernie suggested a £50 fee, and Eric added, 'We'll also supply the train fares and the digs.' By the late Eighties, Eric Morecambe was dead. The need for a younger version was more pressing then ever.

For Bob things seemed to have come full circle. As a schoolboy he and his mates used to look forward all week to Thursday nights because it was the night that *Monty Python's Flying Circus* was on. Now they looked forward to Thursday nights because of *Big Night Out*. Bob's accommodation problems, and the fact that his day job was so demanding, meant that he began to live for those Thursday nights all over again. One week when he spoke to Keith on the telephone, he said: 'If you are coming down, come down on a Thursday. I'm going to go up onstage.' Keith laughed at Bob's plans to take part, but made sure that he would be there just in case he wasn't joking.

Keith felt that *Big Night Out* had the same sort of energy as the punk scene in the late Seventies: 'Nothing comes out of nothing. In the Seventies punk had been reacting against Bowie and the stuff that came before it. Jim seemed to be reacting against Ben Elton and that wave of comedy.' Eventually Keith met Jim too and was struck by the way he seemed to talk about different things from everybody else. 'I remember one time he just started talking about the fact that somebody owned the rights to a particular colour.'

Everybody who went to the *Big Night Out* was struck by the combination of energy, enthusiasm and free-flowing madness. This was largely down to the way that Jim structured it, according to John Irvine: 'Jim would write sketches, mostly with characters and a point, but in terms of dialogue he would make it completely up on the spot. I did sound effects on different tapes – I wanted a sampler but they cost £25,000 back then – and those were pegs around which he improvised, which was why it seemed so mad. That was his great talent. It was unplanned until he gave me the cue.'

It was only after watching the show for about six weeks that Bob plucked up the courage to perform himself – by this time word of mouth meant that the back room of the bar was full. Bob says his first act was to present Vic with a cheque for a million pounds 'in recognition of all the work he has done for the starving children of Africa'. Keith Bridgewood, however, suggests that Bob's first turn was in a legal capacity: 'He was called the Singing Lawyer at the time and his role was to repeal the rock laws.' At first his contributions seemed fairly spontaneous – he would come out of the audience to present Vic with a cup for 'being extra special' – but gradually he became more integrated into the performance. If observers thought that his post-Live Aid gag meant that Bob was about to inject an element of topical social satire into the act, they were quickly disabused of that notion. Bob's next addition was The Man with the Stick, a short northern man who would come on bearing a stick, his true identity concealed by illustrated headgear.

Guest acts had a habit of talking about subjects that they were vaguely familiar with. Dorian Crook, for instance, did a weather report in a so'wester because of his air traffic control background. Another time Jim asked him to pretend to be the inventor of the Hovercraft. Bob used to wear some pretty scruffy suits, but he could still adopt a fairly authoritative air, and one time at Malcolm Hardee's Tunnel Club in Mitre Road, near to the entrance of the Blackwell Tunnel, Jim got him to impersonate a Blackwall Tunnel security officer. They still hadn't come up with a good regular character for Bob, though they felt they had come close when Bob used to get up and talk about his work at the Camberwell Courts. Sitting around in John and Jim's flat in Deptford one night, Jim and Bob thought of something related to Bob's day job as a solicitor. The character of Judge Nutmeg was hardly based on any real judges at the Camberwell courts, but, rumour had it, Bob did play the part in his own robes that he wore when fighting for Southwark tenant's rights – 'He was hardly organized enough to spend the time looking for theatrical robes,' laughs an old colleague. Nutmeg would hand out the punishments dictated by the wheel of justice, which prompted two crucial catchphrases – 'Comb its hair' and 'Spin the wheel of justice'.

The catchphrase culture that developed was central to the show's growing popularity. There was a sense of community because the audience was encouraged to join in. Along with 'Very poor', 'What's on the end of the stick, Vic?' was one of the first lines that the audience could contribute. Alan King suggests that this enquiry was inspired by

Sesame Street: 'It was just a way of parroting any old comedy, it was hardly the kind of phrase that tripped off your tongue, but that seemed to work in its favour.' The Man with the Stick was perfect for Bob. Wearing a mask helped him cope with early nerves, and the illustrations on the helmet helped Jim remember his lines.

King was worried that certain catchphrases could be double-edged. If an audience member shouted out 'Very poor' at the wrong moment it could have a devastating effect on the atmosphere. 'But Jim had a technique of control and turning the phrases in his favour that very few other performers have.' The result was a heady cocktail of daftness, deftness and drunkenness. The secret of their success seemed to be a magical blend of not seeming to care and yet taking great pride in their performance. Each week they grew in confidence and produced a whole new show, a potty, potted history of light entertainment.

Having seen the show at Winstons, Jools Holland became both a fan and a friend. Jim had always been a snappy dresser, but Jools' style impressed him and as soon as he started to make some money he got his suits tailor-made by Sidney Charles at 36 Deptford High Street. Velvet collars and vents started to sprout and the *Big Night Out* took on a slicker, more professional appearance. Though not completely professional. As Jim freely admits today, 'We were invariably drunk when we did it.' As a result things did go wrong. On one occasion he accidentally set his hand on fire; on another, playing The Price Slasher, he literally slashed his hand open with a toy sword.

The friendship with Holland gave Jim's career what looked like a terrific boost in 1986 when Jools got him a spot on *The Tube*, the Channel 4 music programme that Holland used to record in Newcastle every week. Suspended on ropes, Reeves presented Square Celebrities, a very loose spoof of the ITV game show *Celebrity Squares* in which doors would open and minor celebrities would appear to answer inane, insane questions. It didn't quite work – possibly because he didn't yet have Bob's stabilizing presence – but it was a quantum leap in the right direction. 'Jim was suspended on wires and asked questions,' remembers Holland. 'He was always very good at asking questions, which is more important than answering them. It was quite a laborious process and lasted about twelve minutes. I can remember Malcolm Gerrie, the producer, saying there was no way Vic Reeves was worth twelve minutes of television time.'

For the first time Jim seemed to feel something really special was happening. He had an early chance to show off his new status when he had to go to Newcastle to do some filming on a Thursday that clashed with the *Big Night Out*. That night he had some flyers printed up that said that the show was presented by 'TV Personality' Vic Reeves. In fact it very nearly wasn't. He wasn't able to get to south London in time for the beginning of the show and in his absence Paul Kennedy had to fill in. When Jim did arrive he was proudly clutching that day's edition of the *Northern Mail* to show where he had just come from.

The Goldsmiths Tavern was Vic and Bob's equivalent of the Star Club, Hamburg. It was the place where they built up a tremendous sense that they could achieve *something*, not to mention a tremendous body of work. They appeared there almost every week for a year, sometimes on Thursdays and sometimes on Saturdays. The change of nights could sometimes result in an odd turn-out, because on the nights that they weren't on Goldsmiths was a gay pub. One night a transvestite who used to appear on other nights died a death appearing with Vic. Jim and John's phone number was listed in *Time Out*'s comedy section, enabling all sorts of oddballs to get a slot on the show: 'Jim would book anyone,' says John Irvine. 'If they were bad it made him look better.'

When not performing, the group seemed to shuttle between pubs in Deptford and the Grove House Tavern in Camberwell, close to Bob's flat. On Saturday afternoons they would often meet up in a café and cook up ideas. There was a strong retro feel about the gatherings, long before nostalgia became fashionable. Jim and Jools Holland had got into old motorbikes, forming the Gentleman's Motorcycle Club and having meetings in Jools' garage in Greenwich. Holland recalls how the club launched itself in style: 'We cut our thumbs and signed up in blood on a piece of blotting paper. It was the kind of organization where more effort went into the planning than the practice. It was rather pathetic. We only ever went on one rally, from my office to Greenwich [less than a mile] for an official dinner. Then it turned out somebody's light wasn't working and we went back. We decided to get a cab so that we could drink.' Around the same time Dorian Crook had bought an old Hillman Minx. Crook recalls that Jim threw himself into this new pastime with typical gusto: 'We would go to car rallies and never do things half-heartedly. Because it was a Sixties car we used to wear

Sixties suits and make a big day out of it. Went to a rally in Burford near Oxford. It was full of bearded men in Austins wearing jumpers and they took pictures of us because we stood out.' Jim made sure that even the soundtrack on the trip was authentic for the period they were attempting to evoke. 'We used to listen to his tapes of plinky-plonk Sixties music in the car because it was a kind of *Carry On* image. Jim never does anything half-heartedly.' Everything was an event for Jim. Later when he moved into his flat at IB Westgrove Lane in Blackheath he bought a black fez and used to have Black Fez nights. Jim and other men would gather, no women were allowed, cigars and wine were brought out and outrageous opinions were voiced.

With Bob in the show, however, things got ever more serious. Bob had a way of grounding Jim's more arcane flights of fancy in something resembling reality. There was more of a structure to the mayhem and less larking about. Bob helped Jim come up with ideas such as consumer testing products such as crisps. Bob particularly recalls a consumer test of fertilizer: 'We did the manure trials, didn't we? Different droppings from animals and you had to identify them. I remember very clearly one of those pictures from a butcher's that shows the different cuts of meat and I was supposed to be this professor of meat cuts and all that happened was Jim said "What's that bit?" and I said "That's the rump – isn't it?" which was quite clear for everyone to see.'

There was still a strong feeling that this was a family affair rather than a professional operation, even when rising celebrities started to turn up. As well as the Squeeze contingent, actor Tim Roth, who had lived nearby, came down. He ended up on stage one night, and Jim, worse for drink, followed him into the toilets and proceeded to harrass Roth at the urinal. Jack Dent was living in Leeds in 1988, but he would come down to London three Thursdays out of every four to see the show. 'I'd tell my friends I was going down to see a comedian called Vic Reeves. They said, "Never heard of him." I said, "You will."' Sometimes Dent would perform, too. In a nod to his own dodgy early Eighties clubbing past, he sometimes came on in a string vest and claimed to be a new romantic whose clothes had all been stolen. Everyone had a chance to do a turn. Their reputation spread. They were even booked to do a special wedding party at Goldsmiths in September 1988.

Even with Bob's stabilizing influence the shows were always strange, unpredictable affairs. At the Goldsmiths Tavern they were particularly ridiculous, because Vic's ideas were so grand and the venue was so small. One night he did an easy-listening duet with Ben Addison from punky pop group Boys Wonder. Jim joined his guest onstage to do a version of 'You Only Live Twice', but with Vic's lectern on one side of the stage and various props on the other, there was barely enough room for one of their stools, let alone two.

For a show that seemed incredibly haphazard and fuelled by alcohol, it was remarkably well put together. The show would start with John Irvine at the back cueing up James Last's *Swingtime* LP, the intro to 'I'm a Believer' would play and Jim would get his timing just right, walking to the microphone just in time to sing the first line. Jim's background meant that he was streetwise enough to handle anything the audience threw at him. Violence often erupted when it was least expected. One night a member of the hillbilly band that had been booked to play threw a guitar into the audience for no apparent reason and split someone's head open.

It would be nice to say that the causes of the fights were redolent of the punch-ups that greeted Picasso's first cubist exhibitions – great new art always provoking a violent response and all that – but it was probably more a case of too much Holsten Pils. Here it is worth noting a parallel with the evolution of punk rock. That scene was also marred by a glass-smashing incident at the 100 Club in Oxford Street, where the Sex Pistols had enjoyed a successful residency during the summer of 1976.

Jim and Bob now found themselves at the cutting edge of comedy, certainly a cult, but getting bigger by the week. This was an act that made the new wave of comedy seem like the old wave by simply recreating the spirit of a northern working men's club, where you got a meal, a singer and a comic in one evening. *Time Out* described it as 'not so much alternative cabaret, more a Butlins-type TV variety show'. Fortunately for Jim's career, what he was doing also looked remarkably like a ready-made television show.

While Jim and Bob were becoming established at the Goldsmiths Tavern, Jim also started working on his stand-up skills at the Rub-a-Dub Club on Thursday nights at the Greyhound Pub in Sydenham. After a few spots which went down quite well, the promoter, Simon

Palmer, who had played in a band called the Swinging Plonkers at the Parrot Café, offered Jim the job of compèring every week. It was only thirty pounds a night, but it would give Jim a chance to try out new material away from his usual fans. Or so he thought. A mark of Jim's growing popularity was the fact that soon after he started, in May 1988, the tiny back-room venue began to fill up with his New Cross acolytes. This meant that sometimes even very good visiting acts, including promising turns such as Frank Skinner, struggled. Most of the rising stars of the circuit came south of the river to the Rub-a-Dub Club, but, in a complete reversal of Jim's experiences outside south-east London, they often had a hard time. Mark Lamarr recalls comics talking about 'this fucking compère who cuts you off before you get on'.

There was a kind of symmetry to this strange regionalist phenomenon. Jim also did some dates at colleges in north London as part of a Rub-a-Dub Roadshow. Student unions could book three acts and Jim as compère for £175. One night at Imperial College, only Jim and Felix Dexter stayed around for the gig. Felix did his turn, then Jim, in typically provocative mood, spun things out alone to make absolutely sure that they were entitled to their fee. 'It was a catastrophe. He did a mammoth set to groans,' recalls Palmer.

Jim compèred at the Rub-a-Dub for over a year, growing in confidence all the time. Sometimes Bob would come along too. Often they just messed around, tapping into a collective juvenile unconscious and the post-modern obsession with trivia. Jim would peep through a crack in the wall, wondering if Nelson Mandela or some other major political figure was behind there and speculating on what he was up to. Out of these embryonic improvised pieces, parts of the *Big Night Out* would emerge. Palmer even thinks that Bob did The Man with the Stick for the first time at his club, after a session of larking about with a paper hat.

Sometimes the *Big Night Out* and the Rub-a-Dub overlapped and Jim couldn't fulfil both commitments. One week, though, he had a bright idea. In Simon Palmer's lounge one day they knocked up a tape so that it would sound as if he was introducing the acts live but via a telephone. 'The first satellite link at the Rub-a-Dub,' announced Vic, via a concealed cassette. Unfortunately during the gig Palmer forgot his feed lines before the taped segments: 'I came out with some nonsense, which made Jim sound even funnier.' With a classical orchestra in the background, Jim introduced the night's headliner following a preamble about melting cheese and balancing some beetroot on a piece of hardboard: 'Ladies and Gentlemen. He has very long, flowing, billowing hair and a tiny little beak – please pay attention to Nick Hancock.'

The Rub-a-Dub Club was odd at the best of times. I can remember seeing Jim introduce Jerry Sadowitz there. It was a very strange night indeed, with Reeves having to placate a crowd who were slightly unsettled by Sadowitz's twisted anti-political correctness routines. There was no denying that Sadowitz was clever, but the irony of his gags wasn't always clear. In a variant of an old racist joke, he used to ask the audience, 'How do you get eight Pakistanis in a Datsun?' His answer was, 'Fuck knows, but they manage it, don't they?' – which wasn't as offensive as the usual explanation of putting two in the front, two in the back and four in the ashtray, but was still skating on thin ice in front of a liberal audience.

Jim's *Tube* appearances hadn't led to anything directly, but he would soon find another influential patron. In early 1988 Jim had managed to find a new outlet for his creative talents, although he had to go all the way into the centre of London again. Gossips, in Meard Street, was one of Soho's longest established nightclubs. In the early Eighties the new romantic scene had suddenly made these ageing nighteries, formerly viewed as little more than pick-up joints, socially acceptable again. Young, business-minded entrepreneurs started to rent out rooms for one-night specials. Jim had got to know some of the people involved through a sharp young Londoner called Adam Ross. Adam was introduced to Jim by a friend who was the manager of Boys Wonder, the wannabee cool proto-Brit-pop band which included the twins Ben and Scott Addison, residents of Blackheath and occasional performers at the *Big Night Out*.

Adam liked Boys Wonder and had a band himself, called Loot after the Joe Orton play, and wanted to set up a club at Gossips called The Swag on Wednesday nights. 'The idea was for Loot to have the residency, but we changed shape and decided to add a Seventies retro night because we were playing the Sex Pistols and following it up with Barry White records. We wanted to get a bit of a scene going like the early days of punk.'

Darlington cemetary, 1976: Jim and Graham Bristow brave the winter cold. Jim's beloved striped blazer would see him through his heavy rock phase and well into his late '70s northern provincial punk mode. © Jack Dent

Jim (left), John Irvine (squatting) and and Rob Colbrook (right) with members of pomp rockers The Enid, at Redcar Coatham Bowl, 1977. Jim used to follow the band around and one night after a gig he ended up sleeping on the floor of their run-down Rolls Royce. © Jack Dent

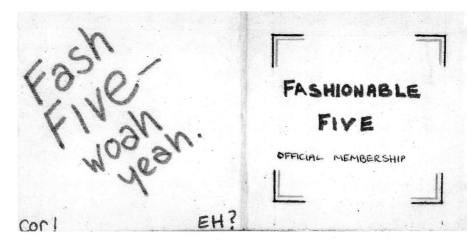

The Fashionable Five membership card. Holders of this card felt that they were members of one of Darlington's most élite clubs. With only a quintet of members it was certainly one of the smallest. © Jack Dent

The Official Fashionable Five Salute. The original line-up left to right: Jack Dent, Rob Colbrook, Graham Bristow, Jim Moir, John Irvine. © Jack Dent

Left 1978. *That* car coat. Jim's taste in clothes always set him apart from his friends. When the others wore jeans and leather gear for gigs, he turned up in a coat that his father might have worn, and looked more like Sid James than someone on the cutting edge of style. © Jack Dent

Below Darlington City Centre. By 1978 Jim had succumbed to a shorter haircut and in keeping with the standard pose of punk times, had taken to wearing drainpipe jeans and leaning aimlessly against furniture shop windows. © Jack Dent

Brixton, summer, 1979. 67 Arodene Road, SW2, Jim's bedroom. Newly settled in London, Jim revelled in the freedom and started to toy with different looks. This Gallic one didn't quite catch on. © Jack Dent

Brixton, Christmas 1979. The Fashionable Five's first Christmas away from home. The group went out and bought as much of the cheapest lager as they could find and afford. Hi-jinx ensued and Jim ended up decorating his face with burnt cork. © Jack Dent

Dig Me I'm Django, 1980. An early gig back in the north, with Jim on saxophone and Jack Dent in the background. An early review in the Middlesbrough fanzine *Jesus Idiot* was fairly scathing about Jim: 'I think the sax player looks like a frog when he blows out his cheeks.' Prophetically the review also decribed Jim's dancing as 'hilarious'. © Jack Dent

Left Sing Hi! The New Romantic, Notting Hill, Summer 1981. Jim has always had a habit of homing in on celebrities. At a party at the Notting Hill Carnival he hooked up with Phillip Salon, the new romantic club-runner and early mentor of Boy George, who had been to one of Jim's parties in Brixton.
© William Wilding

Right Crystal Palace Park, 1981. With distressed denim and 'hard times' chic dominating the style press, Jim does it the budget way, donning Oxfam threads and opting for the Polish peasant look.
© Jack Dent

Bob and Middlesbrough chum Keith 'Kags' Bridgewood larking about in photo-booths 1977/78. © Keith Bridgewood

Above Nick Cave meets Edna Everage 1983. © John Irvine

Above right Bob playing the fool with objects stuffed down his trousers, Caversham near Reading, 1978. © Keith Bridgewood

Bob at his mother's house in Tollesbey Road, 1979. Billy the cat was noted for his ability to stand on his back legs. Bob's mocassins were a well-kept secret. © Keith Bridgewood, 1977

Bob revisiting the derelict remains of Head Wrightsons, the steel foundry in Thornaby where he worked before going to university, 1979. © Keith Bridgewood.

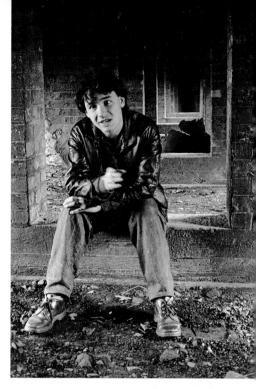

Bob on Alpine Expedition, 1980. Actually a café in Brighton during his Sussex University days. © Keith Bridgewood

Adam Ross can still remember being told about 'this bloke who sings Rod Stewart songs with a horse brass round his neck', and being introduced to Jim in the Hawley Arms pub in Camden Town. 'He looked like a scruffy student then, but you could tell he had style because another time he turned up wearing tweeds and a flat cap like a country gent.' Jim agreed to do some DJing at the club, says Adam: 'He was so enthusiastic about getting up with all these props. He had an old furry wheel that he would spin. In the first weeks we stormed it. Then things started to tail off. Wednesdays was the worst night of the week. Most weeks I didn't pay him so I felt a bit bad that he had brought all these props and records.'

The Swag was an opportunity for Jim to take some risks, says Adam: 'A lot of the material was stuff you saw on TV. He liked the place because he could do what he liked. It was far more beneficial for him than us. When he was on there was a great atmosphere, a buzz in the air that something was happening.'

In a way that would be typical of his ventures in later years, Jim made a special effort to make the club feel like a real event, putting 110 per cent into the preparation and teasing punters with the promise of big stars: 'I used to hire lookalikes to sit in the corners so that it would seem as if there were real celebrities. People would come in and see Arnold Schwarzenegger there.' Jim, decked out in a denim jacket covered in horse brasses, also brought his own records along. By now he had built up a huge collection of naff early Seventies pop, and would take great pleasure in regaling punters with the *Greatest Hits of Clodagh Rodgers*, picked up in Deptford market for ten pence. Other albums contained Hammond organ instrumentals. Jim would put them on and – prefiguring the karaoke boom – invite the audience up to provide the vocal accompaniment. One night only seven people turned up, but they were Japanese, so they seemed to appreciate the singalong tapes.

Adam got to know Jim and they used to go to parties together and get stoned. But there was always a guarded side to Jim. Adam was shocked when he realized how old he and Bob were – they were hardly ancient, but they were pushing thirty when many clubbers were only just into their twenties. It wasn't exactly a generation gap, but it did make a difference when people were choosing what music to put on at parties: 'I can remember Jim in the back room at one party giving it the full monty to Bad Company.'

Jim soon realized that Adam's brother was Jonathan Ross, who was rapidly making a name for himself with the Channel 4 series *The Last Resort with Jonathan Ross*, and was keen to meet him. Adam asked Jonathan to come down to the club and see this strange performer – half DJ, half comedian – but things didn't quite work out. 'Eventually I pulled out, and one night Jim turned up and they said I wasn't doing it any more, so he picked up his bags and went home. And that was the night that Jonathan turned up.'

Jonathan Ross recalls Adam telling him about Jim because he thought Jim's sense of humour was in tune with Jonathan's fondness for the trivial and the bizarre. He also showed Jonathan a plate with one of Jim's intricate yet childlike paintings of Elvis Presley on it. 'Adam said he's a really strange fella who loves early rock and wears a horse brass around his neck and comes out and does full-on rock posturing. So we met up at a Japanese restaurant in Brewer Street. It was a strange meeting. I liked him immediately and I think he liked me, but was quite wary of me. I didn't know he had done any performing. I looked at his pictures of Elvis Presley. He asked for ten pounds for each and I said, "Don't be stupid." It was a bit condescending and gauche but I gave him a hundred for each of them and later commissioned one of Bruce Forsyth and one of Ronnie Corbett. He seemed quite pleased for the cash. I said, "You should try performing", not knowing he was already doing a fully formed show and had more ideas than I had ever had in my life.'

Eventually Jonathan did get to see Jim perform, in March 1988, but after three months The Swag was in free-fall: 'I went down with my wife and there was about four people there. They all looked like secretaries. Jim was DJing, oblivious to the lack of crowd. At one stage he stopped the music, put on a backing track, came to the front of the stage and sang "Thunderball". People were completely bemused.'

Jonathan invited Jim to appear on his TV show, a themed edition based around a country fayre. Jim's role was to talk about his funny-shaped vegetables. After dreaming of having Jack Hargreaves as his own guest, he now seemed to be impersonating Hargreaves himself, incorporating him into one of his old routines. 'He did Silas Proudharvest the farmer and died on his arse. It was a very strange show, but I was delighted to have him on. I knew he would be huge if he wanted to be, but he didn't seem to have a fierce desire to do stuff, he was happy to do bits that he was doing. Backstage after the show someone said, "It was shit tonight. That farmer was useless. The only thing that saved him was the cucumber flute.'"

Undaunted, Jim seemed happy to have another bash on *The Last Resort*, as Ross recalls: 'Then he did something as Leslie Cooper – he always like traditional English names. We wanted to have a street artist and had been looking for someone but could never find someone bad enough. I told Jim and he said, "I'll do it." He painted Malcolm McLaren's face on a plate and did pictures of the other guests, but at the end members of the audience rushed up and grabbed the plates and they all disappeared.'

While Jim was moonlighting, Bob, displaying characteristic shrewdness, had continued with his day job. He had started out extremely committed to social justice, but by now any residual glamour had all but evaporated, and it seemed to be a job that he was doing purely for the security until something better came along. He later talked to journalist Carol Sarler about his day job: 'When you're working in Peckham doing legal aid divorce cases, housing and criminal law, you've always got half an eye on what you'll do next, because it is exhausting and badly paid.' It did have its heroic moments, though, and it got Bob into the papers long before his TV success. On 4 March 1988 a large feature in the *South London Press* reported that Robert Mortimer had been victorious in winning a case against Southwark Council over cockroach infestation.

The story said that in one night an unnamed mother had trapped over six hundred bugs in the kitchen of her ground-floor flat. With Bob's help, she took Southwark Council to court and the council had finally admitted a public health offence at Camberwell Court. The *South London Press* had clearly got the bit between its teeth. The following Friday it followed up the initial story of the unnamed mother of three's five-year campaign with 'Battle of the Bugs' – a full-page feature on the plague, which included an interview with one of the men from Rentokil, another with Dave Clark, a London zoo entomologist who said that 'as far as I'm concerned cockroaches are great', and an update on the latest technology being used to eradicate the problem – apparently endemic in south London. But the main part of the feature was an interview with 'Robert Mortimer ... who had paved the way for that historic victory'. Bob's advice to others with the same problem was 'go out and sue'.

By October, Bob's advice was clearly being taken. Fifty-four-year-old Gwendolyn Wallace, who lived on the Cossal Estate, had also notched up a victory against Southwark Council at Camberwell Magistrates Court thanks to Bob. Southwark admitted liability and was ordered to pay £917.12 costs and carry out a thorough treatment in the new year. According to Bob, if the cockroaches weren't cleared from her house by the first week in April, the court would be duty bound to close it under the 1936 Public Heath Act. There was even a risk that the whole estate might have to be shut down.

In the meantime, the Goldsmiths Tavern had problems of its own. Jim and Bob started to look around for another viable venue. It was a strange time for alternative comedy. After the initial boom, it was now entering a kind of post-alternative era, which in numerous places involved a return to variety roots, but with a contemporary twist. In Brixton there was the sinisterly named *Room 16* at the George IV pub on Brixton Hill, close to Jim's old house in Arodene Road. These shows also featured weird acts and art-inspired installations. At *Room 16* one night the entire auditorium was covered in dirty washing. There were acrobatic acts, contortionists, people who sang while standing in buckets. But what these other clubs lacked, which the *Big Night Out* had in spades, was a sense of occasion – the *Big Night Out* pulled it off because the evening seemed to have a coherent vision. Even if some of the ideas came from some of the other performers, Vic's constant presence and name in the title lent the evening a consistency.

But even Jim was unable to do much about the drunks that would wander in from the other bar and cause trouble. One night a man just wandered straight on to the stage and had to be forcibly pulled away from the microphone. Fights caused by drunks would break out with alarming regularity. Sometimes with fans who maybe stared too long at someone's pint, sometimes with each other, just as a matter of ritual. Something had to be done about the trouble, but in fact the growing success of the show resolved the issue. The Goldsmiths Tavern only had a capacity of one hundred. In the autumn of 1988 Jim moved the operation to Sunday nights at the Albany Empire, a bigger, more professionally run venue on Douglas Way, just round the corner off Deptford High Street.

Chapter Four

Making the Grade at the Empire

There was an element of risk about moving, but at least Jim was taking his own establishment show with him this time. Not every gig he did was such a success. In fact it was a pretty good rule of thumb that the further Jim Moir travelled, the worse his experience was. While he was still finding his feet he had done a few open spots at Malcolm Hardee's Tunnel Club in Mitre Road, a desolate stretch of south London near the Blackwall Tunnel. This was a notoriously rough venue – as people used to say about the Glasgow Empire, if they liked you they let you live. One night, after he had started working with Bob, Jim was booed off, but after leaving the stage he heard cheers for an encore. He came back to do an encore of his rock and roll food anthem 'Meals on Wheels', only to find out that he had been the victim of a sadistic Tunnel Club speciality. He had been cheered back on so that the audience could pelt him with cans. Bob was in his Man with the Stick mask and could not see well enough to dodge the missiles.

Hardee wasn't a big fan of Jim's comedy. In fact he was more impressed by Jim's suits than by his act: 'I never ever saw him looking scruffy,' recalls Hardee. One night at the Tunnel did go better than others. 'He came on and did a punk version of an old Bing Crosby song and that seemed to impress the audience. I still think he sort of struck it lucky in a way. I've since seen people doing similar things, but he was pushed on by ambition.'

Malcolm Hardee's patronage was very much a mixed blessing, as

Jim recalls: 'In early 1987 he asked me to compère a fucking awful Grand Talent Night at the Tunnel. Malcolm had said that the prize was a spot on Jools Holland's TV show, but Jools didn't know anything about it. Malcolm would go off and leave me to do it all, and he never left any prize money, so at the end of the night there were these sad cases from the talent circuit with no prize money and no TV appearance.'

The Grand Talent Nights moved to the Goldsmiths Tavern in 1987, and became *Vic Reeves' Talent Bonanza*. The kind of acts that appeared made Jim despair, but also feel that he was doing something special himself. These were the kind of people that had missed the alternative comedy gravy train and, unlike Jim, had no sense of irony about their middle-of-the-road aspirations. As John Irvine recalls, 'It was just an endless run of hopeful nightclub singers and out-of-work actresses.'

Peter Brooke Turner, a six-foot-two singer, was one of the few entrants who Jim liked. His stage character, Brooke Turner, also known as Easy-Listening Man, crooned suave cruise ship ballads. He remembers the event as 'a complete shambles, not so much a talent night as Jim and his mates' and lost to one of Alan King's acts, 'Les Pantalons', a string of underwear which sang in French, but Jim had decided to book him on a regular basis anyway.

Malcolm Hardee was also on the bill when Jim did a solo set in Blackburn. They had travelled up together on a train and Hardee had found the journey rather awkward. He felt that Jim had been talking nonsense for most of the journey. By the time they got to the venue they both needed to unwind, and they went across the road to a nearby pub and started to play on the fruit machine. Hardee completely missed his gig, and in the book *Ha Bloody Ha* by William Cook, Jim claims to have missed his own spot too.

Gaining confidence, Jim and Bob had once tried their luck in Twickenham, but from the moment they came onstage they knew they had a problem, says Jim: 'I came on with a pot of yoghurt and Bob came on with a spoon and said, "Come on, give us some," and this huge cry of "Fuck off" went up.' 'They hated us,' recalls Bob. The incident reveals a bloody-minded side to Jim – when the going got tough he got so pissed off he refused to be defeated, much to Bob's chagrin. 'Jim also had some peas and I was supposed to ask him for some. Instead I said to Jim, "Get off," and he just said, "No way." Meanwhile I'm saying "Pass us these fucking peas" – just so that I can get off.'

It was just one of those nights when the audience didn't seem interested in comedy. Astonishingly, says Jim, the evening went even more badly for someone else on the bill: 'This other act said, "I've done forty nights which have gone very well, and this was the night I invited my family down to see me." He had to crawl out of the toilet window to escape.'

Yet despite these disasters Vic Reeves was starting to attract media attention. On 18 September 1987, Jim compèred a *Biggest Night Out* show at the Albany Empire. The journalist Caroline Sullivan saw the show and reviewed it for *Melody Maker*. Bob was not performing and things had clearly not yet fallen into place. Sullivan saw that something was happening, but was unimpressed by Vic, the variety acts, Boys Wonder, Easy-Listening Man, The Bay City Rollers cover versions and Doctor of Dr and the Medics blowing 'the world's longest raspberry'. Her conclusion was fairly damning: 'I can only speculate that the performance art craze of 82 travelled south at a veritable crawl.'

But Jim's most notorious gig was in Bracknell, to the west of London. Malcolm Hardee was involved again, booking them to do a turn at *The Friday Alternative* at the Cellar Bar at the South Hill Park Arts Centre on 9 October 1987. Although according to Hardee the audience had a unique way of expressing their dissatisfaction. Rather than simply heckling, they signed a petition demanding that Vic and Bob never darken their doors again. Although according to Simon Hoolihan, who ran the club, 'The petition was to stop me retaining some of their fee to refund money to people who complained.' Hardee also claims that despite this disaster Hoolihan later tried to book them for the larger Wilde Theatre, but Hoolihan maintains it was Dick Witts, the theatre's artistic director, who wanted them back.

Steering clear of the conventional comedy circuit, Jim and Bob also tried their hand as a gigging band for a while. They got a support slot with local band Oh Oh Chongo at the Royal Albert pub in New Cross, but billed themselves as The Potters Wheel and performed selected highlights from the *Big Night Out*. Through Simon Palmer, who ran the Rub-a-Dub Club, they managed to get some bookings at colleges in London, but they always ran up against the problem that students who didn't know them were more interested in cheap beer than innovative comedy.

Stevo recalls that The Potter's Wheel was another of Jim's perverse attempts at being a rock star: 'It was a joke band. I played guitar, a guy from *Kerrang* magazine was joint singer with Jim and Bob was on bass. The few rehearsals we had ended in drinking sessions, but we got mentioned in *Kerrang*.' In the end, the band performed to backing tapes put together by John Irvine and pretended to be crafts fanatics, coming onstage and buffing vases to music. They specialized in send-ups of the Stars on 45 compilation singles and wore border twist tweed suits. Eventually Stevo left, but the remaining members fulfilled a contractual appearence at a debutante's ball at the Hilton. Stevo went along as a fan this time: 'Everybody talked throughout the set, but it was one of Jim's best-ever gigs. Afterwards we were given £500 in token chips to play at the casino.' Bob was convinced they were legal tender and asked to cash them in straight away, only to be told they were strictly for fun.

Jim soon realized that their most successful shows were their own: 'That's because we controlled it. If people came they were coming to see us, so they can't complain.' But this didn't offer them any easy way to broaden their appeal. To attract a bigger audience they had to play second fiddle to well-known acts sometimes, but they seemed to choose the wrong times, the wrong venue and the wrong headliner.

Somehow they found themselves opening for erstwhile New York folkie Suzanne Vega at Regent's Park Open Air Theatre in June 1987. Bob says that there was an administrative mishap and seven comedy acts turned up by mistake. 'We stood there and whistled the theme from *Grandstand* while two bears wandered around in the background.' According to Alan King, who was also there, the most frustrating aspect of the night was the fact that they did a second set later which went really well, but Jim forgot to say who he was – 'and this was at a time when most of his act consisted of "I'm Vic Reeves, the north-east's top light entertainer".'

Sometimes, however, things went wrong through no fault of their own. During one show Jim brought a member of the audience up onstage. Bob, as Judge Nutmeg, was supposed to say something cruel about him. Unfortunately Bob didn't realize that the audience member was blind and said to Jim, 'Look into his eyes – there's nothing there.' It could have happened to any performer, but with Jim and Bob it revealed two different facets of their professional personality. On the one hand it showed that anything really could happen when they were onstage. On the other hand, it showed that they still had some way to go to get a well-oiled, television-friendly version of their creation ready for mass consumption.

After Winstons and the Goldsmiths Tavern, the Albany Empire in Douglas Way was more like the London Palladium. It had proper facilities, dressing-rooms, a balcony, more than one bar and, best of all, it was only a five-minute walk from Jim's flat on Bronze Street. The weekly residency was booked in seasonal blocks, and Jim set to work on preparing the shows. There was more space to manoeuvre, more time to perform; everything seemed bigger and more professional. There was a desk onstage now, rather than a lectern. For the original performers there was a change of mood: 'It stopped being a private party and became a comedy gig. I miss the weekly party, we all lived for that. It was just as much fun when we were doing it in the lounge. Getting ready for it was always a laugh,' says John Irvine.

Despite knowing how popular they were becoming, it still came as a surprise to Jim on the opening night, when he arrived at the Albany long before opening on the first Sunday evening in November 1988 to deliver some home-made props, to find that there was already a queue forming outside. Deptford hadn't seen anything like it in a long time, if ever. And this was all through word of mouth.

The show became more elaborate, which meant that more acts than ever had the chance to appear with Jim. Bob's creative role increased, but it was still very much an ensemble rather than Vic and Bob and a supporting cast. The larger scale of the performance meant that there were opportunities for comedians from the circuit as well as friends. Johnny Immaterial, a likeable comic with a nice line in Kenneth Williams impersonations, fitted in quite nicely, while others did less well. Jim, Bob and Alan King came up with The Three Scrutineers, who came on and 'looked about for a bit'. And there was a house band, featuring Steve McGuire of Doctor and the Medics on guitar. McGuire was a kind of musical director, co-writing Vic's regular big finale number 'Oh! Mr Songwriter'. If some sketches seemed like padding, there was no doubt that Jim was taking things more seriously. There is a thin line between a parody of a light entertainer and a light entertainer, and Jim seemed to cross backwards and forwards. At one show, audience members were given free copies of a Vic Reeves annual, a photocopied fanzine containing examples of his artwork and humour – a rather grand gesture for an act barely known outside the borough.

At another show a copy of a flexidisc, 'Howlin' Wind', was handed out. According to Alan King, this featured Jim, a blind piano player and a drummer, who looked like Captain Birdseye, from the Montague Arms on the corner just before New Cross Road began. This was a notoriously bizarre pub, frequently used by foreign coaches as a stopping-off point before the drive to Dover. John Irvine and Jim used to drink in the Montague Arms in the early Eighties after band rehearsals and Jim had already become a minor local celebrity even then: 'In around 1982 to 1984 the pub musicians would coax him up onstage to do some club singing. He usually did a cover version of "You've Lost That Loving Feeling" by the Righteous Brothers.'

The Albany shows began to attract a following from beyond south London. Having been told how good the show was by his colleagues at his production company Channel X, Jonathan Ross came down regularly and even attempted a few sketches on stage. The loyal audience didn't take too kindly to this interloper from across the river, spontaneously greeting him with the variant on a theme, 'Fuck off, Ross.'

Graham Smith, who was working at Channel X in the late Eighties, recalls being inspired by the *Big Night Out* and went on a regular basis: 'They were so prolific that every week it was a different show. So many comedians work the opposite way, honing their act until you get a perfect act. Their idea was the opposite – once they had done something they then would move on to do something else, which generates an enormous amount of confidence that you can do stuff live and people will love it. They never had any sort of self-doubt in that respect. They have ultimate belief in what they are doing, which is crucial. It is all about having certain beliefs which the audience buys into.'

But the price of success meant swapping the family, party atmosphere for a more ruthless streak of professionalism, as established comedy names became involved. Paul Whitehouse and Charlie Higson both turned up regularly at the Albany. By now they had made a name for themselves as writers for Harry Enfield, but had yet to do much performing themselves. Charlie Higson had met Jim at the beginning of the decade when their mutual friend Alan Davidson from Darlington had been at the University of East Anglia with Higson, and Moir had been up to Norwich to visit him. 'I knew Jim vaguely,' recalls Higson, who by now had also had some pop success as the lead singer with the Higsons. 'I had been involved in music and art in those days and I met him at parties in Norwich. He used to hang out with the art school mob and do strange art stuff. Then Alan moved down to London and I didn't think much of it for a few years. Then I heard Jim was doing comedy and I saw him do some stuff on *The Tube*. I caught the last show at the Goldsmiths Tavern and thought it was amazing and got Paul to come with me to the Albany.'

Paul Whitehouse remembers the conversation well. 'Charlie said to me, "You've got to come and see them, they've got a man who flattens a piece of brie on a carpet tile." This was at a time when there was a lot of worthy comedy about.' Jim had already made an impression on Paul anyway: 'I remembered him on *The Tube*. He had a dead eye like a shark.' He was particularly attracted by the accents. 'They stuck out because there weren't any northern, working-class voices in comedy then. And Jim came out with all this stuff about early Seventies rock and managed to make a band like Free sound hip.'

Whitehouse and Higson were both keen to become involved with the *Big Night Out*, partly because they thought it was brilliant and partly because by appearing in it they hoped to get their Equity cards. Paul Whitehouse was the most forthcoming, coming up with a spoof stand-up comic called Johnny Vitriol. 'I did it with Jim at the Rub-a-Dub Club. It was just an awful observational comic who would say things like "Nigel Lawson, he's fat, isn't he ... and a Tory". He would sneer but that was about as vicious as it was.'

Higson, the quieter of the two, asked Alan Davidson to ask Jim and Bob if he could be involved. They tried him out and he ended up doing a few characters at the Albany. Both he and Whitehouse made up the numbers as contestants on Novelty Island, the increasingly popular talent show send-up in which contestants had to reveal their strange skills from within a small paddock. This didn't always work out, however. The arrival of Higson and Whitehouse, created some tension among some of the people involved who had been around in the early days. A stage seemed to have been reached where skill and experience counted for more than having bumped into Jim in the bar in the early Eighties. It wasn't so much a lack of loyalty to his earlier friends, more a drive to produce the best show possible.

Paul Whitehouse admits that he and Charlie 'never really got it right. It is difficult living in their little world. They present their world and they let you in and you feel fairly privileged. They are the best thing on television even when they are crap. They freely admit they nick stuff from everywhere, they just get away with it quicker than everyone else.'

At the Albany the show may have been more serious, and the entrance fee raised to three pounds, but it still had a spontaneous feel, often out of necessity. By April 1989 *Time Out* was billing it as 'traditionalish variety show with guest acts and bands (still to be announced). Quiz games, lookalike contests and much else.' If that sounded vague it was probably because Jim and Bob were still writing the show when the listings deadline arrived.

Charlie Higson and Paul Whitehouse's contributions helped, but their own writing was never completely in tune with Jim and Bob, as Higson recalls: 'The best bits were always Jim and Bob's ideas. I did The Man with Two Bodies, a man with forty-foot long trousers painted with scenes of canals – that was one of Jim's ideas. I also did a ventriloquism act with a corpse called David Dudd and his Dead Dad, and I impersonated Tanita Tikaram.'

The move to the Albany coincided with an increasingly close relationship between Jim and Bob and Channel X. By 1989 Ross was one of the most influential personalities at Channel 4. He had effectively been discovered by the channel, which was now keen to promote him as their brightest star.

While *The Last Resort* had been a late-night Friday programme, his new series was an attempt to push him into the weekend mainstream. *One Hour with Jonathan Ross* seemed to echo the *Big Night Out's* love of old-fashioned variety in its jamboree bag of chat, music and downright oddities. It was a shameless attempt to appeal to the young, hip audience and at the same time reposition Ross as an all-round family entertainer.

One Hour with Jonathan Ross also found a sizeable role for Jim. In the same way that Michael Miles used to present a cheesy quiz show in the middle of *Sunday Night at the London Palladium*, so Jim as Vic became the host of Knock Down Ginger. The name was taken from the old schoolboy prank of knocking on a neighbour's door and then running away before they opened it, but in this version Jim stuck around to ask frankly ludicrous questions. 'We wanted a quiz show,' says Ross, 'and we came up with an approximation of the American quiz *Remote Control*. We had a huge set built with nine doors, three up three across, and various people as characters.' In essence, it was 'Square Celebrities' without Jim strung up on wires.

Behind every door there was a celebrity, sometimes a group of them huddled together. Often they were people who had become part of Ross's posse, such as Kathy Burke and Rowland Rivron. Rivron and Jools Holland were chums, and Holland had played piano on Ross's shows. Paul Whitehouse and Charlie Higson also used to join in, and whichever guest was on that week might get a chance to take the mickey out of themselves too. Phil Collins was a station-master. Bob played a bearded, baby-carrying social worker.

Jim and Bob were new to television studios and even their appearances were the stuff of comedy, says Ross: 'I remember one time Tom Jones was in the studio next door doing Dame Edna's show. He came in to say hello and said, "What the fuck are you doing there?" as Bob walked past with a side of beef on his back. Gilbert and George were on and at the end Bob ran over with the side of beef and we all started stomping on it.'

Jonathan Ross gave Jim and Bob as many opportunities as possible to try different things out. On one show Bob impersonated Roger Moore, on another he sang the Ken Dodd song 'Tears', replacing the word 'jubilation' with 'constipation' to general merriment. A lot of old-style comedy was creeping into their work. One show was set on a train as it travelled from Euston to Coventry. In a stunt that could have come straight out of an old Will Hay movie, Jim and Bob played fare dodgers who pretended to be inspectors. In one scripted scene they asked a woman in the toilet for her ticket and then ran away with it when she slid it under the door.

Off-camera, an incident on the train prefigured the future difficult relationship with Channel 4. One of Jim's favourite bands, the Fall, were also on the train and Jim was clearly in awe of vocalist Mark E. Smith. At one point Seamus Cassidy, the Channel 4 commissioning editor who would sign up Jim and Bob, appeared in the carriage. Andy

Darling, a journalist who had worked with Jonathan Ross and would later work with Jim and Bob, decided to play a stunt. He claimed to be able to tell if an orange had pips just by looking at it. Jim played along by claiming that he could tell whether a bus had open doors at the back by the sound it made when it went past. Mark E. Smith said he could tell what religion someone was by their face. At this point Seamus Cassidy said, 'What am I then?' and Mark E. Smith said, 'You are a cunt.' It was an odd, awkward moment during an even odder television event, recalls Darling. 'In Coventry everyone stayed on the train to go back to London, but Mark E. Smith got off and that was the last we ever saw of him.'

Jim had been a vegetarian, but now that was well and truly a thing of the past. He had come across some ham in a fridge at a New Year's Eve party and had lapsed badly (though John Irvine thinks it may have been bacon). As if to make up for lost time he was developing a particularly keen interest in meat. On one show he met Ian Astbury of the Cult and got the rock star to autograph a side of beef for him. Unlike most comedy of the day there was a complete absence of any mention of sex and politics, but plenty of gags about meat paste and most of the major food groups. As Jim told the *New Musical Express* in 1990, 'We started on spreads and meat pastes and then went on to crispbreads.' The recordings were great fun and much lager was drunk. There was less responsibility than usual because he didn't have to prepare the entire show and he was paid £300 a night too.

As funny as they were, these comic interludes didn't work quite as well as his own live show. Once again they seemed to hark back to Jim's ropey performances on *The Tube*. Reeves could only ever really be funny when he was the ruler of his own universe. Place him in something else, even a show hosted by a sympathetic fan such as Ross, and he could fall ominously flat. Unlike the generic political or observational stand-up comics of the era, Reeves and Mortimer could not appear as guests on someone else's show and do a five-minute 'turn'. It was something they would strive to resolve as they become more and more successful, more and more in demand and more and more keen to promote themselves and attract an audience that hadn't seen their own shows.

The year 1989 found Jim and Bob in a strange kind of limbo between fame and obscurity. They were well-known in south London, and starting to get plenty of mentions in the music press. People were even becoming familiar with Jim's pasty complexion, thanks to Knock Down Ginger. But he was still something of a not very well-kept secret. Part of the reason for this was the inaccessibility – not of the material, but of the venue. For anyone in north London, Deptford seemed like the end of the world. There was an underground station – in fact two, New Cross and New Cross Gate – but they were part of an odd little branch of the Metropolitan Line which went from the east end of London directly south of the river. For potential fans in other parts of London, it was a challenge just to get to the Albany, but it was worth it. Peter Orton, who directed *One Hour with Jonathan Ross*, had seen Jim there, but only after some cajoling. 'I was living in Hackney, so I put off going down there for ages, but when I did I loved the show.'

This probably exlained why the only people who seemed to cross London to see the show were car-driving television executives. Jonathan Ross's unfailing support prompted other people at Channel 4 to see what the fuss was about. Mike Bolland, the Head of Light Entertainment, was enthusiastic (he had been responsible for *The Tube* and had championed Jim then), and got the person who had taken over as his commissioning editor, Seamus Cassidy, to go down.

Cassidy, a sharp Irishman who had worked his way up from script editor at C4, seemed to have mixed feelings about Jim and Bob. On the one hand he could clearly see that they were talented; on the other, he wondered whether they would work on television. The first time he saw Jim he was compèring a night at the Rub-a-Dub Club and they were fairly shambolic: 'Bob wasn't there and it didn't have a lot of connection with what I saw later. If Channel X hadn't taken me to the Albany I probably wouldn't have remembered it was the same guy.' When Cassidy saw the full show it was immediately clear that they were doing something very distinctive indeed: 'At that time the vast majority of stand-up comics lived on twenty minutes of material and it was something that bothered me. Vic and Bob changed that.'

Like others, Cassidy was certainly drawn to the fact that they were so prolific: 'You could go and see them a month later and they had a completely different two-hour show.' This seemed perfect for TV, which had a voracious appetite for material. Cassidy was also impressed by their use of language: 'I liked the fact that Vic can find the word courgette funny.' However, he still had some reservations, says Jonathan Ross: 'He didn't take convincing of their talent, he took convincing of their parlaying it to the screen and, looking back on it now, its influence *is* far greater than its ratings.'

Impressed by the *Big Night Out*, Channel 4 set up a meeting with the duo's management. By now Jim and Bob were being handled by PBJ Management, the prestigious, influential agency that also had Harry Enfield and Rowan Atkinson on its books. Rumours, however, started to fly about that the BBC was also interested in signing them, recalls Cassidy with a rueful smile – 'which was partly why we decided if we were going to slap dicks on the table we were going to slap Michael Grade's [Head of Channel 4 at the time] down. He was a very large penis at that time. At the time BBC2 was nicking everything we had and we were quite combative about it.'

The cigar-smoking impresario took a pair of jeans into the office to change into before heading south of the river. By all accounts Grade was duly impressed. One story even suggested he was up and dancing on the table. This seems unlikely, but eye-witnesses do confirm that he was waving his arms about and shouting out the catchphrases with everybody else. His family had a background in variety, and Grade believed that whether Jim and Bob realized it or not, they were tapping into a long, respected vaudevillian tradition. According to Cassidy, Grade turned to him and Mike Bolland after the show 'and said, "Shall we go and do the deal then?" and we said, "We've already done it," and he said "Good," rubbing his hands. He loved them, he was a big, big supporter.' Bob, however, was never too sure about Seamus's commitment: 'We felt that Seamus took us on reluctantly. We never really saw him. Michael Grade was more involved.'

According to Jim today, the BBC's Alan Yentob had been due to see the show, but a sudden family bereavement prevented him from making the trip. In May 1995, however, he told the *Mail on Sunday* that Grade and Yentob were both present on the same night: 'I think they went round the back and had a scrap.' In fact Yentob did get down to the Albany on a different night – ever the sharp entrepreneur, Jonathan Ross was negotiating with him too: 'Jim and Bob were linked to Channel X from day one because we were the only people championing them. Jools and Harry Enfield had seen it and loved it but hadn't thought about moving it on,' says Ross. Although Yentob was a fan, he was not so interested in televising the *Big Night Out*. Rather presciently, as it would turn out, he wanted Jim to present a lighthearted panel game, the latest revival of *Juke Box Jury*. In the end Jools Holland got the job. One week Jim appeared as a guest. He wore a loud checked suit like an old variety hall comedian and was introduced as Britain's top light entertainer, despite the fact that nobody knew who he was.

Alan Marke, co-founder of Channel X, who ended up looking after Jim and Bob because Jonathan Ross was involved in his own projects, remembers a meeting with Alan Yentob which may have swayed the duo's decision to sign with Channel 4. Apparently they went to see the BBC head and were kept waiting for about thirty minutes. Having finally been ushered in, they were just about to discuss things when Alan Yentob's secretary said that Arthur Miller was on the line. Yentob apologized, went next door to take the telephone call and, according to Marke, Jim and Bob got fed up waiting for him to return and left.

Jim and Bob agreed to go to Channel 4 through Channel X, and Alan Yentob would have to wait a few more years to get his revenge. In the meantime a development deal was done through Channel X, which basically said that Channel 4 would put the *Big Night Out* on to the small screen. Cassidy was keen to have director Geoff Posner on board because he had worked wonders with other young comedians: 'Geoff was hot at the time. He had worked with French and Saunders, Victoria Wood and Lenny Henry and had shown that he could take a performer and make them into a star. We figured he would be good at presenting them to the public.'

By the late Eighties Channel 4 were desperately in need of new comedy talent. They had led the way in discovering big names, but the BBC had systematically taken their best names away from them. The Comic Strip team, for instance, had recently changed channels, and Channel 4 needed to reassert itself. Seamus Cassidy put a bullish face on: 'We were never sorry when we lost a star, we just said we would go out and discover another one. Vic and Bob were very important to C4 because they were the cutting edge – it is a hackneyed phrase, but they were. They were the thing that said we were setting the pace. There was a lot of shit being said at the time, which was ninety per cent bitchy and ten per cent right, that comedians were getting on TV too fast, but I think Vic and Bob got on quicker than a lot of wankers who had been honing the same fifteen minutes at the Comedy Store for the last five years.'

That December I attempted to interview Vic Reeves for the first time, for the *Guardian*, to coincide with their special Christmas live Albany show, which was to include a seasonal panto, an attempt at mind regression, and an appearance by their alter egos Donald and Davey Stott, 'who will be trying to cut someone's leg off and then pour some hot oil on a bird'.

It was an encounter that Jim would be driven to duplicate for countless other journalists in the forthcoming years. Asking him what made Vic tick, the response wasn't so much an explanation as an obfuscation. Over the years, his views on his craft would become as oblique as Eric Cantona's outpourings on soccer. His humour, he explained, was 'like a shopfront with a little bit of dust in the corner'. This, however, was positively articulate compared with his opinion of the contemporary comedy scene: 'I see it as a very, very long trench with a worm and a piece of hot bacon near by.' What he was less oblique about was the fundamental fact that his and Bob's sense of humour came from their upbringings in Darlington and Middlesbrough respectively. The first time we ever talked we discussed accents and, funnily, the last time we met, the first thing Jim started talking about was the accent of the student from the north-east in Mike Leigh's film *Career Girls*. Jim has always been aware that their accent was, and still is, a priceless asset in the south, where it helps them to stand out. Paul Whitehouse agrees: 'I'm convinced the accent helps. In the late Eighties there were no northern accents in comedy and that made them interesting straight away.'

Bob thinks this is something that happened by accident. 'I think, unbeknownst to us, our accents were very distinctive, because we are not Geordies. It is hard to imitate, but there is something vaguely appealing about the accent. People would hear it and take a look.'

More significant than the accent, though, is the sense of humour, which, like Jim, Bob also thinks has a sense of place. 'There is a very definite sense of humour from where we come from which is hard to describe. Maybe it's being overly sensitive about petty things' – they used to do a gag about panicking because they had left a fork in the knife compartment, which certainly fell into that category – 'they can be taking the piss or having a laugh but you might not be sure. People from the north-east haven't got that chirpy tone that Liverpudlians have – they don't want to be clowns, more characters. And I don't think I've ever heard anyone complain about hard times in the north-east. Because it is such a big industrial place there isn't the collective sense of area that you get in Yorkshire or Newcastle and because we don't have that identity maybe we don't feel we've been shat on over the years.' Jim agrees: 'If there is any area of the country where people are least likely to moan, it's where we come from.' They had been funny in the north of England, they had been funny in south London. There was no earthly reason to imagine that they wouldn't be funny everywhere else.

Chapter Five

'A Cult of Monster Proportions'

Jim Moir had been unwittingly shrewd in the way that he had built up his following. By hiring the venues himself he had got people to come specifically to see him. Other comics tended to turn up on bills, and even the best acts could fall foul of a dodgy, moody audience. As Malcolm Hardee observed, 'When he did do the circuit, generally speaking he didn't go down that well.'

Now Jim and Bob were becoming involved in the world of television. On the one hand this meant huge potential, on the other it meant handing over control, something which has always been precious to Jim. Dorian Crook was around at the time and remembers a feeling of inevitability about the *Big Night Out* series: 'Jim had been doing his stuff with Jonathan Ross, he had to move on in some way.' It was also a very exciting time. Nearly a decade on, Bob still looks back on those early days at the studios with a great deal of affection: 'I loved the early television stuff. The first time I went into a television studio that was great. It was fantastic being down in Wandsworth seeing the props arrive.'

For the core of people who had been involved since the mid-Eighties this may not have seemed like an overnight success, but one has to think back to what the television world was like at the turn of the decade. As Crook says, 'to get your own TV show was something special'. Nowadays there is a joke in the industry that is constantly crying out for new talent: 'One good gig and you get a series on

Channel 4. One bad gig and you get a series on Channel 5.' Either way there seem to be a lot of places for new comedians to get TV exposure. Apart from the terrestrial channels there is now cable and satellite too. Back then, Channel 4 was really the only place a new comedian could expect to be signed to. The satellite channel BSB had a commitment to comedy – in fact Jim and Bob appeared on Jools' satellite programme *The Happening* – but hardly anyone was watching it and it would soon be swallowed up by Rupert Murdoch's Sky Television. It was only in the early Nineties that BBC2 started to get its act together and commit itself to discovering and nurturing new talent. There was a sense of excitement in the air as Jim and Bob prepared for their big television début. Jim tried to keep things in perspective, however, with an unusually modest observation: 'I thought we might as well do one show, then when I'm an old man I would be able to tell my grandchildren that I had been on television.'

Maybe he was partly worried about what Paul Whitehouse calls being found out as a 'fraud'. Maybe the public would see through his comic juxtapositions and cease to laugh at them. Even on the eve of *Big Night Out's* Channel 4 debut, Jim and Bob were still testing out their material around the pub table with drinking mates. There was no other way of deciding if something would work. As Bob told *City Limits*: 'We don't try and analyse it, because once that happens it's lost completely.'

Before the first series of *Vic Reeves Big Night Out* started on Channel 4, however, there was one last attempt to get things absolutely right. In the closing months of 1989, a pilot was filmed by Channel X (executively produced by both Jonathan Ross and Alan Marke) which was never broadcast. This was a strange period. The contracts had been signed, the shows had been scheduled, but nothing had been transmitted. In fact they still had those seasonal shows lined up at the Albany Empire that Christmas.

The final pilot directed by Geoff Posner attempted to condense the best elements of the live show into a shorter running time. This had worried some of the people involved. Paul Whitehouse recalls thinking, 'You can't turn three hours into thirty minutes. What about the purity? As it happens, I think they got it right.'

There was still a fair amount of honing to do, but then again, there was a rough and ready feel to the TV version that lent it some street credibility. When a toy mole fell off a bit of string as it whizzed around Vic's head, it felt as if this show wasn't that different from the live show. It didn't matter how haphazard it looked, though *Vic Reeves Big Night Out* was scripted to within an inch of its life. There was an attention to detail that, given the time and the opportunity, Jim and Bob would always put into their work.

From the moment the now familiar music started, the tone of cartoon juxtaposition was set. The opening credits saw a chop being prodded by a stick, a trumpet being tickled with a feather and some Branston pickle being spread on a shin by a spatula. This was swiftly followed by an introduction that would soon become legendary: 'Ladies and gentlemen, Britain's top light entertainer, Vic Reeves.' The man who had once dubbed himself the north-east's top light entertainer was clearly thinking nationally now. The star entered on a modest chariot pulled by Tom Selleck (actually Bob in a wig). His black hair gleaming and freshly greased, resplendent in a white suit, not to mention an ashen-white face, Reeves resembled the missing link between Martin Bell and Marty Hopkirk of *Randall and Hopkirk (Deceased)*. Without further ado he explained that he was going to sing a song about things he liked to sniff. This was a routine that was never used in *Big Night Out*, but this ditty was destined to end up as the theme tune to *The Smell of Reeves and Mortimer*. Vic danced along what looked like a couple of trestle tables quickly bolted together, singing the praises of objects ranging from manure to Frank Muir, from an oak panel to the hair of a spaniel, and culminating in Lulu's hairdos and Eno's espadrilles.

The mood was set for something that was neither a chat show nor a variety show, but a mutant hybrid of prime-time light entertainment. Vic went to sit behind his desk (festooned with giant horse brasses with Elvis Presley's face on them, designed, as most of the props were, by Jim himself) and proceeded to mutter about spotting Richard Stilgoe pushing a wheelbarrow full of milk, with little finches hovering above, before introducing his assistant, Les, played by Fred Aylward. At this stage Bob was never introduced – he never played himself, only a variety of characters in various disguises or, in the case of Rick Astley, no disguise at all. An initiate might have thought that Les was the other half of the double act. We were promptly informed, via Les Facts coming out of the tickertape machine on Vic's desk, that Les (1) was formerly the lead singer in Japan, (2) loves a spirit level, and (3) has a terrible fear of chives. Somewhere the counting went astray, because another 'third Les Fact' turned out to be the fact that he was under the power of a mysterious voodoo chile from Peterlee. Vic produced a Les-lookalike doll from the table, and whenever he moved the doll's arm, Les's arm would move too.

Seated at the desk, surrounded by a red telephone, countless microphones and a Harpo Marx-style hooter, Vic pressed on. Given the set, and Vic's helpful tones, the next item seemed like a drug-induced episode of *That's Life*, as Vic provided the audience with some ideas for making use of old denim. A tea-bag carrier, for instance. Harking back to Tappy Lappy and his Elvis film with Brett Turnbull, he donned a cardboard Sean Connery mask (from the *Untouchables* period) and attempted to scrub a ray gun. It was the kind of humour that over the coming years would either repel viewers or attract them.

The next gag introduced The Man with the Stick. The audience had been well-primed to cry, 'What's on the end of the stick, Vic?', but Bob, lurking beneath a huge paper mask, was not telling just yet. Instead he told us about some of the illustrations on his headgear. A few rippling waves depicted 'the feeling you get on a sunny day listening to Level 42'; another picture drawn by Vic revealed a leech drinking port out of a test tube. The Man with the Stick went on to discuss safety standards in the studio, though it was quite difficult to understand him – partly because of the unusually thick accent and partly because the mask tended to muffle his voice. Before he left the stage, though, he pointed to the spot on Vic's neck, cueing Vic's near-apoplectic response of 'You couldn't let it lie.'

Some set-pieces clearly worked better than others. After the break a couple of old men could be seen at the back of the stage tossing a blow-up globe to each other. By the time the series reached the air they would be replaced by one old man at an easel crying, 'You're wasting your time'. It still didn't work, but at least it halved the cost of extras. Novelty Island, on the other hand, survived intact. In the pilot, Bob introduced wretched Little Englander Graham Lister, who got laughs by pushing lard through holes in Mickey Rourke's face, which had been stuck on to the side of a cereal packet. The winner, however, was Mr Wobbly Hand – a character who simply wandered the stage with an outstretched oscillating hand – also played by Bob.

As with the live shows, any promise of special guests usually meant Bob in disguise, or Bob's girlfriend Emma Cafferty, who lived with Nicky Smedley who ran the Parrot Café (and recently became a Teletubbie). Paul Whitehouse appeared pretending to be cookery writer Egon Ronay dressed as a monk. Mike Wattam, a mate with an Equity card, was also in it.

The longest-running characters in the Reeves and Mortimer repertoire, Donald and Davey Stott, also did a turn here, hosting their own cack-handed version of *The Generation Game*. Two victims had to pass some lard from hand to hand, before the retarded brothers scuttled off the stage in embarrassment. The final routine was lifted pretty much lock, stock and barrel from the live show. Via the fluffy Wheel of Justice Judge Nutmeg dealt out some punishments to members of the audience brought before him on trumped-up charges. The audience had to remind Vic to 'comb its hair' before he span it and, in the pilot, the victim was accused of 'fannying about on a yacht wearing Midge Ure's deodorant'. Having sentenced him to be sellotaped to a bear, Bob asked Vic if he had squeezed that spot. There was another chorus of 'You couldn't let it lie', before Vic swung into the final song, 'Oh! Mr Songwriter', that always closed the live shows. Where, in Deptford, the cast would tend to return for this scene, here Vic did the honours on his own, with only Les lurking in the background. Bob came on quickly as The Man with the Stick and revealed a lump of wax with a picture on it that Vic, in all the excitement, couldn't make out, but with the mike twirling around his head and the audience at his mercy, this was very much Vic's show.

The pilot was deemed a success of sorts, though some changes were made. Geoff Posner had chosen to do some location filming. Jim played a soul singer guzzling food from a trough on a farm, and the duo pretended to be Simon and Garfunkel. It didn't work quite as well and made the show more like a conventional sketch show, whereas the intention had been to replicate the live experience as closely as possible. There was some thought that, as talented as Posner was, he wasn't really on the same wavelength as Jim and Bob. Later on, when the duo were more experienced with television, this wouldn't matter, and could even be an asset, because it meant they had total editorial control, but it was felt that someone more familiar with their style might be better. Peter Orton, who had worked with Jim on Jonathan

Ross's shows, was brought in to direct and produce the series. The studio in Wandsworth was booked for filming to go ahead on the first series of *Big Night Out* in the spring of 1990. It was not a case of would Vic and Bob make it big, but how would they handle making it big?

For Bob it was a real turning-point. But he was still cautious, mixing his day job with performing. Finally he took twelve weeks off, but he never returned. The cockroaches of Camberwell could sleep easier in their beds. His plastic briefcase and some cake crumbs were all that remained at his desk.

The changes when the series started were cosmetic but also significant. Les was introduced no longer as Vic's 'partner', just as his 'assistant'. 'Couldn't let it lie' became 'wouldn't let it lie'. The tickertape machine on Jim's desk became more hi-tech. But apart from that things stayed pretty much the same. Orton even made sure there was a stage and curtains on the studio floor to give the sense of still being in a club rather than a recording studio.

Like a first album, the first series was, in some respects, the easiest. Jim and Bob simply had to distil everything they had done so far. On the one hand there was a hell of a lot to distil, on the other there was no pressure to come up with new material just yet. Seamus Cassidy's only worry was whether they would be too esoteric even for trendy Channel 4. He decided to tackle this problem by hiring Scottish comic Jack Docherty, from the mildly Pythonesque sketch show *Absolutely*, to be script editor. This was basically a fancy job title for someone who read the jokes and decided whether they would be funny on television or not, but Jack did come up with some original ideas about the dynamic of the show, according to Cassidy: 'The impression I've always had is that Jack and producer Alan Marke constantly tried to keep them roughly within what people can understand, but nobody, apart from maybe Charlie Higson, when he was script editor for them at the BBC, has been able to say, "Nobody is going to get this, just don't fucking do it." But Jack was the one that spotted they were a double act. Everybody else had been talking about it as Vic's show and his sidekicks. But Bob was clearly a major comedy brain behind it. Jack pointed it out with characteristic directness, but he didn't do much to the scripts, he loved them so much he didn't feel the need.'

The real challenge was cutting the excess of material down to make a thirty-minute show, recalls Peter Orton: 'It wasn't easy, but Jim and

Bob learnt very quickly that there was only a certain amount of time.' It was an embarrassment of riches, as opposed to a shortage of usable material, which was the case with other comics on the live circuit. 'It was really a case of finding the more accessible material among the really weird surreal stuff that they had,' says Orton. 'It was a case of finding stuff that wasn't too off the wall. There were also decisions that were taken to make it more of a stage presentation as opposed to a TV presentation, which was what they went on to do with *The Smell of Reeves and Mortimer*. We recorded it as live and it only ever overran by about five or six minutes.'

Orton's aim was to have watertight scripts but retain Paul Whitehouse's beloved purity: 'I didn't want them to compromise too much really, so I just shot it in a very live way and gave them a lot of freedom. We didn't rehearse a lot. We rehearsed before the night, but not lots of cameras, which they did later on. It was tightly scripted in terms of blocks. We knew that Novelty Island would happen there, for instance. It was scripted in terms of plot changes and costume changes. It was scripted in terms of structure, but a lot of ad libs I didn't see until the show, which I thought was the best way of doing it.'

To newcomers it may have seemed esoteric, but this was Vic and Bob at their most accessible to date. There were showbiz elements which anyone could relate to. When Bob Mortimer closed one show as Rick Astley, Jim came out from the wings in overcoat and glasses pretending to be Eric Morecambe. They had been described as Morecambe and Wise on acid, the first post-modern double act, but this was a snippet that would have been recognizably funny to anyone who had grown up watching television in the Seventies. There was even an early sighting of a genuine joke when Jim said, 'I put so much petrol in my car the other day, I couldn't get in.' This was prima-facie evidence that Vic and Bob weren't being weird because they couldn't come up with conventional jokes – they *didn't want* to come up with conventional jokes.

Orton's strongest memory is the feeling that this was something completely new: 'Absolutely no doubt. I'd never seen anything like it, and that was what was so good.' It was so different, though, it also created a certain amount of friction: 'There were a couple of times I was very anxious about one or two of the items.' There was a heated exchange of views in the Green Room over Talcum and Turnip, two very bad silent knockabout clowns played by Jim and Bob. Orton wasn't convinced, and the scene very nearly wasn't filmed: 'They were just arsing around in the middle of the stage. It didn't have a point, which I thought was too far off the wall. I thought it was too loony.'

Jim and Bob were quickly getting to grips with the workings of television and wanted to be involved at every level, recalls Orton: 'They were pretty exact about things. They used to fax me very specific drawings for props and scripts. We had quite a lot of discussion, but they knew what they wanted.'

Orton was a very sympathetic programme-maker, but Jim and Bob did suddenly find that they had to deal with people who didn't necessarily understand what they were attempting to achieve. Alan King had drifted away from the group, Dorian Crook's involvement in performing was smaller – because his Toff could not be broadcast, for obvious reasons. Easy-Listening Man hadn't made it onto the TV version. Instead there were new people to make the props, new set designers to create the look of the show. Jim had wanted a stark, plain background, but when it appeared, the designers had insisted on jazzing it up with sparkling stars. Jim's first fight was to get them to revert to the plain lines that he had in mind. For virtually the first time, Jim and Bob saved their drinking until after the show and performed for the cameras sober.

The main thing in their favour, though, was that Orton allowed them to retain the world that they had created onstage. It was a magical place where childlike things could happen. The secret of Jim's humour was a wit that was as innocent as it was infantile. Bob had been the catalyst that had made it palatable for a wider audience at the Goldsmiths Tavern. The challenge now was to retain enough of that weirdness but make it palatable to an even wider audience. Not that Jim was necessarily thinking this way. In fact the last thing on his mind at this stage was ratings, which was probably fortunate, because while the show had an enormous cultural impact, its ratings were nothing to write home about. Michael Grade, however, was undaunted, and determined to stick by the duo. Seamus Cassidy recalls meeting him at a Christmas party at the end of 1990, and rather sheepishly broaching the subject of this strange mix of Crackerjack and Sunday Night at the London Palladium, which he thought might be a bit sensitive, since, at around a million viewers a week, the ratings hadn't so much gone through the roof as limped up a couple of steps. 'Michael looked at me and said, "If nobody watches this show we should carry on doing it."'

There is no denying that the series had an enormous impact, completely disproportionate to its viewing figures. Tom Fawcett remembers that Jim used to 'virtually explode with delight' whenever he saw his name mentioned in the *New Musical Express*, so it is not hard to imagine how he felt when he saw his shiny face peering out from the cover of their edition of 26 May 1990. It was the week that the band of the moment, the Stone Roses, played their historic gig at Spike Island, but thanks to journalist James Brown, who had vociferously championed Jim and Bob, Vic was put on the cover of a special comedy issue. Inside Danny Kelly's feature confidently predicted that Reeves and Mortimer would have an impact as great as the first series of *Monty Python* or *The Young Ones* and would be 'a cult of monster proportions'.

Cassidy suddenly saw that comedy was becoming the new rock and roll. Despite the low viewing figures it was hipper than ever: 'Vic, Bob and Sean Hughes took comedy into the rock press. The music press is a relatively small constituency but its influence is greater. *The Tube* also had a much greater influence than its viewing figures suggested and *Big Night Out* was the same. But the ratings system isn't representative. It doesn't have meters in kids' bedrooms, or count video recordings, common rooms, or second sets. Ratings are based on the idea that the family gathers round the telly and we all know that hasn't been true for at least twenty years.'

The *New Musical Express* wasn't exactly unfamiliar with hyperbole, but this edition was unusual for two reasons. Firstly, they weren't accustomed to championing comedians. Secondly, for once the hype was correct. Danny Kelly still felt that it was necessary to clarify the situation with a black warning box at the top of his fawning feature: 'The article below contains unusually high levels of journalistic hype, drooling anticipation and unquestioning devotion.' The following two pages were basically a beginners' guide to R&M on the eve of *Big Night Out's* television début. Readers were instructed when to shout 'What's on the end of your stick, Vic?', they were told about Les, and they were informed about 'You wouldn't let it lie'.

One can get an idea of how excited the music press was by the following article in which the paper's writers assessed the comedians of the day. The best TV shows of all time were *Fawlty Towers*, *Whatever*

Happened to the Likely Lads? and *The Fall and Rise of Reginald Perrin. Vic Reeves Big Night Out* was rated at number fourteen, which was pretty good for a show that had not even been transmitted yet. The best comedy records were by Derek and Clive (Peter Cook and Dudley Moore), National Lampoon and Peter Sellers. The selection revealed the pitiful standing of contemporary comedy. Could one imagine a critics' choice of music being so lacking in up-to-the-minute releases? Vic and Bob were clearly something to get excited about.

When the series actually aired, there was still an element of shock among the original group who had been working together during the late Eighties. Dorian Crook recalls that although they had known there was going to be a series for quite a long time by then, the actual evidence on the screen was still pretty memorable. 'Jim had gone from mucking about on the dole to a television series in five years and I think we were quite taken aback. More so than we would be now because there are so many channels making comedy programmes today.'

Even though they had done bits with Jonathan Ross, it was only when they did their own series that the realization dawned on them that this was for real: 'At the Albany we were just not of this world,' says Bob, alluding to the TV industry that seemed to be clamouring for them now. Even Jim, who had been doing dress rehearsals for stardom throughout the Eighties, suddenly seemed taken aback that it was actually happening. Surely they would be rumbled after one show and promptly sent back to south London.

It was only after the first series had aired on Channel 4 that Jim and Bob decided they needed some office space to work in. That June they started to rent Jools' office at his studios in Greenwich High Road, known as Helicon. It was an eccentric building, something of a south London folly with the façade of a country railway station. Sometimes unsuspecting members of the public would turn up there in the forlorn hope of catching a train. Others swore blind that it used to be a station, but it had basically been little more than a derelict row of garages until Holland had renovated it. At first Jools was working in New York, but when he returned Jim used to claim that they used to pay £50 a week and Holland used to listen to them working through the keyhole.

They would turn up every day and attempt to write something, although things did not always work out. Jim and Bob have never been computer-literate. One day, when they were still using a primitive

Amstrad computer, Bob took out the disc, wiping off the day's work in the process. It was an unconventional working arrangement at Helicon. When they fell behind with their rent Jim and Bob agreed to appear in the video for Jools' single *Holy Cow* in lieu. As the video had a farming theme they decided to sit in a mudbath. They thought it was rather funny, but didn't realize how long filming took and ended up sitting up to their waists in mud for most of the day. They would finally leave in 1993, but every now and again, Holland still finds remnants of their time there: 'airgun magazines, pornography ...'

There was a lot of luck about the way Jim and Bob got involved in TV. In retrospect they were relieved that Channel X got to them first. Another company with more of the Oxbridge/BBC pedigree, a Hat Trick (who made *Have I Got News For You*) or a Talkback (the company formed by Mel Smith and Griff Rhys Jones), might have tried to mould them more, but Channel X, being fairly new to the television game themselves, was prepared to let them have that crucial bit of freedom. According to Bob, their long-time regular producer Alan Marke 'is just a facilitator. If you've got a vision he couldn't give a fuck, so you get total control.' As Alan Marke puts it: 'We just thought "They're nuts, let's stick 'em on telly as they are."' While more recently the duo – and Jim in particular – have been very keen to make sure that the programme-makers do what they want, back then they weren't quite so confident with their demands. However, as it was something of a unique programme, nobody at Channel X was prepared to mess with a winning format, thinks Jim: 'Even with the *Big Night Out* they were never really convinced they knew what was going on, so things were left in our hands.'

The news of a new comedy sensation had even got round to the broadsheets. There was a genuine sense that this series, which started on 25 May 1990, marked a watershed in TV comedy history. There was a freshness to Reeves and Mortimer. They weren't from Oxbridge, they weren't from the Edinburgh Festival, they weren't even originally from London. No wonder the press was confused – the comedy world hadn't seen anything like them in decades. Jim was interviewed by Carol Sarler in the *Sunday Telegraph*. From the moment Sarler called him at home the answerphone message hinted that this was not your off-the-peg, standard stand-up but a far more rarefied bespoke variety: 'Hello. Thank you for dialling the right number. In a few seconds' time, your voice will be etched on to the inside of a scallop shell with an extinct labrador's fingernail for posterity. Please remain seated.'

Jim explained his motives for cleverly remaining in Deptford when touring might have given him national exposure earlier. 'It would have cost too much to drag the show around, so we stayed in the one venue,' he told Sarler. 'Anyway, I thought if anyone wanted to see it, they could make the journey down to south London.'

Given the right circumstances, however, Jim would venture out of south London. That spring he appeared at the Hackney Empire alongside Jools Holland and a very young Steve Coogan in a charity concert, *Nothing Like a Royal Show*. The performance was recorded by ITV and screened in April, effectively giving Jim some mainstream television exposure to whet the appetites of potential fans of his Channel 4 series.

Jim had given the impression that he didn't expect television success, but he now seemed excited by it, and quietly confident. In his spare time he had become more and more involved in the Gentleman's Motorcycle Club with Bob, Jools Holland and Andy Morse, and he was now looking forward to being able to buy more British motorbikes so that he could indulge in his hobby. He would painstakingly explain the code of conduct of the club — current membership four — to anyone who would listen: 'Courtesy, consideration and care at all times.' No Hell's Angels they, they rode English bikes such as Velocettes and Ariel Leaders. 'We wear tweeds at all times, we ride at sensible speeds, and we take our helmets off whenever we pass a lady on the pavement.' Jim was deadly serious, but this all contributed to his image as a great British eccentric. No one, not even the people who found him funny, could get to the bottom of Jim Moir, and this made him all the more appealing. Why was Wendy Richards pulling a cup out of a policeman's stomach? Why were Spandau Ballet laughing at an orphan who'd fallen off his bike? Why were Milli Vanilli trying to create negative gravity in their tights? The growing fanbase didn't care — they just knew that when Vic Reeves said these things they were, inexplicably, inescapably funny.

Chapter Six

England's Merriest Men

After the event, of course, it is easy to see why *Vic Reeves Big Night Out* was such a success. It combined the free-form spirit of punk rock with an unashamed love of the variety circuit and, in particular, the working men's clubs of the north-east, where both Reeves and Mortimer's families had been entertained over the generations. Jim was happy to acknowledge the comparison with the night out when you got 'a three-piece band, a comic, a woman dancer and the Jack Jones singer'. You could argue that the duo were transcending barriers of age and class and reflecting the fragmented post-modern culture of Thatcher's Britain in the late Eighties, but for Jim his act was not something to be dissected. That was the kind of thing you did with corpses, and their comedy was very much alive. 'Our comedy isn't making any point. It's just daft,' he explained to an endless queue of inquisitive journalists keen to put a label on him.

For John Irvine, though, it was not free-form enough. John had always been the big fan of experimental music in the early Eighties and now he wanted to keep the comedy closer to the avant-garde: 'I argued for those things that were not accessible – a lot of the stuff could have gone in if that format wasn't forced on them. I didn't have a clue why it was done, they didn't seem to have a problem with it. But they were no longer totally free until the cue, they were rushed, which took freedom away from what they did. Channel 4 should have shot loads and cut it.'

But despite their old friend's misgivings the television show also had a huge amount of confidence about it, something that reflected the fact that it was already an established live success. Who else would have had the nerve to enter at the beginning of the very first transmitted episode accompanied by a man (Mortimer) dressed as Isambard Kingdom Brunel, who held a stuffed Alsatian in his arms while he sang the Monkees' 'I'm a Believer'?

Vic Reeves Big Night Out gave the world not just two new stars, but an entire galaxy of characters. While Harry Enfield might have been content to portray cartoon-like creations that were easily recognizable archetypes, Vic and Bob came at comedy from a quite frighteningly different tangent. Sometimes it was dark, sometimes it was cruel, sometimes it was simply absurd, as in the case of the cheeky foul-mouthed fox named Alan Davidson, after Jim's non-performing chum from Darlington (on TV, of course, he was a lot less foul-mouthed). The supercilious Graham Lister, played by Bob, may have been a distant cousin of Harry Enfield's 'You Don't Wanna Do That', and Mr Dennis the sweetshop owner, with his strange customers and views on the world, was manageable, but from that point Reeves and Mortimer went off the scale with their menagerie of madmen. There were the Stott brothers for instance: Donald and Davey had bald wigs and were terrible at everything in a high-pitched whining voice. They attempted to present mock shows themselves, but were held back by the fact that they could barely complete a sentence, let alone an idea.

Alan King had once described Jim's crowd at Winstons as all 'a bit wonky', and the same could be said for the show; everything was out of kilter within the world of Vic Reeves. On Novelty Island, Jim did the hosting with the aid of a bell inside a handbag, the first of many examples of gender disruption. Graham Lister often felt he ought to have won, but his performances were consistently awful. One week he burned paper; another week, as in the never-screened pilot, he thought victory was assured when he pushed lard through the facial orifices of a picture of Mickey Rourke the film star. A singing mound was disqualified for not being able to enter the picket-fenced paddock. The winner would be announced to Reeves by a different method each week. The message sometimes came tied to a seagull's leg, sometimes carved inside a kebab, sometimes phoned in by Jean-Paul Gaultier from a hiding place in Torquay. The proceedings did seem somewhat toned-down compared with the anarchic bearpit of the early live shows in Deptford, but only just. One audience member back then had asked if he could take part in Novelty Island. He stood onstage, put a coffee jar on his head and hit it with a hammer. Despite the copious blood and the novelty element of the act, the punter failed to win.

No detail was overlooked in an effort to squeeze humour out of every situation. The only things missing were real celebrities, but cardboard cut-outs seemed to be a more than acceptable substitute. As arts theatre combo Action, Image, Exchange – inspired in part by the dance-based theatre company called Geographical Duvet that used to run the Parrot Café – the duo donned masks of Sean Connery and pranced about at the front of the stage and no one was heard to feel short-changed.

The budget seemed low, but it was enough. Bob claims that one of the reasons Channel 4 was keen on them was that they were so cheap. He thinks there was a budget of around a million pounds, but says Peter Orton brought the series in for around £110,000, which is quite an extraordinary difference. Orton couldn't confirm the figures but says, 'The budget at Channel 4 was fine for me for that show.' Location shoots would have bumped the costs up, but Orton didn't want to do that anyway. 'That would have taken away from it. I wanted to do a representation of the live show. That's why I put up a stage in the studio and put curtains across it.'

Granada Television's Mark Robson had got to know Jim and Bob during the end of their run at the Albany and saw immediately that they would work on television. 'The gift to any television commissioner was that it was presented in the form of a television programme. You had the combination of brilliantly original talent and something that was based on traditional television variety. That thing they used to do where Bob would come out and say to Vic, "Look, you're making us look like a cheap music-hall act" – I think that always encapsulated everything their humour was about. They were and are in love with cheap music-hall acts and they had always seen themselves as that, and that is one of the reasons why they retained a certain humility and decency in the profession where some of their contemporaries have turned out to be right cunts. All they've ever wanted was to be the best of today's variety double acts.'

The result was a show that was at odds with everything else on television at the time. It was more like a black Ealing comedy, or an episode of *Dr Who* directed by Spike Milligan. There was something camp about it, too. It wasn't just the foppish suits, or even the white handbag that Vic carried when he presented Novelty Island. It was something to do with the relationship between Vic and Bob. It wasn't exactly homoerotic, but it was strangely ambiguous. Neither was the straight man in the comedic sense, but in the sexual sense they both emphatically were. And yet there was something that bonded them together. The way they bickered with each other but then ganged up on anyone else who tried to assert themselves onstage was reminiscent of a marriage. When Jonathan Ross had first seen Jim and Bob together in a club he had thought they were lovers. 'Bob turned up and I thought they were gay. Bob was saying to Jim, "You weren't happy tonight, were you?" When Jim said to me, "I want my mate Bob to be in the show," I thought, Oh God, he's got a talentless lover who he wants to elbow into the act. In fact Jim and Bob both had girlfriends, but when they were together there was a definite chemistry between them.'

By July 1990, the world could be divided into two types of people: those that got Vic Reeves, and those that didn't have a clue what was funny about a Brylcreemed, besuited, possibly insane parody of a TV personality. Most of Canada probably fell into the second half. Charlie Higson recalls that in the summer of 1989, he and Paul Whitehouse had wangled their way out to Montreal's Just For Laughs Comedy Festival. Jim and Bob were also out there and decided to test the waters with a gig at the small Club Soda with a view to coming back and doing a big show at what had become comedy's most important international trade fair. 'It was a most extraordinary night. There was a handful of us who knew them – most of the audience had no idea who Vic and Bob were. Then there were some problems with Bob's work permit, which meant that he wasn't allowed to speak, so they had to come up with an act without Bob saying anything.' As with the Twickenham yoghurt incident, this was the kind of scenario that made Jim more determined then ever to stand his ground. Not surprisingly, Higson recalls it with crystal clarity.

'There was this whole club full of completely bemused Canadians, but Jim rises to the occasion at times like this. He gets very belligerent and bloody-minded and he will make things more extreme rather than make compromises even if they hate it. Bob was shitting himself and it was the year when all comedians started to get a social conscience: they weren't doing drugs stuff, they were talking about marriage and kids, and Jim came out and said, "I'm Vic Reeves, I've just had a boy," and the audience clapped and cheered and whooped. Then he continued. 'He's called Ian and he's a crab," at which point he pulled out a crab and a stony silence descended on these people. Jim proceeded to interview the crab with the help of offstage tapes about the arboreal rainforests of Scotland.' Seamus Cassidy was also there and took a perverse delight in the show: 'Going very badly in Canada was very funny, almost as funny as they were.' Cassidy recalls Jim doing his MOR new wave tribute 'I Remember Punk Rock' to 'jaw-dropped silence'. While the Canadians were too speechless to heckle, the British contingent found it perversely hilarious, remembers Higson: 'It was so funny to see an audience completely confused.'

There were still a fair number of English viewers who were confused too, and the press seemed to take it in turns to crack this new comedy conundrum. In October *The Independent* dispatched high-brow arts critic Adam Mars-Jones to interview the duo. He immediately established his upmarket credentials, by suggesting that in their three-piece suits they looked more like right-wing journalists from the *Spectator* than comics, 'but then Magritte looked like a businessman'. As in the case of punk rock's Dickensian urchin lookalike Johnny Rotten it was part of the very essence of breakthrough artists that they don't resemble their immediate antecedents. And neither do they behave how you expect them to behave. Over the years Jim and Bob could be crude, rude or erudite, depending on the rapport they had with the journalist or what mood they were in on that particular day.

Mars-Jones felt that the duo were concealing something in not acknowledging their artistic influences. His speculation may well have been informed by the fact that earlier in the year Jim had actually written a short review in *The Independent* of Turner's seascape *Snow Storm*, which was being exhibited at the Tate Gallery. The review was a mix of the juvenile and the autobiographical: 'As a child I always wanted to be a deep-sea fisherman.' He went on to reveal that 'one critic wrote: "Turner paints with cream, chocolate, egg yolk and currant jelly: here he uses his whole array of kitchen stuff." So even if you don't like the painting I suppose you can always eat it.' In a touching gesture, the nature lover donated his fee to the Royal Society for the Protection of Birds.

Mars-Jones had his suspicions about the fag-pulling laddishness, however, drawing attention to the fact that in conversation Moir referred to his younger fans as fourteen-year-old 'women'. There may not have been a political agenda onstage, but was he a champion of political correctness at heart? As for Bob, he had done legal aid work; did he have a conscience too?

They seemed particularly skilful at reinventing themselves depending on the market of the newspaper they were speaking to. In the *Daily Star* they revealed to Ollie Wilson that the secret of their success was booze. Bob claimed to drink sixty-four pints of lager during the week and fifty more at the weekend, getting into the pub at 6 p.m., staying until 11, before hitting a club and ending up with the market workers in the early pubs at Smithfield at dawn.

The drink references were exaggerated, but maybe not that much. Alcohol had always helped people appreciate the duo's humour, so why shouldn't it help them come up with the gags in the first place? Rational, clear-headed thought might make one realize how silly, infantile and pointless it was. Drunk, one could let rip.

It also helped them to relax on tour, and they would soon find that they needed to relax. In the autumn of 1990 they undertook a small college tour. They suddenly found that local cult fame had become national cult fame as 1,000-seat venues were selling out well in advance. People were turning up at campus venues across the land ready to shout the catchphrases that until then had only been uttered by a modest coterie of south Londoners. One of the people who joined them on the tour was Simon Day. They had 'discovered' him during a talent night at the Rub-a-Dub Club. Like them, Day, a south Londoner by birth, had not wanted to be part of the Comedy Store circuit. 'My local venue was the Tunnel, which was too scary, otherwise I might have tried stand-up earlier.' Jim and Bob invited Day to join them on tour. 'I came on in the middle of their set to talk about acid house and Robert de Niro, things like that. It was all very new to me. I had been a landscape gardener.'

Day had been impressed by the nerve of Jim and Bob. He felt that they were courageous even to set up a club in south London in the first place: 'It was like me going to Wigan and starting a cockney knees-up.

It was a rough area and quite brave.' Day soon realized that Jim was pretty fearless when it came to performing, even in the early days. As other people have also observed, he has absolute self-belief: 'If anyone else did a bad gig they would go home. Jim would step off the stage and go straight to the bar. There was no humiliation whatsoever.'

It was an indication of how quickly the duo had established themselves and how proud Channel 4 was of them that by the end of 1990 they were chosen to see in the New Year with a TV special. Their New Year's Eve show was like no other special before it. Reeves told the *Daily Mirror*: 'I can assure you that there will be no men in kilts singing about how sad they are to be away from bonnie Scotland.'

Success put Jim under pressure to justify his art in a way that he had never had to when he was performing live. *Time Out* tried to get at his motivations and there were the first rumbles of a personality crisis. Was Vic a creation, or was he basically Jim Moir? 'A lot of it's me. The majority is me,' he said. Bob agreed: 'You never go through the process of saying, "What would Vic do, what would Vic say?"'

For once they were prepared to give their comedic processes some thought, though. Bob explained that they avoided observational comedy. Jim explained how they revisited the old traditions of falling down, dressing up and putting on strange voices, and went on to elaborate on why they shied away from the joke set-up, punchline rubric: 'The joke is whatever you make it in your mind without it being laid on a plate for you. It's just ironic juxtaposition at the end of the day, really. It's the oldest form of comedy going.' As if realizing that maybe they had given away a trade secret and revealed too much, they soon became wilfully obtuse. Asked for a list of who they admired they came up with Elizabeth Arden, Ruth Rendell, Jeremey Irons, the proprietor of Smith's crisps and Toilet Duck. None were known for their comedy.

By the end of 1990, however, they were firmly esconced as Channel 4's most prestigious performers. The chance to go 'first footing with England's Merriest Man' was the high point of the schedules on the last day of the year, with Vic in dandyish jacket and ruffles and Bob in a neat pin-stripe number. The show combined the best elements of the series to date with a hint of seasonal magic. As ever, there were little touches to delight and attention to detail that others might not have bothered with. Vic entered leaning on a false arm that looked like his real one until he got up and left it at the table. It wasn't clear whether the gag was inspired by the *trompe-l'oeils* of surrealist art or Rod Hull's bogus limb that used to enable him to support Emu. While another star's desk might have been covered in tinsel, Vic's was decked out in Dalmatian-style spots. In fact stuffed dogs positively littered the set. During Novelty Island – direct from King Herod's fitted kitchen – Vic perched on one as the acts paraded in front of him. Wavey Davey (an unwitting nod to a similarly named character in the old radio show *Round the Horne*) saw off the Kennedy family with a gentle 'see ya', Judith Grant revealed her hobby of dressing fruit by burning a pear in a velvet jacket and a Jacobean ruff. Bob returned as Barnes Wallace, and there were two Stompers who jumped up and down to tunes ranging from the theme from *Steptoe and Son* – a musical leitmotif that would keep returning throughout their career – to the Rolling Stones.

There was a Hogmanay supper with the Living Carpets, which culminated in Bob announcing that he was completely unaffected by explosions that happen on the stroke of midnight. With the aid of a pause in filming and a replacement dummy being put in his seat, he promptly exploded – except that, as Vic pointed out, it wasn't quite midnight yet. The usual gags were nicely stretched and distorted. There was a running gag about *Honey You Shrunk the Kids* ('No, I shrunk the kids', 'What, you as well?') and to continue the joke The Man with the Stick was played by a smaller person concealed in the hat, Bob doing the voice backstage.

The pre-recorded New Year's Eve show was also the first time the duo's fame and status meant that they could call on genuine celebrities to spice up the proceedings. Mark Wingett, a co-star of *Quadrophenia* who had become better known as a copper-haired copper in ITV's *The Bill*, tried to arrest Vic from behind the desk and left the stage with a gag, 'I'm a centaur parting', revealing that his bottom half was a cloven-hooved mythical animal. Vic argued that it was a satyr, which rather blunted a joke which was obscure enough at the outset.

There was a very early echo of *Shooting Stars*, when Kim Wilde and Michael Starke (corpulent window-cleaner Sinbad from *Brookside*) appeared in a game to find out who was the best pop star, called Pop Plumbs. In a series of rounds Starke was presented with difficult tasks, while Kim, when not being swooned at by Vic or Bob, was given an easy ride. In the opening round, for instance, both contestants had to saw a wooden leg off an old man. The difference was that Wilde's leg was made of balsa wood while Starke's leg was made of teak. There was also a precursor of the non-sequitur style questions of *Shooting Stars*. In the showdown Starke was asked to supply the name of a popular harbour. He replied 'Liverpool', but the correct answer, for no particular reason except that Vic wanted Kim Wilde to win, was Hartlepool. Unfortunately, when Vic turned round to present Wilde with her prize she had disappeared backstage with Bob.

If a highlight was Bob's comedy fall, a lowlight was the That's Justice finale, which seemed unusually under-rehearsed. There was some confusion over Judge Nutmeg's first name, Bob saying it was Neville and Vic saying it was Lionel. A member of the audience was selected and condemned to be a paperweight for the Fonz, but with time running out, the stage was suddenly overcrowded with the special guests crammed on stage for a quick chorus of 'Oh! Mr Songwriter'. As the credits came up, the copyright of '1990-stroke-1991' showed that Jim and Bob, given the space and time, were still keen on those little details that made their old shows so special. The programme was followed, rather poetically, by Squeeze, featuring Jim's chums Jools Holland and Glenn Tilbrook in concert at Newcastle City Hall.

By February 1991 Jim was able to enjoy the spoils of success. He and Jools Holland had a spectacular joint birthday party at Malcolm Hardee's new Up The Creek Club, on Creek Road, near to Winstons. The theme of the night was 1791, and guests had to turn up in period costume. Among those in attendance were Jonathan Ross and his wife Jane and Dave Gilmour of Pink Floyd. Jim turned up as a scurvy knave in a tricorn and long black wig, while Holland came as Nelson, which meant that there was a nervous moment when Bob turned up as Napoleon, but things went swimmingly all round.

It is the nature of celebrity that it has its good side and its bad side. Jim in particular found that he had to juggle working on a second series of *Big Night Out* with a seemingly endless round of promotional interviews. At the same time he was becoming keener on the London party scene, spending less time in Blackheath and more time in the centre of London, the medialand around Soho, near to the offices of Channel X. With a new series due to start on 27 February, the *TV Times* was lucky to find Jim at home and able to give them a guided tour of his Westgrove Lane residence to accompany a feature on the forthcoming series. His large first-floor flat seemed to confirm everything people were thinking about Reeves, that he was eccentric and odd. It was a sign of his hectic lifestyle that he hadn't really done much decorating since he moved in. All he had to show for himself was a matching green pin-striped armchair and sofa, and shelves containing some miniature motorbike kits given to him by Bob. The walls featured pictures that had followed him from flat to flat throughout the Eighties. An eerie portrait of Elvis Presley having his pocket picked by Frank Sinatra looked down on visitors.

In the bedroom his clothes were strewn about, while his suits hung from the wardrobe door. If Loyd Grossman had been going through the keyhole he would not have been impressed, but would have concluded that this was somebody who did not care about food very much. The fridge contained beer, eggs and butter.

The shelves were also full of atlases, reference books and bird-watching manuals, reflecting what he claimed was his second favourite hobby. He claimed he liked nothing better than getting on to his motorbike, putting his binoculars around his neck and heading for the country. Unfortunately there was little time for twitching, with a new series and further commitments in London to fulfil.

In the spring of 1991 when the BBC's *Comic Relief* came round, it was inevitable that Reeves and Mortimer would be invited to take part. Contractual obligations to certain channels were always suspended for good causes, but Channel 4 did not have an exclusivity clause on Jim and Bob anyway. The nature of their involvement was more problematic. Once again, outside their own universe, they struggled to make an impact. Their best jokes were alternative ideas for the charity's Red Noses – crash helmets for carrier pigeons was a particularly good one – but there was a general awkwardness about their act. A spot of late-night free-form word association had them standing onstage talking about getting 'irate', to which the other started talking about 'high rates' in Peckham. It was all strangely parochial, but not very funny, except to the most committed Reeves and Mortimer fan. Paul Whitehouse revealed why he was probably not the best choice as script editor on the second series: 'I'm a complete fan. Even when they were crap they were the best thing on Comic Relief.'

Ben Elton, who introduced them, probably summed up the national position on Reeves and Mortimer. As they left the stage to a rough approximation of baffled applause, Elton remarked: 'One half of the audience in hysterics, the other half don't know what's going on.' It seemed to encapsulate the way that Reeves and Mortimer had divided the comedy nation.

Stardom had changed them and yet not changed them. They still lived in modest flats (Bob had recently bought a place in Camberwell), with the only extravagance being new CD players. They still liked to go down the pub and drink pints. When they were invited to celebrity parties they felt rather like gatecrashers, though this didn't stop them from becoming positively ubiquitous on the London social scene. Jim had always liked having his picture taken, and now there were more chances for snappers than ever. He did feel less comfortable about the fan mail they received. In March 1991 he told the *Daily Mirror*: 'We've been sent hair, diving gloves, and of course, loads of meat products. Very poor.' They already felt like pop stars, though.

Jim in particular was much in demand for other events wanting a spot of credibility. He appeared in the celebrity gathering for ITV's *An Audience with Jackie Mason* and at the Brit Awards when they were still known as the BPI Awards. Jim's distinctive image had always singled him out even before two Channel 4 series. Back in May 1989 he had been invited to take part in a BBC2 pilot dinner party-based discussion programme about comedy, made by the Late Show team in which celebrity guests had a meal and a drink seated at a large round table that was quite obviously in the middle of a television studio. Jim was unusually quiet, but then he was rather overshadowed by Keith Allen standing up and storming off in the middle of the meal, complaining that the event was too middle-class.

Comedian Morwenna Banks was also on the programme, which was called *The Comedy Café*: 'It was a prime example of how not to make a TV Show. Various writers from very different backgrounds were brought together to come up with a sitcom.' The only option open to a number of people involved was to get very drunk. Banks, who was sitting next to Jim, had to go offstage in the middle of filming to throw up. Vomit had to be blowdried out of her hair. When she returned Jim decided to chip in with his idea for a plot: 'about three dwarves who live in a septic tank.'

Comedy had given Jim the stardom he had never achieved when he was in a succession of bands. 'Our last tour was like being in a rock band. There were screaming girls at some shows who had to be held back by crash barriers. Not that I'm grumbling, some of them were very nice.'

In the *News of the World*, however, he played down the sexual perks of being a star: 'My sex life is dull and straightforward. Even when I played in bands when I was younger I was more interested in going for a pint with the lads than picking up girls. I must have a very low libido. I'm more interested in riding a motorbike.'

Stardom, of course, brought with it absurd tabloid scare stories. On 24 March 1991 the *News of the World* revealed how Jim had been on a giant ferris wheel in Montreal and had only been saved from certain death by Bob Mortimer grabbing him. The truth was that it had been little more than a minor panic attack at the Just For Laughs Festival, brought on by being stuck at the top, 150 feet from the ground, when the wheel stopped: 'I had this insane urge to escape over the side, although I'd have been killed if I'd tried. I almost certainly would have jumped if Bob hadn't been there.'

The second series of *Vic Reeves Big Night Out*, which started on 27 February 1991, built on their following. It was essentially the same as the first series, with Peter Orton still at the helm, but Jim was finding things a bit repetitive. They spiced things up, however, with a few new characters, some taken from the old live show, some especially concocted for Channel 4. There were the Ponderers – the two big-chinned Swiss men (played by Jim and Bob) who would silently debate the merits of pointless acts such as injecting ink into a Battenberg cake. Then there was Morrissey the Consumer Monkey, the rather scrawny puppet, who offered reports on the safety of various products. Back in the Albany days he had been known as Pippin the Consumer Monkey, and there had been some talk of renaming him Freddie Mercury, but Morrissey 'sounded right'. Jim's interest in Bryan Ferry was still there: he opened one show with a strutting version of 'The In Crowd', the old mod classic that had been a hit for the Roxy Music vocalist in the Seventies.

The catchphrases which they had already been doing in Deptford for a couple of years before Channel 4 signed them up were now wearing a little thin and there were rumours that they actually had to be convinced to do a second series. 'They were getting fed up with doing Man with the Stick,' confirms Orton. By his own admission Paul

Whitehouse was too much of a fan to be of any real use as script editor: 'I just turned up and laughed and said, "Learn your lines and don't forget to fall over".' Reeves still sat at his desk like a madman abandoned in an IKEA crèche, with the addition of more comic falls from Bob, but their humour was just as hard as ever to fathom for many non-believers. Journalists would turn up to interview them and come away more bemused then ever. A *Guardian* questionnaire, published that June, shed as much light on Jim's motivations as any interview to date. He confessed that his idea of perfect happiness was 'bells tolling in the distance'. He claimed that he relaxed by wearing a sequinned mask and cloak and reciting episodes of *Bonanza* to a group of elderly Dutch totters, and would like to be remembered 'as a mad Moorish swordsman of the late eighteenth century'.

Chapter Seven

Dizzy Times

The year 1991 was when things snowballed for Reeves and Mortimer. It started well with the second series of *Vic Reeves Big Night Out*, but perhaps they took too much on. In July they were preoccupied by the filming of *The Weekenders*, their Channel 4 sitcom pilot. There was no date planned for broadcast yet, but *The Weekenders* would prove to be a pivotal moment in their career. It wouldn't be transmitted for another year – a year that would mark some of the most significant events in Jim and Bob's life to date.

Maybe there was a feeling that the success had to be milked – there was no way of knowing how long it would last. Jim and Bob had made it big without following the well-trod path of university, stand-up, Edinburgh Fringe Festival that had become the standard route for most successful alternative comedians. They had no role models to guide them, but they seemed content to make it up as they went along, defining their own approach to the comedy business on an almost day-to-day basis.

Unlike the stars who came immediately before them – Mayall, Edmondson, etc. – they didn't have any background in drama, nor did they feel the need, like Ben Elton, to address a particular agenda. They just continued to do what they used to do for a laugh on a larger budget. It made perfect sense for them to start their career together in a pub – they had been working on it unconsciously in pubs for the previous decade, long before they had even met. Bob has his own modest theory: 'It's all about just growing up in a rural area and farting about with mates.'

Not that they were completely averse to doing something conventional in comedy terms. Having never appeared at the Edinburgh Fringe before, they booked themselves into the small Gilded Balloon theatre for five nights at the end of August. The tickets were only released a week before the show and, given the fact that the venue only had a capacity of 250, it was no surprise that young fans chose to queue up all night rather than miss the opportunity of seeing their heroes in the flesh. Bob was rather taken aback by the attention: 'It was nice when they came because you think, "Oh, maybe we can make a living doing this." But we'd turn up and there would be five hundred fans outside trying to get at us. It was unbelievable.'

The shows were a chance to try out new material for their autumn tour. Karen Koren, who runs the Gilded Balloon, recalls that it was touch and go at the start of the run: 'When they went onstage I don't think they knew what they were going to do, it took them a few nights to get into it.' Proof of their genius is probably the fact that they can be funny even when the material is thin, and things *were* a bit rocky in Edinburgh. Jim's mobile face and Bob's short, stocky frame seemed able to transcend a mundane script, but it was a close thing. Matt Lucas, a fan then, but soon to work with them, agrees: 'I think the best comics are better than their material and sometimes that is true of Jim and Bob.'

Eventually things began to fall into place. Jim and Bob were able to enjoy themselves in Scotland and even judge the 'So You Think You Are Funny' competition for new comedians. It was a way for Bob in particular to stay in touch with new acts. He was always enthusiastic about discovering emerging talent and this was the perfect way of tapping into it at the very source. They didn't even ask for any payment, as long as they could be put up in a nice flat for the duration.

Jim and Bob loved the atmosphere of the Festival, but if history had been different Jim might already have been a Fringe veteran. According to Karen Koren, Malcolm Hardee offered her Vic Reeves when he was a solo act about five years earlier. Koren wasn't sure if he was right for her venue: 'He was very middle of the road, completely different to anybody else at the time.' As it happened, Malcolm confused the issue by also attempting to book Jim into the rival venue, The Pleasance.

Things started to look messy, but were resolved when Jim decided he didn't want to perform at the Festival at all. In retrospect, given his track record as a solo performer outside south London, it was probably one of the shrewdest moves of his career.

In early 1991 Jim had also been approached to make a record. He had struck up a friendship with journalist Paul Morley, who helped to secure a contract for Jim with Island Records via his own new quasi-independent offshoot, Sense. Ever since his exploits in the early Eighties Jim had never quite let go of his desperate desire to be a rock star. The nearest he had come to this sort of fame had been as an extra in a Shakin' Stevens video for the single 'What Do You Want to Make Those Eyes at Me For?' in 1987. Jim claimed to have been approached to appear in it while walking through Leicester Square, but the fact that he looked so much like a classic rock and roller in his leather jacket, black Harley Davidson T-shirt and quiff suggested that things were not as spontaneous as they seemed. In fact, Peter Brooke Turner confirms that he and Jim were hired for the shoot, and paid £10 each.

Apart from his own rock-and-roll flexidisc of 'Howlin' Wind' he had also appeared as Vic (complete with unusual piratical earring) in a video for New Cross balladeers Band of Holy Joy in 1989, which had been featured on an *NME*/CND compilation video *Carry On Disarming*. In the film Vic introduced the band as they did a gig on a seaside pier and could be seen during the promo nodding approvingly at the bar — the scene was actually filmed back in Deptford! In 1990 he and Bob had also contributed backing vocals to a cover version of the old R&B standard 'Holy Cow', which was featured on Jools Holland's album, *World of his Own*, but with comedy being compared to the music industry by countless critics and with Vic having been 'discovered' by the *NME*, the stage was set for a bigger comedy-rock cross-fertilization.

Jim had already renewed his involvement in pop earlier in the year, providing backing vocals for Morrissey when the former Smiths singer had covered the Jam's 'That's Entertainment' on the B side of 'Sing Your Life'. Unfortunately it was not one of the Mancunian moaner's bigger hits, stalling at number thirty-three in April 1991, but it had given Jim a taste of pop success beyond selling a few tapes through the classified ads of the *NME* or giving away his own single at shows. Jim had found that he had so many copies of 'Howlin' Wind' still cluttering up his home that he had given them to his old friend Ian 'Wally'

Wallis, who had formed a thrash rock band called Dan. Wally gave away copies of 'Howlin' Wind' free with his band's album.

In fact Jim soon outstripped Morrissey's effort with his own début single which charted at the end of April and reached number six. 'Born Free' was a cover version of the classic John Barry epic, previously performed by Matt Monroe (listeners unaware of this fact would soon discover it during a Mark E. Smith-style rap in the middle of the number). As well as harking back to Jim's early efforts at karaoke at The Swag and his musical interludes at the Goldsmiths Tavern, it was also the nearest he came to singing a song straight. His performances on *Vic Reeves Big Night Out* had had a strange ambiguity about them. Off-camera, people wondered whether he was sending up singers or trying to be one, but felt too embarrassed to ask. He seemed to believe he was a real balladeer, but there was always an unconventional kink in his vocals – mainly owing to the fact that he usually retained his Darlington accent – which made him instantly recognizable. It also made it difficult to take him seriously as a crooner, but it did make his music highly entertaining.

For the début single release of 'Born Free', Jim had been billed as Vic Reeves and the Roman Numerals. The album, however, was very much Jim's project. The front sleeve featured Jim alone, looking very sultry in spectacles and waistcoat, while on the back he was in full fop mode, complete with cravat and walking cane. Other musicians played on it, and Bob helped out here and there on vocal duties, but this was Jim's chance to commit his musical talents to vinyl for posterity and he wanted to show the full range of his interests. *I Will Cure You* was not so much an album, more a musical CV, the commercial equivalent of inviting a girlfriend up to his bedroom and playing her his Hendrix guitar solos.

To help him achieve the required results, jazz experimentalist Steve Beresford was hired to programme the drums and ended up bringing in his own coterie of musicians and producing a number of tracks too. Beresford has seen *Vic Reeves Big Night Out* and had been rather taken by Jim's style. In fact the programme had been recommended to him by seasoned saxophonist Evan Parker, who adored the programme so much he had gone out and bought a video recorder just so that he could tape it. 'I loved the bad singing and the wordplay,' recalls Beresford. It struck a number of other chords for him too. The free-flowing language had an improvised jazz feel to it, but it also recalled the old northern humour of music-hall star Frank Randall. Most intriguingly, both Beresford and Evan Parker – who was immediately brought on board for the recording sessions – saw comparisons between Vic and Bob and the Kipper Kids, an Anglo-American performance art duo who were big on the European festival circuits in the Seventies. The Kipper Kids used to appear onstage in odd clothes such as jock-straps and flying helmets and spout verbal gobbledegook, and were compared to old vaudeville acts. They would also stage elaborate fights – a growing element of Vic and Bob's act – which would often end in the participants being cut and bleeding. Jim and Bob may have been more mainstream, but they seemed to be subverting conventional entertainment genres in much the same way.

Jim and Bob's penchant for elaborate, bizarre and imaginative props also reminded Beresford of the old American comedian Ernie Kovacs, one of the earliest television comedy pioneers who specialized in ingenious visual gags. Kovacs would construct a set at a 20 degree angle and then film it at that angle, so that everything would seem level except for liquids. Anything round would roll down to one end, but on the screen it was hard to work out why because to the viewer everything seemed to be level.

Steve Beresford also felt that Jim and Bob's wordgames were a kind of ritual, developed to cope with the grind of daily life. It reminded him of the time he had worked in Dillons bookstore in the Seventies and had come up with similarly silly ways of making the days pass more quickly. Paul Morley had worked with Beresford on his own underrated Channel 4 television series, *The Thing Is*. In that show Beresford had come up with unlikely variations on musical genres and between them they set out to repeat the trick here, going through the songs that Jim had done on *Big Night Out*, adding a little depth and coming up with ways to rearrange them. The sessions took place over a week during the summer of 1991 at Dave Hunt's studios at 30 Stronsa Road, just north of Hammersmith. It was a civilized working arrangement, just like going into a very relaxed office, starting at eleven o'clock in the morning and always finishing by seven in the evening. Beresford's abiding memory of the sessions was the total lack of comic eccentricity, but a couple of things did stick in his mind. 'I remember Jim talking about the car crash in the Jacques Tati film

Traffic. He was very impressed that it featured such a weedy car crash. And Jim and Jonathan Ross had perfect skin, as if they had just come straight from a health club.'

In the autumn Jim's second bona fide single, 'Dizzy', was released. Jim was backed on the cover of the old Tommy Roe pop anthem by the Midlands band the Wonderstuff. Part novelty record, part straight pop-retread, no one knew how it would fare in the intensely competitive pop market. Even the record company seemed to have underestimated the pulling power of Reeves as the single slowly but surely began to climb the charts.

In September Jim and Bob set off on their second live tour, dubbed the Brown Tour. If the short, college-based tour of 1990 had given them a small taste of what it was like to be a pop star, complete with entourage and screaming fans, this tour would make them have second thoughts about what they were doing. Jim may have been overly modest when he thought *Big Night Out* might only have been a one-off to tell the grandchildren about, but even he didn't expect to be at the top of the charts and appearing at the Hammersmith Odeon for ten nights less than eighteen months later.

Dorian Crook was on tour with Jim and Bob when it was confirmed that 'Dizzy' was number one at the beginning of November. He remembers the chart conquerers being typically subdued about it: 'They were not the kind of people to say, "Hey we've got a TV show, let's have a champagne party," and they were the same about this. They were very relaxed about it. I said "Well done", but they tend not to go in for those platitudes. They didn't behave like others would.' In fact Jim did mark his long-awaited chart success in a characteristically unusual fashion – he buried three pairs of Chelsea boots.

By the time the tour was well under way, the success of 'Dizzy' was having some weird spin-offs. The now-defunct newspaper *Today* claimed that because Vic had featured a bank of Whirlpool washing machines in the video and on *Top of the Pops* – the lyrics compared the lovestruck singer's spinning head to a whirlpool – the manufacturers were now 'cleaning up', with demand higher than ever.

By 1991 success had contributed to the demise of Jim's long-term relationship with Lucie. They had got used to underwear arriving in the post, but were still taken aback when someone sent pickled bullocks' eyeballs. Persistent fans in public places were a constant problem. It even prompted Jim to go out in a disguise – he once donned a wig in Liverpool to avoid signing some meat products – but it was hard to sustain a conventional relationship when you couldn't comfortably walk the streets together. Jim and Bob had needed a police escort to escape from a venue in Nottingham. Support act Simon Day recalls that he had just one fan: 'a fat bloke clutching loads of tiny cuttings about me'. Day was shocked by the response they were getting on and off the stage: 'I remember it all being very bad. Security had never seen anything like it, even in terms of bands. All this wonderful crafted comedy was lost, you couldn't even hear it for the screaming.'

Jim and Bob also had constant attention from women, which was hard to resist. According to an interview in *Today*, both had their adoring fans in similar measures: 'The women chase us both down the street equally and at exactly the same speed,' said Bob. Jim tried to be more settled, and he started to see Sarah Vincent, a social economics student based in south London, on a regular basis. They had got to know each other in a pub when she had accidentally poured a pint of lager over him.

After the single, *I Will Cure You* made its way up the charts. It was a peculiar album, put together with Jim's usual care. On the sleeve there was even advice for fans planning to have a family, with Jim drawing in his longstanding fondness for thinking up bland names: 'Thinking of having a child? Then why not try these names: Doug Watson, Ralph Kendall, Ann Mitchell and Grace Williams.' Inside there were illustrations. Jim also suggested some walks people might like to take, including the 1977 Diamond Jubilee London Walk and map references and pictures of the places where he had buried his Chelsea boots in September. There was also a decidedly Pythonesque list of cheeses inappropriate for grilling: 'Edam, Jarlsberg, Emmental, Gruyère, Parmesan (no chance).'

If the advice was odd, the songs were distinctly strange. It showed that Jim's tastes were about as broad as they came. He also seemed determined to shake off some of his past. The *Big Night Out* theme was rendered in a disposable middle-of-the-road style, while the *Big Night Out's* showstopper 'Oh! Mr Songwriter' got a funky James Brownish pastiche (a slight return, 'Oh! Mr Hairdresser', opted for a rock pastiche). The most sublime Reeves moment on the album comes in the middle of this track when Evan Parker gets stuck into a free-form solo. After some sax tootling that seems to have lasted an eternity, involving the unusual, highly skilled techniques of 'circular breathing', Jim can be heard to shout, 'Pack it in, Parker.' Much to Parker's chagrin, he never met Jim, who recorded his spontaneous outburst at a later session. Most unlikely of all, Jim's interpretation of the old Deep Purple stomper 'Black Night' was produced by Phil Oakey of the Human League and inevitably sounded more like an out-take from his synthesizer combo's forthcoming album.

Any thoughts that this album was meant to be taken seriously appeared to be dashed by two ditties that harked back to two of Jim's old musical dabblings. 'I Remember Punk Rock', dubbed 'Test Card Swing' by Steven Beresford, waxed nostalgic about the Buzzcocks and Co. to the theme tune of some long-lost sitcom. Paul Morley had to act as mediator when Jim described Beresford's original arrangement as too much like Frank Zappa. In the end it got the distinctively bland MOR treatment, with Jim and Jonathan Ross providing an easy-listening whistling chorus. 'Sing Hi! The New Romantic' was his ode to a generation of tea-towel wearers presented in a marching-band style.

There was definitely an air of indulgence about the project, a feeling that above all Jim was having fun and making the most of his pop star fame by enjoying a singalong with his new pop chums plus Bob and Jonathan Ross. 'Empty Kennel' was a sentimental spoof of the standard canine tearjerker 'Old Shep', only this time his faithful dog had died and he was inviting listeners to join him in the kennel. 'Summer of '75', previously performed by Jim and Bob's rambling duo Tinker's Rucksack on *Big Night Out*, had now been transformed into a jaunty yet murderously dark bar-room anthem that the Pogues in their pomp might have been proud of. 'Meals on Wheels' was another old favourite, a rock-and-roll retort about sending food to geriatric celebrities such as Jimmy Savile and Cliff Michelmore.

Some songs didn't make the final cut for the album. According to Beresford, '"Lost Island" was a showbizzy uptempo piece about Jules Verne's mother making shoes out of melons and police helmets out of cheese. The verses were like Kurt Weill and the chorus was a kind of music-hall patter.' In which case, perhaps it would have gilded the lily. The twelve songs already included boasted a dozen different musical styles. One more might have scared all but the most passionate fans away.

The highlight, however, apart from 'Dizzy', which did have a genuine pop fizz to it, was Jim's interpretation of 'Born Free'. For fans who hadn't bought it as a single, this was worth the purchase price alone. If *I Will Cure You* is a novelty album, it certainly withstands more repeated plays than most novelty albums.

With a record in the charts and a tour traversing Britain, the shock waves of Reevesmania could be felt up and down the land. In Blackburn a boy had reportedly been expelled from school for carrying a handbag while shouting 'Look at the size of that sausage.' Bald people were now frequently known as Les, and future captains of industry could be heard disturbing the peace of student unions up and down the land with cries of 'You wouldn't let it lie.'

Two people even attempted to find Jim's buried Chelsea boots, following the map references and polaroids on the inner sleeve of *I Will Cure You.* Iain Muirhead and stalwart companion Mark Wilson set out on 7 December. Further details of the following story can be found on the Internet (http://www.users.zetnet.co.uk/vic_and_bob/found.html), complete with added pictures:

'Soon after buying the album, we resolved to go after the Scottish boots. But we weren't fired into action until Vic and Bob pitched up on Jonathan Ross's chat show one Friday night and revealed that no one had yet found any of the boots. So we bought the necessary Landranger map and identified the grid reference as a spot in Glen Etive in the Highlands. And the next morning – a cold but sunny Saturday – Mark and I set off on what we were convinced would be an enjoyable but fruitless road trip.

'We arrived in Glen Etive around three hours later and immediately recognized the wee bridge pictured on Vic's polaroid. So Mark positioned himself on the spot where Vic was shown standing and I tried to find the location from which the picture was taken. We had brought a spade with us, believing that the boots would probably be buried. But, within seconds, we found we were wrong. Glancing under the right-hand side of the bridge, Mark spotted a white Safeways carrier bag. He quickly dragged it out, opened it up, and there they were, in all their glory.

'We went mental. Jumping around, whooping and hollering. And, as we made total tits of ourself in the midst of all this serene Scottish scenery, a load of ramblers from a Rolls-Royce factory in the west of

Scotland came round the corner. Intrigued, they demanded to know what was going on, and – although they hadn't a clue who we were talking about – they were bemused but excited for us as well and proceeded to take about 100 pictures of us, the boots and themselves. From there, we returned home, stopping off at a hotel for a swift celebratory beer.

'We also took the chance to telephone a number printed on the rear of the polaroid we had just found in the boots. It was the answering machine of a management company (presumably R&M's) in London, and Mark happily registered the find. We never heard a damn thing from them afterwards. Mark and I phoned a few times to see if Vic or Bob had ever been informed of our triumph, but they were never interested in talking to us. Miserable sods. Still, that was the only disappointment of one of the most joyous days of our lives.'

Jim was also brightening up his mother's life. His parents had seen the show in Glasgow and finally realized that comedy was no longer a hobby for their son. And, according to Jim, his mother was benefiting from her new-found vicarious fame: 'The corner shop now knocks a couple of pence off the fish.'

But for everyone who appreciated Jim's humour, there would always be another who was completely dumbstruck by it. An appearance on *This Morning with Richard and Judy* was a dream come true for Jim and Bob – they used to watch the ITV show before settling down to work – but things didn't go to plan. When the chat show couple asked them what they thought was funny, Jim started to wax lyrical about *Dad's Army*. Judy Finnegan seemed to think he was trying to be ironic and, as Jim told the *Mail*, 'Judy suddenly went mad. She threw up her arms, cried, "I cannot take any more of this," and cut us short. It was heartbreaking.'

And following the success of 'Dizzy', the record company decided to release Jim's dance reworking of 'Abide With Me', remixed by the Grid as a single in the hope of having a big Christmas hit. The song didn't go down very well in Brixham in Devon, the home town of the original writer, vicar Henry Francis Lyte. One of the locals contacted Island Records to complain that the disc ought to be withdrawn, commenting that 'putting a dance beat to a hymn was like dancing on someone's grave'. The fans had misgivings about this simplistic parody too – it only reached number forty-seven in the charts.

According to reports, Jim was planning to kill off The Man with the Stick, Morrissey the Consumer Monkey, Judge Nutmeg and Mr Wobbly Hands after the tour. It had become a bit of a Loadsamoney syndrome, with the catchphrases that made them now threatening to break them. The prospect of saying 'You wouldn't let it lie' again was distinctly unappetizing. Jim told the *Daily Mail*: 'Viewers may have heard them five, maybe six times. I've heard them sixty million times and they are getting very tiresome.' The risk of burn-out was tangible. 'We're bored stiff with it and we've got better things to do,' he moaned. 'I'm so sick of saying "You wouldn't let it lie" or "Look at the size of that sausage" and having to look as if I am enjoying myself.'

To the public it seemed like a sudden, abrupt decision, but Jim and Bob had been doing these characters in one form or another for nearly seven years now, so it was no surprise that they felt they had run their course. As Jim told *The Independent*, 'For your own sanity you've got to change it ... I don't know how people do plays, saying the same things over and over again.' Where there were once people at parties reciting *Python* scripts, their children were now reciting *Big Night Out* lines.

The reality was always different from the dream. After the dust had settled, Jim was able to take stock of the absurdity of topping the charts: 'Suddenly you think you're a bit of a rock star and you can't really get out of it. You sort of puff your chest out. You can show off being a rock star. It's much better than being a comedian, when you tell jokes and there's no leg kicks.'

But things weren't ever as simple as this. When they did 'Dizzy' for *Top of the Pops*, Jim recalls how they had to do six takes. The Wonderstuff would have a tequila slammer each time, so thirty seconds into the take it would hit everyone. Jim remembered that they were going to place a camera inside one of the washing machines onstage, and that he was supposed to open a door and sing the line into it. But when he opened the door they had taken away the camera, so he rushed around opening all the doors. It was one of those classic performances that didn't go exactly to plan, but it didn't stop 'Dizzy' from staying at number one for two weeks.

By the end of 1991, the success of *Big Night Out* had taken its toll on the duo. That November the tour teached Newcastle City Hall. What should have been an emotional northern homecoming, particularly as the gig was being filmed for video posterity, was a fraught occasion.

While there were no complaints from the paying punters, there was definitely an air of exhaustion offstage. Back at the Copthorne Hotel Michael Heseltine was also in residence, which made for tight security and a tense atmosphere. Malcolm Hardee had travelled up with Jim, and, for reasons best known to himself, he decided to crawl along the balcony that ran along the front of the building, dressed only in his socks and a long leather overcoat, to give Simon Day, who he thought was staying in a nearby room, a surprise. This might have been dismissed as comedic high jinks if Michael Heseltine's room hadn't been near by as well. Instead Hardee was taken away by Special Branch until one of Jim's party could confirm that he was not a threat to national security. Jim, meanwhile, was oblivious to this. As ever, he had spotted someone famous and was in the bar chatting to local celebrity Jimmy Nail.

Bob had problems too. Around the time that he had met Jim he had been diagnosed as having a type of arthritis. He explained what happened in the *Daily Mail*: 'I woke one morning in agonizing pain and couldn't move.' It had taken over a year before it was properly diagnosed, and he had his back strapped and had been on pills. At times on the tour it was so bad he had to hobble to the theatre. The change of climate meant that the end of the year, when the air was moist, was a particularly bad time for the condition, but he refused to let it affect him.

That night's show bore all the hallmarks of a show at the back end of a long tour. Jim looked more lardy-faced than usual and the show was more shambolic than ever. Part of the problem was the fact that Jim and Bob's sudden chart attack had caught them unawares. They didn't know whether they were a pop group or a comedy turn. Before the show even opened the professional schizophrenia was apparent; there was the theme from *Swan Lake* and fireworks and dry ice, pyrotechnic affectations more usually associated with rock gigs. At the Goldsmiths Tavern this kind of grand gesture was perceived as a tongue-in-cheek critique of celebrity. This was the real thing.

Somehow they had to marry a rock show with a comedy show. 'Dizzy' was clearly a pop song, but what about their other material? 'Meals on Wheels', for instance, was a supercharged rock number, but it was basically about delivering food to the elderly; Jimmy Savile having to have his muesli was hardly classic rock lyricism. Jim seemed to be revelling in the stardom and performed it as if he was Rod Stewart, swinging the microphone stand and preening himself at the front of the stage. The song, however, was essentially daft, and, as if to hammer home the point, in the background a half chicken/half bear swung a bucket at a BMX bike. When he took off his headgear he revealed himself to be Simon Day, now christened Tommy Cockles ('They stuck a note under my hotel door with a couple of suggestions on it. The other one was Peter Peanut'), playing an American actor and telling the duo: 'You guys are a pair of goddam sickos.'

Day recalls the duo having mixed feelings about their pop success. Although he was getting as fed up with 'Dizzy' as he was with his catchphrases, Jim loved the stardom, but realized its demands were keeping him away from comedy, which he adored even more. Bob was also uncomfortable with it. He was worried that the pop thing might distract from the fact that Jim was a comic genius: 'I sit next to him when we work and I'm just amazed ... it's a real privilege.'

By now Simon Day was growing in confidence as a performer, even though the partisan crowd could give him a hard time. Earlier in the year he won the Hackney Empire New Act of the Year award and was developing his own style, cultivating the character of variety veteran Tommy Cockles. At his early gigs Day used to ramble and say whatever came into his head in the hope that it would be funny: above all, he didn't want to be seen as a Reeves and Mortimer clone. 'I couldn't try to copy their sense of humour. They wanted me to come on in cowboy boots shouting "Boiled onions", but I preferred to do my music hall character.' The audience didn't always appreciate Cockles. 'As soon as they realized I was not part of their show I got off. Bob tried to reassure me. He used to say, "There will always be ten per cent of the audience who will find you funnier than us and think that we are shit." After that I wasn't afraid of any gig.'

Travelling from town to town on the coach was often just as nerve-racking. It was certainly not what Day expected. Although they shared the same sense of humour, Jim and Bob appeared to have very distinct personalities. Bob would talk about comedy, Jim would talk about Todd Rundgren. 'I thought I was part of this Haight Ashbury thing, I'd gone from being a gardener to this. Listening to them talk was just delightful. They were more funny offstage than on, doing quizzes, just sitting around. But I'd try to be funny and they just wouldn't laugh.

Then I'd start talking normally and they would burst out laughing. They had a completely different idea of what was funny to everybody else. You try and do their humour and they'd look at you as if to say "how dare you". I loved working with them, but in a way you can't ever *work* with them.'

It was an irony that a show that had started off as a live event was now defined by its TV incarnation. Jim had once said that he didn't take the *Big Night Out* on the road – if people wanted to see it they could come to Deptford. The reality was rather different now. Two years earlier the show had been too big for the Albany; now it was a squeeze at the major rock venues of every city in the country. As a consequence the Newcastle show seemed devoid of the subtleties that the television version had been able to play up. Vic's facial expressions were only really for the benefit of the first few rows. It was the visual humour painted by broad strokes which got the largest laughs. A giant dummy of Les, popping out from behind the curtains, got a huge cheer. In fact the cult of Les was more popular then ever, with a bald lookalike even in the audience. With its audience participation the *Big Night Out* seemed to be the *Rocky Horror Show* it was hip to like.

If Les had the cheers, Bob's Graham Lister got the jeers, coming on and accusing Vic of being a workshy fop. Vic, however, got his revenge. When Lister produced a placard announcing that Vic was 'Absolutely Queer' (a reference to the recent outing campaign by militant gay groups), Vic pulled off Lister's wig, revealing him to be hairless, and produced a placard announcing that Lister was 'Absolutely Bald'.

Jim's onstage madness reflected the offstage hysteria. At one point Vic couldn't get Morrissey the Consumer Monkey on to his hand and became frustrated with it. He claimed to have heard all of its current consumer tests via John Stapleton and his wife on *Watchdog*, making the monkey redundant.

Novelty Island was the cue for Lister to return, this time with Simon the Seasonal Seabird, a cardboard gull who could echo the changing years, by dropping leaves from its neck for autumn or shooting an orange out of its mouth to signify the summer sun. Lister looked as if he had been upstaged by a steam-powered bra which bolted across the stage, but the judge, a giant digestive biscuit with an eye which looked as if it had been painted by Salvador Dali, selected Lister as the victor.

As if there hadn't been enough mayhem already, the Wonderstuff appeared onstage for a finale of 'Dizzy'. It was all really very strange, a hybrid that wasn't completely successful on any level, except a financial one. And even that had a sting in its tail. Because 'Dizzy' was a cover version, the publishing royalties went to Tommy Roe, the original composer. This was a long way from the man who, according to Tom Fawcett, thought he was going to die of excitement when he got his first small mention in the *New Musical Express*.

According to Jim and Bob, though, the problems with the tour had little to do with the actual performance. Nearly a decade on, Bob looks back on it nostalgically: 'That tour was great. "Dizzy" was in the charts, it was like the *Fast Show* with characters like Lister coming on.' Jim recollects that it was the hard work that was the problem: 'We did forty-two nights, so it was pretty draining. We worked it out once that the correct amount of shows for a tour is twenty-six.' Bob: 'It was tiring, but we used to enjoy it. We used to go to bed at three in the morning pissed out of our heads. You'd arrive at 7 p.m., drink three pints before the show, a couple during, then you were just getting started. So you'd have maybe a dozen plus pints every night. We could never stop drinking, that's what did it, not the work.'

Chapter Eight

'Medieval Nepotism'

At the end of 1991 Jim and Bob had been talking about a change, but it was only in the following spring that the extent of that change became apparent. In March they picked up a BAFTA award, confirming that they were redefining the comedy landscape. The following month rumours began to surface that they were in negotiation with the BBC. By 28 April 1992 the rumours proved to be true. The next series would appear on BBC2. Any more than that they weren't telling, although Bob pointed out that they wouldn't be doing anything blue or political.

Having missed out on them the first time round, Alan Yentob had had the last laugh, although Jim delighted in pointing out that one of the top brass at BBC Light Entertainment Group at the time was a man called Jim Moir. They were not related, though apparently it was a very popular name in Aberdeen, and 'maybe if you go back far enough we are related. Maybe it's a case of medieval nepotism.' One of the main attractions at the BBC was artistic freedom, said Jim: 'They leave us alone because they don't have a fucking clue what we are doing. They don't understand us but they know we are funny.'

Jim and Bob still refused to play the corporate game. Despite being wooed by the BBC they still felt like naughty schoolboys when they were summoned to Moir's office: 'It was all rather frightening. We were sat on low chairs in front of this enormous desk and he said,

"Welcome to the BBC. We hope you do well. We're sure you will." In a rather threatening way.'

If the departure from Channel 4 seemed sudden to the public, things had been unsettled behind the scenes for some time. Seamus Cassidy, the man who had never been sure if the *Big Night Out* would work on television in the first place, had clearly had a change of heart. In 1991 he had talked to them about doing a third series, while they wanted to move on to something else, in particular a series of *The Weekenders*, a script they had been toying with for some time. According to Jim: 'It was a case of them knowing what works and wanting to stick with it, without wanting to try anything else. We didn't want to carry on doing the same thing, otherwise we would have ended up being pantomime artistes.' They were keener to take a risk than consolidate. Channel 4, on the other hand, was in great need of a hit comedy series to compete with the BBC.

That June marked the transmission of the pilot of *The Weekenders*, Jim and Bob's sitcom, filmed for Channel 4 the previous July. Scheduled at 10 p.m., it was something of a muted transmission, one of a quintet of sitcom pilots under the umbrella title of *Bunch of Five*. The others were fairly undistinguished, although Charlie Higson and Paul Whitehouse had a reasonable bash at an early lad-based sitcom in *Dead at Thirty*, and Frank Skinner's memoirs of a Midlands childhood, *Blue Heaven*, did get picked up for a series.

The Weekenders may not be the best sitcom pilot ever to be transmitted, but it is certainly one of the oddest, a kind of hybrid of David Lynch directing the Beatles' *Help!* on a budget barely big enough to pay for one of Ringo's drumsticks. In fact it was directed by Sandy Johnson, who directed the Comic Strip team in *Bad News* and more recently lent some of his directional magic to BBC1's *Jonathan Creek*. In *The Weekenders* Jim and Bob played two northern characters called Jim and Bob, whose idea of a good day out is a trip to a meat festival in a field. If it was not so bizarre, it would be tempting to suggest that a lot of their behaviour is autobiographical. In one inexplicable night-time sequence Bob even ends up on top of a wardrobe, just as he did so inexplicably back at school two decades earlier.

Once at the meat festival, Jim buys a sausage from the Human League vocalist Phil Oakey. However, a kind of Fashionable Three – a trio of aliens dressed in identical slacks and pullovers – need the sausage to feed to their queen. Having spotted Jim and Bob with the meat, they set off in hot pursuit. From the opening scenes in which a policeman (Simon Day) chases a man carrying a small bicycle in slow motion, *The Weekenders* is innovative, intelligent and visually striking. In one grisly double take the chief alien rests his cheek in his hand and, when he takes his hand away, the imprint is still there, as if his face is made out of putty. It rather trails off in the finale, suggesting that the title turns out to be an unwitting play on the phrase 'weak ending', but so many original jokes have been delivered by then that one can forgive Jim and Bob almost anything, although at times Jim's nervy overacting tests even the most loyal fan to the limit.

If *The Weekenders* was weird (Jim described it as 'about two very sad men who live for the weekends and their weekends are even sadder') the story behind *The Weekenders* was even weirder. Jim, who tried not to get involved in the politics of the comedy business, was a little vague about what exactly happened about it being turned into a series: 'We went off to the BBC and when we left Channel 4 they were saying no ... it was a bit on and off whether it was going to be a series anyway, because some people liked it and some people didn't at Channel 4. But we wanted to do it, and when we were leaving Channel 4 they said, "If you want to stay you can do *The Weekenders*" – it was sort of a sweetener really, but it never came to anything. There were too many people who didn't know whether they liked it or not.'

In fairness to Channel 4, even Jim wasn't sure what *The Weekenders* actually was. 'I don't know if it is a sitcom really. Sitcom to me means Paul Nicholas in a sitting-room, something indoors. It's more of a comedy drama. A sitcom is about a situation and it is broader than that. And it is very filmic. It's an odd colour because we wanted to get it looking like Eastmancolor, like Fifties films like *The Titfield Thunderbolt*, so we filmed it on a kind of film that we could change in the edit. But we ran out of money so it ended up in sepia. Which was quite nice anyway in an early Seventies *Black Beauty* film sort of style.' The country setting certainly seemed to be another hint that there was an autobiographical element at play here. Producer Mark Robson has always felt that Jim's childhood plays a great part in his comedy: 'Jim always had a fascination for farm life and the country. That was one of the things that used to drive his humour – references to starlings, wheelbarrows, farmers and stuff.' Jim was always the person who went further with a hobby, and in some ways that was what the concept of *The Weekenders* was — people who spent their weekends pursuing their hobbies. The difference was that in *The Weekenders* Jim and Bob were idiots who knew nothing about meat. In reality Jim would want to learn everything about his hobby, whether it was motorbikes, heraldry or progressive rock. Robson thinks that is also something that can be traced back to his childhood. 'When you or I were nine or ten we might have had a fascination with birds and collect a magazine, but he is the sort of person that would pack a bag and go off birdwatching for a couple of days.'

The origins of *The Weekenders* actually predated their very first Channel 4 series. Mark Robson had been interested in working with Jim from the moment he saw him: 'I was producing a pilot for Granada called *2*, by Jonathan Kydd and Christopher Middleton, that featured a number of comedians who were coming through at the time including Steve Coogan, Nick Hancock and John Thomson. It was actually a regional production for the Granada comedy department, and I was looking for somebody to play a postman and I was advised to see Jim by a friend who had seen their live show. He had just been taken on by PBJ Management, who had a rough videotape of his show at the Albany. I watched it and thought it was fantastic and I really wanted him to do the part. It was a really small part, only a cameo, but I was desperate to do something with him. I sent him the script and he said, "I can't do this because it is not my sort of humour, but we have got a script that we've been working on." I said I'd love to see it and we started talking about it.'

Robson met up with Jim and Bob in the Crown, a crowded pub in Wardour Street. 'They gave me the script for *The Weekenders*. It was a different script from the one eventually produced, and at that time they hadn't yet signed a deal for *Big Night Out*, so I was developing *Weekenders* while they were talking with Channel X and Channel 4. I knew everybody at Channel X, so there was no problem there. In fact I had been introduced to Jim by Alan Marke when I was chatting to Alan about something else. Jim wanted to know where to buy a black polo neck jumper and we started discussing where the best place in London to buy black polo necks might be. Eventually we got the script together and we thought Channel 4 might be the natural home. We took it to Seamus Cassidy, went through a couple of revisions with him and he commissioned it as a one-off transmittable pilot, so we went into production as soon as we could.'

So far, it seemed, so good. But then the problems started. 'They obviously hadn't done any location filming before, or any acting before, and some of the things worked and some of the things didn't. But I've spoken to Bob since and he has said it is one of the things on television he has enjoyed doing the most, and he is not just being polite. At some point they want to go back and do it again.'

Although hazy about the fine print, Jim and Bob basically corroborate this version of events. '*The Weekenders* is great, particularly the first half, but then we ran out of money,' says Jim. Bob: 'I loved the first eight minutes, though that's not really a great sales pitch, is it? We had twenty minutes to shoot the last three minutes and we had to change it all round.' This caused further problems. Mike Wattam and John Thomson, playing policemen, ended up in a ditch filled with hospital effluent and had to go off and have tetanus injections.

But even before *The Weekenders* was completed things became rather delicate with Channel 4. There was a feeling that Seamus Cassidy had always been unsure whether they would still be funny outside the confines of the *Big Night Out* format. As a result he may have been predisposed to not liking it when he saw the finished version.

Mark Robson felt that the programme was a success, particularly given the strange set of circumstances under which the pilot was made. 'It was shot on film with first-time actors, it had aliens and a very low budget, and bear in mind that they also tried to do some location material in the *Big Night Out* pilot, which didn't work. I watched it back recently and there are things on it that are very distinctive. I saw Bob about a year after it had gone out, and he said that one of the weird things is that "we've done two series of *Big Night Out*, we've started work at the BBC and I still get people coming up to me in pubs reciting dialogue from *The Weekenders*." And this was a show that went out as part of five pilots in a very late-night slot. Considering it was Reeves and Mortimer, it was treated very badly.'

Jonathan Ross is also a fan of the lost sitcom and was peeved that Channel X had missed out on it: 'Jim and Bob's big obsession was *The Weekenders*. When we were talking about *Big Night Out* they gave me two one-page treatments: one was the *The Weekenders* and one was for *Throatbilly*, about a guy that wins the lottery and spends it all on a strange theme park. And has a small harp-playing hillbilly in his throat. I was always fond of *The Weekenders* and was always vaguely jealous about not being involved.'

Looking back at the cast, it certainly featured an impressive line-up – basically friends of Jim and Bob and Mark Robson. Simon Day was in it, as were John Thomson, Paul Whitehouse, Phil Oakey and Russell from the Human League. Jim had met the Human League in Sheffield during their 1990 tour. It was Paul Whitehouse's proper acting début, and he remembers it for one particularly notable achievement: 'I did have the dubious distinction of making Bob literally piss himself laughing with my schizophrenic Welsh bus driver. Not so funny for him, but very enjoyable for the rest of us.'

Inevitably, Seamus Cassidy's version of events differs, but he does accept that Jim and Bob's departure from Channel 4 was bound up with *The Weekenders*: 'They wanted to do a sitcom and they showed me the script and I thought it was difficult to see. It was very bizarre and I wondered how it would work without an audience. I was instinctively nervous about taking them away from the *Big Night Out* format. Granada bought the script, and I agreed to commission it purely because I wanted to see if they could pull it off. I didn't have a great deal of input because it was quite clear that they didn't want any input.'

Cassidy recalls a number of disagreements in the cutting-room. It was originally going to be forty-five minutes long, but he didn't feel it was strong enough for a longer slot: 'Bits of it were clearly very funny, but bits of it looked like them larking about in front of the camera. I found it very indulgent and said so. We had a couple of anguished meetings about whether we would go with it, but I just knew in my heart of hearts that I didn't want to go on with it. Maybe there would be a time to do it, but it wasn't now, people hadn't quite latched on to *Big Night Out* yet.'

The disagreement seemed to damage Seamus's relationship with Jim. It had always been cordial rather than close, but Jim seemed to take Seamus's comments personally – which, since he had been involved in the decision about whether to commission a series of *The Weekenders*, seemed fair enough. Eventually, while *The Weekenders* was waiting to be scheduled, Seamus met them to decide how to follow the second series of *Big Night Out*: 'We were talking about what they wanted to do next, and they didn't deny they had had an offer and asked me for a plan of what C4 could offer, which was fairly generous, but I understand that Jim rather than Bob had taken my attitude to *The Weekenders* to heart and wanted to go to the BBC. I think they were also tempted with an eventual move to BBC1.' Granada's David Liddiment felt that Channel 4 handled the whole *Weekenders* affair badly. 'If it was intended to tie Vic and Bob closer to the channel, in the end it did the opposite because the channel didn't support it.'

Bob recalls an early meeting that had clinched things: 'We had a meeting with Seamus and said we wanted to do *The Weekenders* next. He wanted another *Big Night Out*, and said if we did another *Big Night Out* he would let us do *The Weekenders*. Then the BBC said we could do a new show, so we went. I think it was implicit that he would only do *The Weekenders* as a series if we did more *Big Nights*.'

Cassidy felt that *The Weekenders* was a case of inexperienced people taking too many liberties with the sitcom rubric: 'By and large sitcoms tend to observe a modified classical structure, and if the jokes are there it will make you laugh and if you are carried along by the story it tends to be all right, but if it is not working you go back to the basic science of it – what it is about? who is the protagonist? are they doing enough to move things along? and *The Weekenders* broke so many rules naively. It didn't ever look as if it was properly choreographed to work at speed, and things based on sight jokes have to go very fast to get their laughs and there were too many longeurs. I would have been happy if it was funny, but at least it didn't cost us as much as the fucking *Cows* by Eddie Izzard.' Cassidy's only consolation was a 'really sweet note' from Michael Grade 'saying "Bad luck, I'm really sorry this has happened."' Jim and Bob's departure would help to give the BBC the upper hand in TV comedy in the 1990s.

Cassidy could not hold them at Channel 4, but he doesn't feel it was a disaster losing them, although others at the station were keen both on Jim and Bob and on *The Weekenders*: '*The Smell* didn't do that many more viewers, it was *Shooting Stars* that changed things. To be honest with you, I regret not commissioning *Dead at Thirty* more. That was a bigger mistake on my part.' For fans of Reeves and Mortimer, though, *The Weekenders* would become the lost masterpiece, the holy grail of strangeness that they would have to live up to on the BBC. Part of the legacy was another script that was never made, in which the duo played fishermen who had no idea how to fish, They would go off at weekends and attempt to attract fish with the aid of kettles and other unlikely implements. Other ideas destined to remain unproduced included the story of the duo going to a health farm run by latchkey children on a council estate and going metal detecting on the Isle of Wight, where they discover a colony of pipe dwellers and a well which has Hitler's diaries, Shergar and the Ark of the Covenant down it.

The duo had started to write their new BBC series in March, even before the ink was dry on the contracts, and spent the first six months of the year on it. After a hectic 1991 when they had a bash at everything that seemed to come their way they wanted to concentrate on this new project. Vic talked to me in June on the eve of the transmission of *The Weekenders*: 'Last year was a complete blur because there was just too much going on at the same time. We've slowed this year down. I think I probably did burn out towards the end of last year. There were just too many things going on at the same time and I was completely knackered.' This time round things were going to be different: 'It'll be along the lines of *Big Night Out*, but mainly just me and Bob.' Catchphrases would be gone, Les would be gone, other characters would be cut back, and there was to be more location filming and some silent comedy, inspired by Jacques Tati – 'characters who fart in a particular way'. And, added Jim, 'Slade at Home, which is going to be like that documentary about those people in Reading, *The Family*, but Slade. There will be lots of arguing and Bob as Dave Hill, very much the matriarch, whereas I'm Noddy, the hard-done-by husband. The other two are the kids and I sort of side more with the kids.'

It was probably the frenzy of 1991 that made them want to draw such a line in the sand when they started work on *The Smell of Reeves and Mortimer*. The decision to ditch the old catchphrases seemed drastic. Mark Robson thought they had dropped them too quickly, but understood their reasons: 'The first national tour they did was inspirational, but the more dates you do year after year, it becomes a grind. The catchphrases seemed new to the audience, but they had been doing them for years. I think they dropped them too quickly, but they had the talent to carry it through.'

That July they went back to Canada for another crack at Montreal's Just For Laughs Festival. Once again, Hardee's Law – the further they travelled from Deptford the worse they went down – seemed to hold true. This time round they were on the big stage and Jim sang the praises of his lucky charm, a twenty-foot roll of Axminster that he carried with him wherever he went. It was so bad it was actually one of the few occasions that Jim would concede were not completely successful since his very first gigs: 'Seven thousand people, one of the biggest audiences we've ever had, and it was absolute silence for twelve minutes.' The Canadian crowd took things a little too literally. 'You could hear people in the audience saying, "That carpet is *too* big." They couldn't accept someone having a twenty-foot roll of carpet for a lucky charm.'

Mark Mylod, who later directed *Shooting Stars*, remembers seeing the performance on Channel 4: 'I remember absolutely pissing myself, but I was watching it on television and there was this absolute wall of silence in the theatre. It certainly didn't translate to Canada, but then Lucky Carpet isn't their most accessible work.' Jim had learnt the hard way that the British sense of humour and the north American sense of humour were separated by more than the Atlantic Ocean: 'It's a very English thing to make an arse of yourself. American comics tend to say, "We're the same as you," whereas with us it's "We're not the same as you, we wear bad shoes and we're completely thick." They didn't have a clue, but they didn't understand Harry Enfield either.' Enfield and Whitehouse had died doing Smashie and Nicey, which sailed right over the Canadian heads, so Jim and Bob were in good company.

It had been a relatively quiet year work-wise, which had enabled Jim to firm up his domestic life. This still didn't prevent him from being taken aback when, in December, his girlfriend Sarah announced that she was pregnant. He told the *Daily Mirror*: 'It was a surprise to me. I didn't know I had it in me. I thought I'd drunk too much beer.' According to the *Sun*, Sarah had pulled out a pregnancy-testing kit in McDonalds and Jim thought it was a pencil. He was relieved to hear that she was pregnant, because he had been wondering why she had been so moody. Planning for the future prompted more upheaval. He started to rent out his small Blackheath bachelor pad in Westgrove Lane and bought an old Victorian house in Lewisham. For the first time Jim could indulge in his passion for pasture. It had a dank shed with mice, and a garden the size of a football pitch which backed on to woods.

It looked as if 1992 was to be the year of brilliant projects that didn't work out. In December Jim and Bob helped out an old friend, Graham Smith, who wanted them to front a pop music pilot his company was making. Smith had been one of the people at Channel X who had coaxed Jonathan Ross south of the river to the *Big Night Out*, and he had always had a good relationship with the comedians. His show was called initially *Pop 1993*, then *Popadoodledandy*, and would feature Jim and Bob chatting to guests in their own inimitable style, doing a few music-based sketches and introducing bands. Notably, Smith raised the money for the show, not from Cassidy's Entertainment department, but from commissioning editor for music Avril McCrory's budget. Despite the fact that *Popadoodledandy* was never screened and never commissioned, he still considers it to be one of the finest programmes he has ever been involved in.

It all happened fairly organically, recalls Smith: 'Through knowing them we would bump into each other, and when I started my own company, TV21, we kicked around this idea with Jim and Bob for ages of their pop show, and gradually we sat down and worked it out. I saw them a lot because we were working with Jools Holland on shows for BSB, and they were using an office at Jools' studios, so we would go down to see Jools and end up arsing about with Jim and Bob. It was one of those shows which is the great unseen Vic and Bob show: the perfect synthesis of Jim and Bob's peculiar world view imposed on a very simple pop show, so it had a video review, guest interviews unlike any others you would see on any other pop show. They had dancers, a silly animated piece in the middle.'

Smith threw ideas at them, but they ended up coming up with their own linking conceits: 'In a way they are unproduceable in the nicest possible sense, but by and large they have such enormous confidence in what they come up with, and by and large it works. It is the best way of getting the pure essence of them. It was absolutely Jim and Bob's take on a pop show. As producers we just shaped their world view and it was a pleasure doing it.'

The acts were a ragbag of pop has-beens and wannabees helping out and hoping for some publicity in return. Nick Heyward, the erstwhile pin-up from Haircut 100, was making a comeback as a solo artist, older, wiser and with the kind of muscles that suggested he had spent the wilderness years in a gym pumping iron; and there was Kym

Mayzelle, a pneumatic session singer who had broken through on the dance scene a couple of years earlier but only had a couple of big hits to her name. Mayzelle and Heyward had to undergo a pop interview like none they had ever experienced before. Mayzelle had a particularly bemused expression when she was asked, with the aid of diagrams, how she would transport some meat. Bob and Jim needed to know if she would use a special harness.

Another band doing their bit at the London Studios near Waterloo was Cud, a self-consciously arty post-punk outfit from Leeds, whose love of kitsch iconography, bad clothes and seedy lyrics consigned them to pop's bargain bins but helped to pave the way for Pulp. They dutifully mimed their current single, 'Rich and Strange', only to be interrupted in mid-flow by Vic and Bob, who barged on to the bright, white stage wearing tiny My Little Pony rucksacks.

As with most recordings, things were laboured at times. Some scenes took a few takes, and it went on long into the evening. But Jim and Bob seemed back on form and ready for fun. After the recording was over, everyone squeezed into cabs to go to a post-production party for Jonathan Ross's show at LWT. While Bob talked about football to whoever would listen, Jim became engrossed in conversation with Nick Heyward, discussing the relative merits of early Eighties pop.

It was the kind of thing that came easily to Jim and Bob. Channel 4 had been pestering them to do a pop show for ages, and this was an easy option. As Jim pointed out, it was simply the kind of pop programme they would want to watch. 'It's just being very irreverent really. If Kym Mayzelle was being interviewed properly by someone I might go off and make a cup of tea, but if I knew it was irreverent I might hang around and take a look.' Bob felt this talk of harnesses revealed more about the subjects than talk of their new single: 'In a way you get a sense of their personality.' Which didn't say much for Nick Heyward's personality. He had to answer similar questions, but when the programme was edited, he didn't make the final cut: 'He made a fatal mistake,' chuckles Smith. 'He tried to be funny with Jim and Bob.'

According to Smith, Channel 4 was 'gagging' for a series of *Popadoodledandy*. Bob thinks they wanted fifty episodes, which seems to be an example of his tendency to exaggerate. Either way, it was not to be. By the time *Popadoodledandy* was completed, events had overtaken them and Jim and Bob were committed to the BBC. It became another great lost show, consigned to the vaults to tantalize fans. Smith was sorry not to make it, but knew that Jim and Bob's priority was a new non-music series. 'To put it into perspective, *Popadoodledandy* was only ever intended to be an additional show. If they had stayed at C4 they would have done *The Smell* or they would have done *The Weekenders*. *Popadoodledandy* would have been additional. By the time they went to the BBC it was no longer relevant, because it was more important that they deliver a brand-new core show for BBC.' Smith does note, however, that some of the ideas in *Popadoodledandy* ended up elsewhere. 'It was the first time they used a big white site, which they followed through with *The Smell*. *Shooting Stars* also echoes that theme of the big white space.'

The best comedy is always about timing, and Jim seemed to have the timing just right in 1993. On 16 May Sarah gave birth to Alice May – named after his grandmother rather than Alice in Wonderland, despite Lewis Carroll's Darlington roots – at the St John and St Elizabeth Hospital in St John's Wood, north London. On the way they had had to stop the car in Oxford Street next to a bus for her to be sick. The pregnancy had lasted almost as long as the preparations for the first series of *The Smell of Reeves and Mortimer*. Filming was now complete, allowing Jim to spend some time on domestic chores and on building a tree house in the garden. He also bought a rowing machine and tried to get fit: there were signs of a modest spare tyre forming around his once-lean frame. Typically he joked about his condition: 'Sex is supposed to get rid of about a thousand calories, but when I do it it's more like eight.'

The move to the BBC was construed in some quarters as Jim joining the establishment. He had been spotted by one journalist having a meeting in Soho's Groucho Club, which was deemed an unlikely place for the old Vic Reeves to have gone. It was an absurd interpretation of events. Apart from anything else, the Groucho in Dean Street was barely a stone's throw from his agent's office, so it seemed like the most convenient place to have business-related assignments. In the years to come the Soho club would become Jim and Bob's favourite West End bolt-hole.

And Jim and Bob were certainly having more business meetings. As well as developing their own BBC series they were also negotiating with the BBC to make a series of short ten-minute films starring Dorian Crook, who was now pursuing his own solo stand-up career. Crook's routine was basically a succession of old-style one-line gags, such as 'I used to work for an origami magazine. It folded.'

The series was to be called *Dot on the Landscape*. Each week they would film him doing his act in six very different places such as a comedy club, a working men's club, a school, a hospital. The gigs would be filmed, and Bob and Jim would also appear as Dorian's tour managers. They would drive him from gig to gig and keep all of his money.

Dot on the Landscape was one of those ideas that started with a brilliant title and went down from there. It never got made and, while everyone remained friends, Dorian missed out on his big break and went back to working in the clubs, under the nickname 'The Human Jokebox'.

Jim and Bob's dealings with the BBC showed that although they preferred not to, choosing instead to remain enigmatic behind a blanket of in-jokes, they could behave in a mature, sensible way if absolutely necessary. On the domestic front, there were also signs of behaviour more in keeping with men in their mid-thirties. Jim was now driving a car rather than a motorbike. On 11 September he married Sarah Vincent. It was a low-key local registry office affair in Greenwich, though in typical Reeves mode he joked that he had had to propose to her because she had found a ring in his car. It was a brief ceremony, with Alice May and his brown mongrel Maggie looking on. Jim was so nervous he reportedly forgot how to spell Moir in the registration book, adding, 'I love Sarah to bits and I'm so glad she was mad enough to become Mrs Reeves.' Despite the confusion over surnames, he was determined that marriage wouldn't change him and he vowed he would attack anyone who asked him if he felt different. Parenthood may not have changed him either, but it did change his hair colour. For the first time since he had been in the public eye he stopped dyeing his hair black and reverted to a natural mousey brown shade. At heart Jim has a strong conventional streak — Alice had ginger hair and he didn't want there to be any doubts about the parentage.

Wedded bliss coincided with an upsurge in Jim's profile. Adverts for Boost chocolate bars boosted the bank balance and he was much in demand. According to a story in the *Daily Telegraph*, he had been approached to appear in Jimmy Nail's BBC drama *Spender* and, most bizarrely, Disney had allegedly approached him and Bob to do the voices of two Bronx-born muskrats. It was a truly strange state of affairs that two comics who had made their name partly because of their accents were now reportedly being asked to put on phoney accents to make an even bigger name for themselves.

The duo did consent to appearing in work by others at two polar extremes of the entertainment industry. They had a meeting with mainstream double act Hale and Pace at the Groucho, got on well and agreed to appear in a sketch on their ITV show. At the other end of the spectrum they appeared in an independent film directed by Jarvis Cocker and Steve Mackey of then-rising Sheffield band Pulp, which was screened to coincide with the release of their single 'The First Time?'. The twenty-six-minute film was called *Do You Remember the First Time?*, and in it various celebrities ranging from Alison Steadman to John Peel to Jim and Bob recalled their first sexual experience. Jim recalled his seduction-by-Hendrix incident and said that he lost his virginity somewhere between the ages of 'twelve and twenty-two'. He summed up the experience as 'week-old liver on a rum-soaked mattress'. Bob's main memory was of tights, bright blue platform boots, 'an overwhelming feeling of "I am doing it" and subsequently "I have done it".'

Chapter Nine

A Strange Smell

Although Jim and Bob had both said that there would be less emphasis on other characters with the new series, they did introduce a new madman into their BBC2 bedlam when *The Smell of Reeves and Mortimer* started on 21 September 1993 at 9.30 p.m. Charlie Chuck – another northerner, real name Dave Kear – had done the pubs and clubs and Butlins for twenty years. Surprisingly, he had ended up at the Edinburgh Fringe Festival. Not so surprisingly, only a handful of punters there had any interest in seeing him. He wasn't represented by one of the major management companies, Avalon or Off the Kerb, who had a virtual monopoly on the crowd-pulling shows and venues, and he had no reputation. Bob, however, came across his act, got Vic and Sarah to see him, and they loved it. Although, according to Jim in 1997, Sarah cried when Charlie Chuck approached her: 'not in laughter, but in absolute terror'. On the night they turned up, Chuck was about to cancel the gig because there were so few people there, but he decided to do it. It was an act that defied description – even more so than *Big Night Out*. Chuck roamed the stage, spouting random words and gibberish, and ended up demolishing his drumkit. It wasn't particularly funny, but it was very scary. Particularly when he started to wave a large plank around.

On *The Smell of Reeves and Mortimer* Chuck was almost toned down. He became Uncle Peter, an eerie, shock-haired sight with a battered face who used to wander on to the stage, like someone out of Samuel

Beckett with Tourette's Syndrome, yell 'Donkey', and beg the duo not to send him back to 'the dark place'. The *New Musical Express* pretty well summed Chuck up: 'less like comedy and more like care in the community gone horribly wrong'.

Jim and Bob always have had a marvellous knack for finding new talent off the beaten track. They were also nurturing a young comedian called Matt Lucas, who, like Chuck, had been discovered by a happy accident. At the beginning of 1992 Bob had gone along to a club called the VD Clinic at the White Horse in Belsize Park in north London, where Dorian Crook was compèring. He had intended to check out somebody else who was doing a set, and Matt was doing an open-spot. Matt was particularly striking because he was eighteen years old and completely bald – a virtual mirror image of the Methusula-wrinkled and tousle-haired Charlie Chuck. He remembers meeting Bob just before the show. 'He came down and was very complimentary. I couldn't believe it, he was one of my comedy idols. I wasn't very good then and Bob was the first person to be encouraging. He sat at the front with a notebook.' Bob later suggested to Paul Whitehouse and Charlie Higson that they should get Matt on to their new series, *The Fast Show*. In the end, though, Vic and Bob ended up using him first.

Matt Lucas had been a huge fan of Reeves and Mortimer almost since the first time he saw them. He was an avid TV watcher, and when *Vic Reeves Big Night Out* started he was interested because he remembered seeing them on the ITV show earlier that year, *Nothing Like a Royal Show*. Apart from that he had no knowledge of them, which intrigued him. 'When I was thirteen I used to record *Friday Night Live* with Ben Elton and Harry Enfield, but Vic and Bob seemed to come out of nowhere.' When *Vic Reeves Big Night Out* started, he didn't get the joke at first. 'They kept saying there would be these special guests and no one turned up. Afterwards I rang the Channel 4 duty log to complain. The next week I watched again, because I thought they would take the show off the air and I wanted to say I had seen the worst show ever on TV. But I began to get the joke and I was hooked. When I went to college in Bristol I based a couple of friendships on a mutual love of that show.'

The BBC series didn't immediately get much higher ratings than their Channel 4 work. Despite good reviews and some elaborate set-pieces, such as building a scree in the studio and spilling cereal on it for their hardrock musical intro 'Don't Step on Loose Muesli', it seemed that they were still too esoteric for the mainstream. Try as hard as they might, they couldn't get away from accusations of art school pretention. *Q Magazine* asked them if they were dadaists, to which Jim replied that they were no different from Morecambe and Wise. 'It's just that they never sang songs about muesli. In fact, we're no different from Little and Large.' They suggested that Greg Mitchell, their resident talking dog, was no more an example of surrealism than Basil Brush was.

Performance artists or not, they were still an intriguing non-conformist double act. The BBC series marked some significant changes in this area, with Bob's profile rising much higher. Now, with The Man with the Stick consigned to the dustbin of comedy, his name was in the titles for the first time and he shared Vic's desk, making them look like two classily dressed newsreaders. Bob didn't get bullied so much, but neither was there a sense in which he was the straight man to Vic's funny man; the roles seemed to rotate by the minute. As Bob told the *Daily Mirror* 'Vic's *Big Night Out* was very much Vic being run down by me; now it's more of a two-hander with both of us getting stick.'

Jim was proud of the effort that had gone into writing the programme. Bob says that they took a conscious decision to write *The Smell* properly, but it was still typically idiosyncratic. Every script had thorough diagrams and explanations of each sketch. He pointed out that the BBC was using their scripts as training scripts for young directors. Charlie Higson, who was a script editor on the first BBC series, had a slightly different explanation: 'I think the scripts were given to trainees because they were so bizarre they were difficult to interpret.'

Higson's role was to liaise between Jim and Bob and everyone else, 'because they are so tied up in their own world. They have very fixed ideas about what they want, and it was usually my task to try and glean from them what it actually was that they were after and explain that to everybody else. Because I knew them quite well I got quite good at it.' The scripts are more elaborate than a Leonardo da Vinci diagram, complete with illustrations harking back to Jim's engineering training. Paul Whitehouse says that they are often funnier than the actual programmes. Higson used to make sure that the props team didn't take things too literally: 'They are enormously readable, but that can cause problems. It might say something like "four foot quiff", and people will be thrown into a huge panic trying to get these measurements exactly right. My job was to go to them and say that that was just Jim mucking about, as long as the quiff is a decent length it will be fine.'

Higson was firmer than Whitehouse and Docherty had been in similar roles, but there were still disagreements, as Bob recalls: 'For instance we had two people who are fighting each other stood on blocks of cat piss and Charlie says, "Does it have to be called cat piss, could it not be urine?" which is a point really, but we just like the words "cat piss". Piss can be funny in one sense and not in another.'

The Smell was directed by John Birkin, a mild-mannered old-school director who had worked with the likes of the Two Ronnies, so knew a lot about getting the dynamics of a double act right. Vic and Bob's desk even recalled Corbett and Barker's admittedly more sedate desk. Birkin did not know much about the duo at the beginning and Bob recalls their first day's filming: 'He saw us doing something and apparently he gave a look which said, "What the fuck have I let myself in for?" But at the end he came up to us and said, "I rather like this."'

There was a polish to the show, whether it was the elegant lighting or the ornate Greek pillars which provided the stage set where there used to be a simple backdrop. Bob admitted that it was a 'toned down' version of their humour, in an attempt to appeal to a wider audience: 'We have made it more accessible but we haven't deviated from the track we originally set off on. We just do what we think is funny. But yes, we hope this show will bring more people in. We've put in more recognizable jokes and parodies, such as our version of *Food and Drink*.' Of course, toning down is all relative. In this world Chris Kelly was impersonated by a man sporting a box of tea bags on his face and with expanding legs. Rebecca Front played an explosively enthusiastic Jilly Goolden, and Bob played wine buff Oz Clarke as a love-struck owl. The influences seemed to be bridging the gap between Bobby Davro and Salvador Dali. Jim agreed: 'Maybe we are more Russ Abbot than French and Saunders, to be honest. I mean, Fry and Laurie wouldn't be doing a song and dance routine, would they?' But however much one pointed out similarities with past comedy (and the fact that Fry and Laurie also liked to lampoon light entertainment in their posh Cambridge way), Jim and Bob were still doing something strikingly new. In the Oxbridge-dominated BBC world of comedy, these two northern accents seemed more subversive than ever.

The main change, however, was that the new series seemed classier, though that wasn't always the intention. They had designed a bleak backdrop for the Channel 4 series and wanted to keep it bleak here. But the designers had other ideas, remembers Bob: 'Once you get a designer in they can't resist putting swirls and lines on things. We got ionic columns instead of doric.' Jim: 'I did drawings of pillars which went down in size and went on for ever, and I don't know if anyone noticed this but the background goes from dawn to dusk as the show goes on.'

The clothes were certainly more expensive. There seemed to be more velvet and brighter colours to contrast with the washed-out background. There were properly choreographed musical numbers, pre-recorded inserts and that theme tune which had first appeared in Geoff Posner's original Channel 4 pilot. But if the duo were plagiarizing their own past, they were also starting to show their influences. *The Smell of Reeves and Mortimer* was really the first time that the duo appeared to be aware of their place in comedy history.

Seated at the desk, they were now including fewer catchphrases and more and more user-friendly jokes in their repartee. The following exchange was typical: Bob: 'I saw *My Left Foot* last night.' Vic: 'What, with Daniel Day Lewis?' Bob: 'No, just me and the wife.' Vic would then honk his Harpo Marx horn. These gags played a crucial part in making the duo more accessible.

The Jacques Tati-influenced addition also made its debut when we met Les Pétomanes, Le Courbusier and Papin. In each sketch Vic and Bob played a couple of mackintosh-clad Frenchmen, who roamed the streets passing wind. Their excessive flatulence could scare animals and small children, but it could also be put to philanthropic use – it had the power to get a kite airborne, albeit ripping it to shreds in the process, or start a small car. If in doubt they could always blow a wig off. Apart from the sound of breaking wind the only accompaniments were some expressive Gallic grunts and some typically French music.

Tati may have been an acknowledged French influence on their flatulent everymen, but there was another influence that lent the characters a degree of credibility. In the late nineteenth century Marcel Pujol was a sensation on the Parisian stage. His act consisted of playing tunes by breaking wind and he was known professionally as Le Pétomane.

Even if they weren't familiar with Pujol, Jim and Bob may well have been acquainted with Le Pétomane through a film of his life with the same title. It was an odd little film that supported some equally dubious British movies in the Seventies. It was hard to know whether it was a serious drama or a spoof, since it told the story with so little direct humour. But it was lent considerable credibility by the fact that the subject was played by the pre-eminent British comedy actor Leonard Rossiter. With a twirl of his moustache and a sombre expression he seemed to capture the essence of his eccentric performer. Update the costume and add the whimsy of Jacques Tati and you had Jim and Bob's contemporary version.

John Birkin (who had also directed *Mr Bean*, so clearly had a love of silent, visual comedy) was particularly keen on these characters. According to the duo he allotted them far more recording time than some of the ideas they were keener on. They felt that Birkin thought the farting was 'a good cheap laugh'. Sigmund Freud said that the highest purpose of jokes and laughter is to help us recapture the mood of our childhood, when we had no need of humour to make us feel happy. The French farters certainly harked back to an age of childlike innocence.

There was no denying that, however striking and original Jim and Bob were, they had their antecedents. One running gag was their inventions. With the aid of Vic's home-made blueprints they revealed various ingenious contraptions, such as the lager duck, the home security dog with a back leg like a vicious scythe and a will-duplicating sink.

This penchant for bizarre indispensable devices had a hint of Heath Robinson about it, but a more direct influence was Spike Milligan. In his BBC series *Q*, which ran sporadically from 1969 to 1980, he also came up with some strange devices, while sending up the BBC show *Tomorrow's World*. In *The Q Annual* some of these inventions were immortalized. Alongside a picture of a machine which looked alarmingly like a printing press mounted on a brickwork plinth, there was a description of a new aid to comfortable sleep: 'This man is going to have a nap by the fireside. When he is asleep his legs will become uncomfortable, and he will normally have to keep crossing them. Not so with the electric leg-crosser. Notice every few seconds the electric appliance automatically crosses his legs for him ...'

While the duo had initially said that there would be fewer characters this time, the reality seemed to be different. There was now a whole raft of regulars who would become household names. There was Mulligan and O'Hare, the folk duo loosely based on Millican and Nesbitt, who had a hit in 1973 with 'Vaya con Dios'. Mulligan and O'Hare's material was darker than your average folk song, due to a combination of domestic strife and hormone cream abuse.

The music world was a particular influence on the series. Jim and Bob blacked up to play Otis Redding and Marvin Gaye as two puppets trapped in a cupboard. Much to Marvin's annoyance, Otis passed the time watching the ships go in and watching them go away again. Marvin just wanted to listen to the grapevine. There was some muttering in politically correct circles, that, like their impression of Barry White (large body, tiny legs, fondness for raw liver), this could be construed as racist, but it was so absurd only the most militant could have taken offence. And there were recent antecedents – in *It Ain't 'Alf Hot Mum* and when their hero Spike Milligan had donned make-up in *Curry and Chips*, his Seventies sitcom in which he played an Indian factory worker.

The audience were also treated to the domesticated Slade spoof that Jim had talked about. Slade in Residence also featured Ozzy Osbourne (played by Neil Morrissey) as a neighbour, Wizzard and Duran Duran were further down the road and they lived on Cup-a-Soup and crisps. Jim was Noddy, Bob was Dave, and Paul Whitehouse and Mark Williams, soon to become stars themselves in *The Fast Show*, played bassist/violinist Jim and drummer Don respectively. The result was rather like a West Midlands version of The Monkees.

Other new characters were as bizarre as ever. In another off-the-wall take on sexual politics, they played the Bra Men, two donkey jacket-wearing Geordies, Pat and Dave Arrowsmith, inspired by the strange people Jim met during his factory work, who wore bras under their pullovers and were constantly convinced that people were trying to sneak a peak at their cleavage. There was more gender playfulness with Jack Dent (the name borrowed from Jim's fellow Fashionable Five member) and Eric Potter, who wore make-up in their British Information Board films which offered advice on subjects such as the Country Code ('No wallpapering ploughs').

Having spent a long time on the series, the duo were now keen to develop new ideas. Bob was still fond of the Throatbilly story that he had shown to Jonathan Ross, and, inspired by his legal triumphs over Southwark Council, he also had an idea about a Rentokil man who plants cockroaches in a bank vault and then robs the bank when he goes back to eradicate them.

The BBC were keen to get Jim and Bob to do something else for them and gave Channel X some development money so that they could come up with a ninety-minute film. Writers Michael Bracewell and Andy Darling were even approached to write a script, but Jim's idea for the story proved to be too esoteric and didn't make it beyond the development stage.

Jim explained it to the *NME*: 'It's about two blokes from Hartlepool who win £18 million on the pools. They decide to build this massive theme park in praise of a former cartoon character called Terry the Tortoise. But they get too enthusiastic over the gate, which is a huge, big steel model of Terry the Tortoise and all the steel works go back into business for a year. So they spend £18 million on this two-mile-long tortoise which can be seen from space. Whenever it winks it drowns the entire region of power.' Besides, he also had other important plans. He had taken a vow to change his hairstyle every week.

The Smell coincided with a new era of domesticity descending upon the duo. Bob had been living with his girlfriend Lisa Matthews, who also made his rather dashing suits, while Jim was happy at home watching his daughter blow raspberries. But they were both in the process of moving out of London. While they still liked to party, the social life and the intrusiveness of the media were beginning to take their toll. There is no doubt that Jim liked to have his picture taken, but he wasn't quite so keen about having his every movement scrutinized. He was also rather distressed by the fact that his back garden in Lewisham had been used as an escape route by armed criminals. Sarah had actually approached one, who was behaving suspiciously with a ladder, and Jim decided it was time to leave London.

In the summer of 1993 Jim and Bob moved out to Kent, to the area around Mersham about six miles south of Ashford. They bought large houses and took their suburban roles very seriously. They even moved out of their offices at Helicon and rented office space above an estate agent in Ashford High Street. A brass plaque outside said 'Mr Reeves and Mr Mortimer'. Inside a plain white room there was a word processor, a map of Ashford, a kettle, a dictionary, a thesaurus and a pair of binoculars by the window. Typically Jim had to get completely stuck into country ways in the same way as he had got completely stuck into motorcycling or hard rock. He started acquiring animals, becoming something of a gentleman farmer and drinking with the other locals in the nearby pub.

They still came up to London to drink and didn't always make the last train, as Jim admitted: 'When I start quaffing white wine on top of lager, I usually know where it's heading. A sleep in a ditch or an eighty-pound cab home.' When he was at home, however, he was in bed by 10.30 p.m. and up at 7 a.m., walking through the fields with Alice.

If the critics were divided about *The Smell of Reeves and Mortimer*, the public soon made up their minds. In December it was voted Best Comedy Series in the *British Comedy Awards* phone-in poll. Bob graciously accepted the award, assuring everyone that 'It will have pride of place under a tin of tuna at our office.' In terms of ratings, though, the programme hadn't been a runaway success, only notching up something in the region of two million viewers. In those terms at least, the move from Channel 4 had not been spectacular. But, as with Michael Grade's attitude at C4, the BBC seemed to realize that they gave the network a credibility which meant more than mere ratings.

Michael Jackson, then head of BBC2, was a huge fan of the duo, and that Christmas he gave them the chance to indulge in a spot of fantasy scheduling, allowing them to decide on a whole evening's viewing on 27 December. *At Home with Vic and Bob*, starting at 7 p.m., gave their critics as much of an insight into the workings of their minds as anything they had ever said in an interview. The BBC had recently latched on to the fact that they had a huge treasure trove of old programmes and the Music and Arts department had set up an archive unit, which was run by John Whiston in Manchester. There had been a trend for these personality-led theme nights which pulled together disparate programmes with the aid of one unifying host. David Attenborough had come up with one theme night, Alan Bennett another, so Jim and Bob were certainly in good company. Part of this theme night, of course, was that the BBC knew that they had potential, but did not know quite how to utilize it. As John Whiston says – no pun intended – 'There was a smell of something about them at the time.'

Jim and Bob agreed to do it, although they weren't particularly flattered by being in such prestigious company. They were torn because on the one hand they wanted to do another series of *The Smell* ... while on the other they had financial commitments and knew that the money would be useful. The result was a two-fold proposition, according to producer David Housham: 'It would let them choose their favourite programmes and link the evening together.'

Once they had agreed to do it, it was a night which allowed them to behave like boys with a new train set. They showed that their interests extended considerably further than old Monty Python repeats. There were clips of favourite haircuts from past editions of *University Challenge*, while spoof Sheffield entertainer John Shuttleworth contributed some inserts. Jim also revealed his enduring love of nature with a screening of the famous BBC *Wildlife on One* documentary about meerkats. There was also a screening of Mike Leigh's BBC film, *Nuts in May*, about the strife that ensues when a camping couple go on holiday. Observant viewers may have noticed a similarity between the look and the antics in Leigh's drama and those of *The Weekenders*.

To make sure that fans had something they would approve of, Les Pétomanes also chipped in, getting involved in a spoof televised *Badgerwatch* which was supposed to be taking place in Jim and Bob's garden (the programme, subtitled 'A Perfect Christmas', was being presented from what purported to be their lounge).

There was one other highlight of the evening. In keeping with his archive-based brief, David Housham had an idea that the way to feature old clips might be through a TV-based quiz show. He put this to them and they very quickly came back with the idea for a celebrity panel game, a cross between *That's Showbusiness* and *Call My Bluff*. Jim described it as '*Blankety Blank* without the pens'. They called it *Shooting Stars* and pulled in some favours from friends such as Jonathan Ross and Danny Baker to make it.

Looking back on it now, Bob can't believe that the BBC picked up on it: 'It was done at such short notice, but then it was repeated and for some reason it got over two million viewers. They were so surprised they suggested we did some more. Boy, must that have been half-arsed when you think about it.' Jim can't even remember who was on the first show: 'Was Ulrika on it? The guests are all very transient for us, but others seem to remember them. And fans get quite upset, quite rightly, when we can't remember what we've done.'

In fact Ulrika *was* on, according to David Housham. There was no George Dawes at this stage. Instead Jim and Bob kept the scores, and Uncle Peter wandered on sporadically to provide a little darkness to counteract their relentless lightness. The other panellists were Noddy Holder, Martin Clunes and Wendy Richard. From the very start, though, Housham felt that the inclusion of Jonsson was inspired: 'Until then she was known as this cheery weathergirl.' By sheer coincidence Ulrika Jonsson had been due to go to Goldsmiths' College to study French and Drama in the late Eighties, but a secretarial course had led her astray. Otherwise she might have come across Jim and Bob in the pubs of New Cross nearly a decade earlier. Ulrika was already a fan and recalls being both shocked and delighted by their job offer, which came about after Bob had seen her doing a sketch with comedian Bob Mills on his late-night ITV comedy show, *In Bed with Medinner*: 'I remember being very excited for the first time in a long time because of my love of their sense of humour. But my thought was "What, they want *me*?"'

Shooting Stars came together just four weeks before transmission and it hasn't really changed that much since. 'They came up with all the elements at the beginning. What impressed me the most was how prolific they were,' reflects Housham. 'I just underpinned the structure.' Housham did get a sense at the time, however, that they did not see a quiz show as part of their career plan.

In the end the archive element became minimal, consisting mainly of a round in which old adverts were screened and the panel had to guess what happened next. There was more emphasis on the finale, when, according to Housham, 'Jonathan Ross was put into a wheelie bin while Vic hit it with a cricket bat. Jonathan had to throw a Brussels sprout out to indicate that he had had enough.'

It was the kind of show that was never intended to become a series. In fact it was lucky that it came about through this theme night. If it had been proposed separately, it probably would never have got made; even if it had, it would have certainly taken a lot longer for it to work its way through the BBC's programming bureaucracy. It was one of those rare happy accidents in broadcasting, where something intended as a one-off goes from strength to strength and develops its own momentum: 'I'm sure they just felt they were having a bit of a laugh and taking the piss out of quizzes,' says Housham.

In reality, the success on the screen was not a true reflection of the making of the very first *Shooting Stars*. Dorian Crook did the warm-up for it and was kept busy because it took four hours to film, an unusually long time for a studio game show. Bob and Jim weren't in the best of spirits by the end of it. When the cameras were on them they were able to perform, but this was one of the few times they could be difficult to work with. Jim in particular seemed to have very fixed ideas about the show and he was reluctant to budge. They had come a long way from their first Channel 4 series, when Bob was in awe of the mere fact that they were in a television studio.

Jonathan Ross took part as a favour to his mates, but he also had misgivings about the concept: 'Danny Baker and myself cornered Jim and Bob and pleaded with them not to turn it into a series.' There was even a rumour that David Liddiment, Jim and Bob's ally at Granada during the *Weekenders* fiasco who was now at BBC Light Entertainment, was unimpressed. Even Ulrika Jonsson had misgivings about the programme's potential longevity: 'I always maintained that I hated the one-off because the questions were to do with the Sixties but I was born in 1967 and came to England in 1979. I sat down and said "This doesn't work", which shows you what I know about comedy.'

Executive producer John Whiston recalls that the response within the BBC was not exactly ecstatic: 'The Programme Review Board had a meeting and said it was a nice one-off but not a series. They didn't think it had any legs. The next thing I heard was the Entertainment Group was going to make it.'

Having been made by the Music and Arts department, the first *Shooting Stars* resulted in something of a political problem within the compartmentalized confines of the BBC. There was certainly a sense that David Liddiment's Light Entertainment department was somewhat put out by the fact that they hadn't been involved in a show that had large elements of comedy in it and perhaps shouldn't have been allowed to fall into the hands of a different department. Housham says that John Whiston definitely felt 'miffed that David Liddiment had poured cold water on the project' because it hadn't come from his department.

Whiston is not too bitter now about losing the hit, and understands that there was a logic to the series being made by the Light Entertainment department: 'Jon Plowman there had championed Vic and Bob in a difficult period. Michael Jackson said that they needed a strong format. They knew that they had something special on their hands when they signed them, but they couldn't work out how to convert that into something bigger until *Shooting Stars*. It was nice to be a midwife and there was a quid pro quo. BBC Manchester got to keep *The Mrs Merton Show*.'

In the event it seemed to make perfect sense. The audience was able to grasp the twisted logic of *Shooting Stars* because it resembled the classic game show structure. In a sense, though, it made one wonder why an audience had never latched on to their previous television work, because everything they had done had been a skewed personal take on a conventional idea. *Big Night Out* had been a perverse old-time variety show, *The Smell* was in the tradition of *The Two Ronnies* and Morecambe and Wise, a sketch show starting and finishing with a big musical number. But *Shooting Stars* definitely seemed more grounded. It had a strong sense of Jim and Bob finally meeting reality somewhere in the middle. It also gave Jim a chance to meet celebrities, a favourite pass-time ever since he had got into the Enid's Rolls-Royce in Redcar.

The success of their BBC transfer and the move to the country seemed to reinvigorate Jim and Bob. In the spring of 1994 they set off on another national tour, a jaunt that would help them find out whether their original fans were still loyal and whether they had attracted a new following. They were determined that everything would work out right and weren't going to take any risks. Even though they had axed them from the series, Lister and Novelty Island were revived, and Jim still encored with 'Dizzy' just to keep the pop fans amused.

These spiritual sons of the Crazy Gang wanted to make sure that the comedy crown was still theirs. Since their emergence the likes of Baddiel and Newman, Jack Dee and Sean Hughes had threatened their status as comedy leaders. The show still faced the same problems as their earlier concert-hall gigs – Vic's gurning didn't quite come off, while Bob's chipmunk grin was lost to all but the front rows – but there were some hilarious larger-than-life moments such as when both of them started vibrating wildly as if holding a pneumatic drill. Like a couple of toddlers they were performing for their own amusement first and for the audience about fifth; they seemed to have reclaimed that early innocence. The turnover of characters and sketches was so swift that if *Viz* magazine ever came to life it would look something like this. As they observed, what they were doing was a manic precursor of *The Fast Show*. At the climax too many things went wrong, as the symphony of surrealism turned into a cacophony of cock-ups, but in their upside-down world the fact that a tightly scripted two-hour show can seem so loose was something that must be seen as a triumph. There was no denying that the hysteria of their 1991 tour had subsided, but this thirty-date jaunt seemed to be a success.

As live performers, however, Jim and Bob were beginning to suffer. They had become stars relatively late, and now in their mid-thirties the strain was beginning to show. Bob would sometimes be out of breath when he was supposed to be delivering a feed line. He commented that maybe they needed to come up with a format which allowed them to sit down more often. *Shooting Stars* sounded increasingly like the answer to a lot of their prayers.

Despite discovering some untapped commercial potential in *Shooting Stars*, Jim and Bob wanted to persevere with *The Smell of Reeves and Mortimer*. This was the series that was most precious to them. This was the series that was the purest example of their unique humour. This was their 'proper job', as Jim called it. This was the series that they had gone to the BBC to make in the first place. The first series, however, had not been a particularly notable ratings success. Any talk in the press of the duo as the new Morecambe and Wise seemed utterly futile when they were only getting two million viewers. With their Christmas specials, Eric and Ernie regularly used to notch up over twenty million viewers. But broadcasting had changed. There were now more stations and more choices. No comedian could ever hope to unite a nation like that. Football and royal funerals apart, there would never be another situation when people would gather together and talk about the previous day's television, though Bob thought they had a fighting chance of uniting different generations: 'When Morecambe and Wise were on, they were watched by everyone from twelve-year-olds to university students to your mum and dad. It was everyone's favourite show. I don't see why that couldn't be done again.'

Jim and Bob had two options. They could either retreat into their fashionable post-punk broadcasting ghetto or try to branch out. Bob believed that they already had a substantial older following thanks to Les Pétomanes: 'Pensioners don't seem to have a problem with people farting and falling over.' Jim, who had always been the more ambitious of the two, was clear that they had to broaden their fanbase: 'Do you think any comic deliberately says, "I always want to remain at 10.30 p.m. on C4"?' The question was how to do it without diluting their product.

By the end of 1994 the BBC was prepared to try out Jim and Bob in a more conventional variety format – as guests on a big seasonal spectacular, *Fry and Laurie Host a Christmas Night with the Stars*. Until 1972 *A Christmas Night with the Stars* had been a BBC institution, hosted by television celebrities from Jack '*Dixon of Dock Green*' Warner to the Two Ronnies. While the two Oxbridge comics played compères, Jim and Bob did their turn alongside Steve Coogan as Alan Partridge, and Paul Whitehouse.

The chasm between Jim and Stephen Fry in terms of class, background and education couldn't have been wider, yet they got on very well, forming a bond which extended from nights at the Groucho club to charity events and Fry's guest appearance on a future *Shooting Stars* (Jim memorably got considerable comic mileage out of Fry's academic track record, boasting that he had been to 'Oxbridge' as well, only to be flummoxed when Bob asked him 'which university?'). There was no doubting that a difficult move to the BBC was beginning to bear fruit in terms of the duo realizing their wider potential.

They were certainly already exerting a huge influence on the media. Comedian Harry Hill was breaking through with the same kind of demented pop-referential stand-up material (his eponymous Channel 4 series in 1997 would be a virtual rerun of *Vic Reeves Big Night Out*, with its characters, songs, oddballs, set-pieces and homages to old kids' shows such as *Crackerjack*). Hill had seen the Albany shows in the late Eighties and had always been a fan; others seemed influenced but less happy to admit it. Bob suggested that the advertising world had been inspired by Reeves and Mortimer. Tango's surreal drinks campaign, complete with slapping rubber glove, certainly seemed to owe a nod to

Mr Wobbly Hand. And *Noel's House Party*, BBC1's Saturday night prime-time entertainment show, also seemed to have utilized the anything-can-happen ethos and repackaged it for a less demanding mainstream audience. (Edmonds had been cruelly lampooned as a bouffant-haired, cowboy boot-wearing reptile in their sketch spoof *Noel's Addicts*.) Bob felt that they had changed the comedy agenda, from political to just plain silly: 'The one thing it has definitely done is make people be a bit daft again.'

The originals and the best now had to reassert their authority. On 5 May 1995 at 9.30 p.m. the second series of *The Smell of Reeves and Mortimer* opened with a dramatic prologue on the links between cottage cheese and evil, harking back over a decade to that ignored Dig Me I'm Django press release. According to the introduction by Patrick Allen, 'in medieval Britain cheese was only extracted from chickens and ducks'. They clearly weren't about to compromise too much. Their suits were a better quality too – in the first show, for instance, Jim sported a well-cut red velvet number and Bob a chalk-stripe grey two-piece: normal, but not very normal. Their comedy was still about the strange things lodged randomly in the subconscious, but they were looking for a way to get it into as many homes as possible. Vic sprayed Bob with a potion to make him attractive to men, and Bob was promptly chased by most of the males in the studio in a twist on the old Benny Hill chases.

They were noticeably reducing the arcane references to Rick Astley and Napalm Death that appealed to *New Musical Express* subscribers and making the programme more accessible than ever with characters that every generation could recognize. The only pop star involved now was fellow northerner Sting, whose albums Jim used to deface, and who had a huge demographic – he appeared on the show and sat on a chair made of lollipop sticks that promptly collapsed.

Now that *The Smell* was bedded in, it was easier to compare it with Channel 4's *Big Night Out*. The main change was in terms of budget. Graham Smith, who had been following the duo since they had been involved with Jonathan Ross, felt that they had been true to their essence: '*The Smell* was not that different to *Vic Reeves Big Night Out*. Essentially it was the same Vic and Bob but slicker. If you go back and look at tapes of *Big Night Out* it is a complete shambles. The BBC was bigger and slicker but essentially they were doing the same sort of thing. It wasn't a drastic evolution, more a natural one.'

Paul Whitehouse was busy, but more than happy to be working with Jim and Bob again, whatever hardships they came up with. He well remembers getting the script for the forthcoming instalment of Slade's adventures. 'I had just finished Harry Enfield's series and I had a good dose of the shits and I thought I don't want to do this. Then I saw in the script that my genitalia were covered with bees and I thought, life can't be that bad then.'

The new series also introduced some new characters. The most notable additions were Councillors Ray Cox (Jim) and Roy Evans (Bob), two balding, corrupt petty bureaucrats determined to put Aldington-on-Sea on to the map as a tourist resort but waging a constantly losing battle. It was pretty broad humour. Much emphasis was put on flapping toupees, and in the very first episode Roy's trousers fell off when he was demonstrating the trajectory of Peter Powell's helicopter, which the councillors were hoping would land in the car-park of the resort's Presto supermarket if they could get permission to turn it into a landing pad. Their crackpot schemes also included placing Fun Bins along the Marine Way seafront bearing the faces of shotputter Geoff Capes, Paul Daniels and Debbie McGee.

The inserts were filmed in Hastings in one intensive, windy day. It had been one of those sketches that Jim and Bob had had to fight for. John Birkin, back on board as director, had not been completely convinced by their ideas on paper. Jim: 'They came out of turmoil as well. We were really behind them as characters, but we were only given a day to do the three sketches that we did. No one else was really into it, so we had to ram them in really quick, whereas we had four days to do Les Pétomanes, which we weren't that bothered about.' It was one of those occasions where Jim and Bob's ideas on paper didn't quite convey how funny it could actually be, agrees Bob: 'No one really trusted us on Cox and Evans, but when we did it John Birkin was fucking beside himself; it suddenly dawned on him what we were on about, that these were the ones we should have been concentrating on.'

Jim and Bob were particularly fond of these new characters. They are still keen on developing them into a spin-off sitcom of their own. Aldington-on-Sea certainly has a nice sitcom-style ring to it, echoing

Walmington-on-Sea, the south coast resort where *Dad's Army* was set. As it happens, though, the fictional location was thought up late on the day. Bob suggested it because Jim had recently moved to an old manor house in the village of Aldington, and it stuck. Jim was really becoming a gentleman farmer now. He soon had cows, sheep, cats, dogs and pigs. And the man whose first job had been to castrate piglets began to take things rather seriously. He had some short-legged Dexter Kerry cows, he called his ducks Edward and Mrs Simpson, and purchased two Tamworth Gilts, named Ginger and Lady Metroland. They were a pedigree breed and there were only 160 in the country.

Jim felt that Cox and Evans had huge potential: 'They're probably slightly more joined to the real world than our other characters, and that means there are more exploits they can get up to. Because they are councillors that means you can have a lot of other people around them – all it would need would be a mayor and a secretary and we'd be up and running. One of our wives would be a lesbian and I quite fancy the idea of Bob's character having seven very wide-eyed identical daughters.' Matt Lucas played Mayor Hobson in the sketches and was blown up in one of them, but hopes that if they do a sitcom spin-off they will be able to use him again: 'Jim said maybe I could be his gay son.' Cox and Evans reflected the duo's love of language, and linguistic precision. They were particularly proud of the scene in which they install a utility post containing a packet of Handie Andies tissues, a tin-opener, a comb and a shoehorn. It was the rather sad seaside scenario juxtaposed with their pathetic aspirations rather than the punchlines that provided the humour. Even at their most accessible, punchlines are thin on the ground, as Bob agrees: 'The thing with us is that if you look at it on paper there aren't really that many jokes there. The most important thing is that every word is really carefully chosen to suit the characters and the context. A lot of our characters just come from voices that really suit us. It's quite a good reflection of the Vic and Bob relationship as well. Councillor Cox has got big ideas and I occasionally deflate them – I question the wisdom of his plans and point out that they won't work.'

Small-town life always inspired them. They were constantly reduced to laughter by the hypocrisy of Little Englanders. One day in Dymchurch, the nearest coastal resort to Aldington, a man had come up to them and told them off for 'bloody swearing'. Graham Lister, the man who knew professional people, doctors and accountants, may have been gone, but this spirit was alive and kicking around Romney Marsh. Perhaps the duo didn't want to offend unnecessarily, though. Otis and Marvin returned, but this time it was noticeable that Jim and Bob had not blacked up for the roles.

Even if they now knew what they were doing, sometimes the production team still took some convincing. Sometimes their ideas were too left-field even for their colleagues, recalls Jim: 'We wanted to do these fellas that did quizzes and lived in a dustbin, but it was turned down for being too bizarre.' Even Alan Marke, the producer who tended to sign the cheques and let them get on with it, said that they had gone too far with that one. Nor was there room for The American Family who Dwelt in the World of Adverts – Dad was like Homer Simpson, Mum was having an affair with Desmond Tutu. The tapes of the sketch were lost when Channel X moved offices, but Matt Lucas vividly recalls how the rehearsals for that particular sketch went right off the logic scale: 'It was Jim, Bob, me and Morwenna Banks. We never knew our lines, what you say in rehearsals has no relevance to what you say on camera, and the scene just got longer and longer until nobody knew what the sketch was. It had started off as an advert, then Jim got up and we're going "Don't shoot!! don't shoot!!" It was four people and none of us working together, all doing our own thing.'

The second series included a classic sketch that was even more bizarre and yet got in because, superficially at least, it was a recognizable spoof of a recognizable programme. In the same way that their *Food and Drink* sketch meant that fans would never look at Chris Kelly in the same light again, so their *Masterchef* deconstructed presenter Loyd Grossman. He had cutlery for fingers, and his head was so large and filled with so much hot air, he seemed to float above the ground. The supporting cast was equally scary. Morwenna Banks played Jean Baptiste, a woman who had cut her ears off to include them in the dish which represented the face of Jesus; Bob played a spiv-like character who had made a shoe out of a cake – or was it a cake out of shoe? – and Matt Lucas played Quentin Mint, a Penguin-suited toff, who removed the silver lid of his dish to reveal Charlie Higson's bare bottom. The *Masterchef* sketch is definitely among Jim and Bob's best work. Matt Lucas remembers that it was a bit of a slog, but worth it in the end: 'It took a whole day, which is quite a long time. I remember

Jim had this amazing head that had cost £2,000 to make; at lunchtime he had to lay down because his head was so heavy. And it had to be supported between takes.' Attention to detail was the perfect garnish on a disturbing montage of grotesqueries: 'Then there was Bob's character with this tiny nose. His own nose had a moustache on it and this one was above it. And actually it wasn't Charlie Higson's bottom. He came out from under the table, but it was actually a prosthetic twelve-year-old child's arse,' points out Lucas.

Morwenna Banks had been approached to appear in their first BBC2 series, but had been too busy, but she made herself available when they approached her this time: 'They sent me drawings of the *Masterchef* sketch and I thought it was magnificent straight away. Jim was very specific about measurements. His Loyd Grossman had to float precisely one-and-a-half inches off the ground. They are the most visually aware comics I know. Most comedians just say "light it bright and shoot it wide" and that's the extent of their ideas about how something should look. Jim and Bob take the visual aesthetic of comedy much much further.'

The props seemed to be becoming more savage than ever. Stage manager Mark Mylod was responsible for getting them all together, and even with Charlie Higson advising them there were problems, remembers Mylod: 'Whenever you work with props and Vic and Bob there's a kind of initiation rite you have to go through. They draw things incredibly specifically, and you go off to the prop-maker and they always do their interpretation of it which is always miles away from what you want, so there is this hardcore of people who make props who actually understand what they want now.' With the aid of a giant prop Jim and Bob had their revenge for being cut off by Judy Finnegan, laughs Mylod. 'The props team once made a giant Judy Finnegan for *Shooting Stars* with the gap on the teeth not quite how Jim had specified it, and they had to go back and do it again. Jarvis Cocker had to throw mini Babybel cheeses through the gap.' As Jim told Ben Thompson in *GQ* in December 1997, he always preferred to draw his ideas: 'If we just tell them what we want it never ends up looking like it does in our minds.'

Other send-ups included Bob as a lusty, shouting John Craven, the presenter of *Country File*, and Jim as a stiletto-wearing Melvyn Bragg, paying tribute to Mulligan and O'Hare on *The South Bank Show*. Most disturbing of all, though, was their take on *Stars in Your Eyes* (at one point they were reportedly going to do *Sties in Their Eyes*, a game show in which people compared infections). Bob's Matthew Kelly boasted a tiny gallows on his head, which only the most observant viewer would ever notice. It revealed how painstaking their comedy could be – and also, for those who did spot it, how dark their comedy could be. Even more dark was a guest on the spoof talent show – a murderer who impersonated George Michael singing 'Faith' with the aid of a cardboard mask in the style of Action, Image, Exchange.

The series seemed more structured than the previous one. There was a real sense that they wanted to break through to a larger audience, Bob paying tribute, in passing, to the masterful Morecambe and Wise: 'They just messed around, their comedy had no message and their timing was superb. We're trying to edge towards their kind of routines in our current show.'

They were also edging towards a more overt knockabout style: any disagreement was usually the cue for them to batter each other over the head with convincingly realistic foam frying pans. This was in stark contrast to a fight in the final run on Channel 4, which consisted of a Chinese burn and ruffled hair. In some ways the more conventional they became, the more extreme they became too. Jim tried to rationalize their work: 'There is a menace underlying it and also an urge to take things to an extreme. So if we are going to present ourselves as being stupid we will be stupid to the absolute nth degree, like when I didn't believe that homosexuality existed.'

With a higher profile than ever, they seemed more prepared to discuss the underlying intentions of their humour and justify it. They even hinted that there was something deeper afoot. 'We've never really done mad for the sake of mad. If we say something which might on the face of it appear completely insane, there's usually something at the tail end of it,' explained Bob. Jim seemed to have had a sudden attack of existential angst: 'People always quote us as saying, "About this time of night I like to put a Caramac under a rabbit." But that was a way of saying, "This is how dreary my life is."' Bob took issue with his fans in modest fashion. Despite admitting to being careful with words in the past, a legacy from his days as a solicitor, this time round he played down any suggestion of verbal sophistication: 'People say we have invented our own language, but we just use more words than is strictly necessary.'

By the summer of 1995 life didn't seem very dreary for the duo. Bob was settled with Lisa, and Jim was enjoying the high life as a country squire. When the duo worked, they worked very hard, but they also liked to have spectacular holidays. In the motorbiking days they rode to France to meet up with Jonathan Ross and his wife Jane, who were renting a château there. Jim used to holiday regularly with the Ross family. Another time he had been to California with him. Jim also liked activity holidays, and as ever he threw himself into the West Coast lifestyle with characteristic gusto, surfing and bodyboarding off Custard Point. When Jim went snowboarding in the French Alps and Austria he wasn't content with simply getting all the gear; he had to bleach his hair blond like a totally rad dude too.

Jonathan and Jim were a kind of mutual appreciation society, enjoying each other's company and testing each other's knowledge of pop trivia. For Jim's thirty-sixth birthday Jonathan bought him a pair of bondage pants. They would often end up talking about the golden age of punk rock and, as many men in their late thirties are wont to do, tried to recreate those happy, naïve days. 'Jim found punk funny rather than a radical, life-changing thing,' says Ross, but that didn't stop him joining in with the spirit. On one eventful night they got very drunk at Jonathan's house in Highgate and ended up cutting each other's hair in a homage to the spiky fashion of two decades earlier. It was an incident that reminded them how far they had come. The following day, with blistering hangovers and terrible haircuts, they went off and had lunch at Simpsons in the Strand. 'Not a very punk thing to do,' continues Ross. Another year Jim gave Jonathan a bass guitar for his birthday and they talked about forming a band called The Fat Punks. 'We would sit onstage playing punk songs in comfortable chairs. Needless to say it never happened.'

But the high life at home and abroad suddenly caught up with Jim and Bob. They had lived a rock-star lifestyle with the inevitable trappings and expensive habits, and now fell into the classic rock-star trap of being landed with a hefty tax bill. It wasn't that they were simply spendthrifts, though; they also weren't as prolific as their peers, taking a painstaking year to write and produce one series. Jim remarked that he was envious of people like Ben Elton and Stephen Fry who seemed to churn out quality comedy: 'Maybe they work all night.'

At the Edinburgh Fringe Festival in the summer of 1995 Bob was looking pretty chirpy in the Assembly Rooms club bar, but he was realistic too. He told me that he and Jim were going to have to go out on tour again to pay the Inland Revenue: 'You can tell how big someone's tax bill is by how long their tour is,' he joked. 'Rik Mayall and Ade Edmondson's tour is eighty dates.' In that context, Jim and Bob's problems didn't seem so serious – their tour was only twenty-two shows, but they didn't really want to do it at all: 'Unfortunately we are not giving up touring and we despise it. But the taxman beckons. We are the poorest people in showbiz.' Apart from their substantial houses – and Jim's required a lot of work and maintenance – they claimed they didn't have a penny. Continued Bob: 'I think at the moment I can honestly say that Jim and I are absolutely skint, in the absolute sense of skintness, except we have our own homes.'

Jim claimed that Bob was having to walk his neighbour's dog for beer money, and he was having to do babysitting and leaflet deliveries to make ends meet. Jim always had to be doing something. Bob said that if the money could be sorted out he would like to retire, whereas Jim would always work: 'I'd have to make key rings with initials on them and set up a market stall. I'm too fidgety.'

But financial worries seemed to have a hand in a flurry of activity too. After the success with 'Dizzy', Jim had largely steered clear of pop, apart from a cover of Ultravox's 'Vienna', which appeared on a free tape, given out with the *New Musical Express* in 1992, but they entered the studios again to record a cover version of 'I'm a Believer' with EMF. The song went back a long way for the duo. Jim used to sing it at the beginning of the show at the Goldsmiths Tavern, and he had opened the Channel 4 series with it. Somewhere along the line, however, the delivery and timing had changed. It had started off ironically, but now it seemed as if Jim was taking it rather more seriously.

The video undercut any sincerity, however. Along with the young pop combo, Jim and Bob impersonated a kind of nightmarish gone-to-seed version of the Monkees, in corny blazers and bad hair. Jim was a gaptoothed Mike Nesmith, Bob played a boyish Davey Jones. The selection of wigs on display made it quite clear that this was a record that should be filed under novelty. Its only redeeming features were financial ones. The duo were prepared to go to any lengths to plug it, even dressing up as their pop heroes Jimi Hendrix, Paul McCartney,

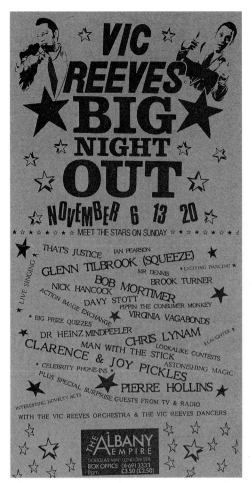

The Vic Reeves promotional bandwagon gathers pace in south London. Flyers from the Big Night Out, 1986, 1987 and 1988: note the disappearing apostrophe. © John Irvine, Rachel House, Jo David

Jim at Swag, 69 Dean Street, Soho. January 1988. While the Big Night Out was building up a following in south London, Jim used his residency at Adam Ross's club to try out new material, along the way 'inventing' both karaoke and easy listening and pioneering a frilly shirt/flat cap combination.
© Adam Ross

The pilot of *Vic Reeves Big Night Out* on Channel Four, 1989. The starry backdrop had to go.
© Chris Ridley

Action Image Exchange.
Political theatre at its most
passionate presents 'The
Facelessness of Bureaucracy'
aka 'Shapes', 1990.
© Tim Ridley

'I swear on the honour of
Clarence The Cross Eyed
Lion that I will tell the
truth, the whole truth and
nothing but the truth.'
The twisted court of Judge
Lionel Nutmeg, 1990.
© Tim Ridley

Top left Eric Morecambe interrupts a gentle ballad by Peter Gabriel, 1990. © Tim Ridley

Above 'A bit of twisted wood with a horrible story to tell'. Jim, complete with clawed paw and fir cone confronts Man With The Stick. © Tim Ridley

Left Jim and Bob outside Helicon Mountain, their office in Greenwich owned by Jools Holland and often mistaken for a real railway station by distracted locals. © Barry Chandler

Right Half of the Gentleman's Motorcycle Club. Jim and Bob motorbiking across Blackheath Common, 1990. Although they loved their bikes they never really got much further. © Steve Double/Retna

Above *The Weekenders*. Passing the time on location outside Manchester, July 1991. © Mark Robson

Left Slade on Holiday. Clockwise from top left: Bob, Jim, Paul Whitehou Mark Williams. © BBC

Right *The Smell Of Reeves And Mortimer*, Series Two, May 1995. Jim, Bob and Charlie Chuck as Uncle Peter. © BBC

Bob as Marvin Gaye, Jim as Otis Redding, 1995. Second series –
note distinctly less blacking up. © BBC

Masterchef, 1995. Jim's finest moment as Loyd Grossman. © BBC

Shooting Stars, Series One, Episode One, September 1995. The birth of a cult. The regulars joined by guests Roland Rivron, Peter Stringfellow, Caryn Franklin and Martine McCutcheon. McCutcheon had been part of the pop group Milan, who had appeared on the duo's music pilot, *Popadoodledandy*. © BBC.

Speculation was rife: would Nicole marry Hugh Grant? In the end, in a spoof of *The Graduate*, Vic lost out to Bob. © Rex Features

David Bowie, Joe Strummer, Tony Hadley and Phil Oakey for teen-mag *Smash Hits*. Andy Fraser of Free seemed to have been forgotten, but the single wasn't. It peaked at an over-generous number three that July.

The second series of *The Smell of Reeves and Mortimer* had not been the big ratings breakthrough hoped for, which made the first full series of *Shooting Stars* more important than ever. There was even a rumour that they had made it because the BBC was reluctant to make another series of *The Smell of Reeves and Mortimer*. This would have been a devastating blow to the duo. Fortunately salvation was round the corner in the shape of a mutant panel game.

Shooting Stars started on Friday 22 September at 9.30 p.m. The format remained pretty much the same as the pilot, with the two regular team captains now Mark Lamarr and Ulrika Jonsson. Country singer Rose Marie and actor Martin Clunes had also been mooted as possible captains. Lamarr had got to know the duo and had a mutual friend in Sean Hughes, whose own series was also made by Channel X (Bob had made a cameo in Hughes' series *Sean's Shorts*); Ulrika was more of a wild card, a Scandinavian blonde – presumed bland – TV personality best known for reading the news on breakfast television. From the start there was a sexual chemistry between Bob, Jim and Ulrika. Mild flirtation soon turned into obsession, and every question she answered correctly was greeted by the Gatling gun cry of 'Ulrikakakaka'. If the series boosted Reeves and Mortimer's standing and helped Mark Lamarr, it completely repositioned Jonsson in the market. It even helped Matt Lucas, who played George Dawes, the drumming, multi-voiced scorekeeper who also happened to be a big baby. ('They just said to me, "You'll be giving the scores out, your name is George Dawes, you're a baby and you wear a nappy."' The compromise was a pink romper suit.) He soon turned up as the face behind the Cadbury's Creme Eggs ad campaign.

Perhaps it was an indication that *Shooting Stars* was not perceived as a ratings priority by the BBC that a relative newcomer was put in charge. Mark Mylod, who had started off as a runner on *The Smell of Reeves and Mortimer*, was brought in to direct, with Charlie Higson acting as an adviser. Mylod got the job with alarming ease: 'I pissed myself when I saw the pilot, and when I heard they were doing the series because Michael Jackson, the Controller of BBC2, really liked it, I went to see

Jon Plowman, who was head of Comedy and Entertainment, and asked him if they had a director. He said no, so I asked if I could direct it. It was as simple as that, and for some reason they said yes.'

Mylod gave the duo a fairly free hand, allowing things to have a loose feel, lengthy scripts were now replaced by an improvisational approach. 'The creative input of me and producer Alan Marke is minimal. The script comes in a few days before we record the show, and it is like half a piece of toilet paper, saying something like "at some point Vic will get up and dance around with a shoe and let's find some nice music for it". There will be a few other set-pieces, so we talk a bit about that, and the end-game needs some preparation, but everything else they just ride it completely, and in my opinion that's what's so good about the show. It gives them space to just go with their energy, and when we get round to editing we usually have to cut it down from an hour to twenty-nine minutes. The bits you would always leave in were these free-flowing bits which were just so spontaneous there's no way they could have come from a script, it was just a case of them having a good time.'

Jim left the serious business of controlling the rounds to Bob, except when it came to the Club Singer section. Jim would draw on his knowledge of working men's clubs to deliver a usually indecipherable rendition of a well-known song. It was one of those ideas that on paper seemed unworkable but, when Jim got stuck into it, could be the highlight of the show. The answers to questions were frequently arbitrary, depending on who pressed the buzzer and the mood of Jim and Bob. Guests didn't arrive on the set until 6 p.m., and then the only advice they got was on how to enter the stage. The team captains only came along early if they had a special routine to rehearse. As Lamarr told me: 'Jim and Bob like to stitch us up as well.'

The guests came from a wide cross-section of that vague notion called celebrity. Lisa Thomas at Channel X would come up with mountains of names, and then Jim and Bob would work through the list saying yes and no and adding their own suggestions. Sometimes their perverse tastes meant that they would choose the lesser-known name, much to the chagrin of the production team, who knew that a big name would nudge up the ratings. Mylod: 'If it was a choice between George Michael and Gordon Burns of *The Krypton Factor* they might choose Gordon Burns, even though me and Alan would love to have George Michael on. Their selection is based on a kind of affection for the guest and/or someone they can get a kind of angle on.'

Often big stars would agree to be on when they met Jim and Bob in person at parties, but the logistics made it difficult to arrange – or perhaps they thought better of it when they sobered up. Noel Gallagher had reportedly been keen to appear, but the show was never able to secure him. Smaller stars tended to be more fun anyway, they tried to avoid anyone who was too obviously kitsch, such as Nicholas Parsons or Jim Bowen, but apart from that anyone was eligible, from pop stars to quizmasters, as long as there was a woman to Jim's right for him to salivate over. A frantic rubbing of his upper thighs whenever a woman appeared in his vision soon became Jim's visual signature. Superficially it wasn't any more sophisticated than Les Dawson's lecherous creation Cosmo Smallpiece or something out of Benny Hill, but Jim managed to lend it the veneer of, if not respectability, at least irony. However, when football players started to copy the gesture when they scored goals, one wondered if they were doing it quite as ironically.

The main thing was that the guests caught the spirit of the programme. Actor Richard E. Grant was reputedly reluctant to do the game at the end but, in the end he was a good sport, allowing himself to be put into a barrel and rolled down a slope to knock some plums into Victorian pots. 'I have a dim recollection of him at the beginning being a bit polite about it, saying, um, he would do it if he had to but he would rather not,' says Mylod. Funnily, this message didn't seem to get through when it came to selecting a victim.

Choosing the guests was something of an art. It never worked when the guests tried to be funny, which is why Jim and Bob preferred Gordon Burns and John (*Country File*) Craven to a motormouth like Danny Baker. Jim claimed that Richard Whiteley was a gem off-camera, telling them some marvellous stories. According to Jim, Whiteley said that when he was on his way down on the train, he went to the toilet and Douglas Hogg MP was in there on his hands and knees looking for his wallet. Danny Baker would not shut up on-camera, but they had their revenge on him. He was selected for the finale and a sweet had to be plucked from his rolls of fat.

The mix of spontaneity and rehearsed humour worked more often than not, and if it didn't it could always be edited out. As Bob told *Time Out*: 'We did write things for it, but we had more fun carping on.

To be honest, most of what we'd written got taken out in the edit.' He was quick to emphasize that although the questions seemed daft, some were serious: 'We didn't want it to be one of those quizzes where you don't care who wins.' Ian Coyle, a young comedy writer, would come up with genuine questions and they would slip their own stupid ones in too. Morrissey lookalike Coyle, in fact, was the real George Dawes: he was the person responsible for telling Matt Lucas how many points each side had notched up, by waving a placard off-camera (if George Dawes sometimes looks like he is squinting, now you know why).

In *Time Out* Bob said that the stunts were 'a bit *Tiswas*', but that flattered them. At the end of each programme a member of the winning team had to undertake a celebrity challenge for a paltry amount of money. A popular one was holding a book with sprouts on top of it while standing on a vibrating platform. The *Tiswas* team would have probably considered such a daft idea beneath them.

The success of *Shooting Stars* seemed to take everyone by surprise. Editions of the first series attracted over 4.5 million viewers – double the ratings of *The Smell of Reeves and Mortimer*, and conclusive proof that, in popularity if not in artistic terms, Jim and Bob had yet to realize their full potential. *Shooting Stars* took off quickly because it was such an instantly recognizable format. Casual viewers who had never noticed anything in *The Smell of Reeves and Mortimer* that they could even get a toehold on found the *Shooting Stars* set-up to be accessible and easy to grasp. There were desks, celebrities, question masters and new silly catchphrases: 'Eranu' and 'Uvavu' and the homage to Hughie Green, 'We really want to see those fingers.' Like a lot of great TV ideas it was not part of any great masterplan – they wanted to broaden their fanbase but they never thought they would do it like this. Charlie Higson agrees: 'Jim has always liked cheesy light entertainment and *Shooting Stars* sort of happened by accident. It was this stupid quiz as part of their night of television and someone at the BBC said, "You could do that as a series." And as they were lazy they thought it was a good idea. I always thought in the back of their minds their plan was to widen their audience and to do something that was more accessible, that people could turn on to and go oh yes, it's a game show.'

The series coincided with the release of another financial injection in the form of a commercially available video, *Reeves & Mortimer's Driving School* (Telstar), a comedy video which could claim it had a serious intent because it was endorsed by the RAC. They were both keen drivers. Bob was learning to drive in a beige Renault 5 automatic, while Jim had a replica Porsche Speedster, the 1952 Austin A40 he bought to get married in (which was more off-the-road than on it), a Landrover and a Range Rover.

In the video Jim and Bob demonstrated how not to drive, having started off by burning the Highway Code manual. The duo offered the kind of advice that no one really needed, such as 'You really shouldn't cook popcorn in your glove compartment as it could pop in your eye and blind you. Or pop out of the car and blind a passing cat or mouse.' Jim attempted to drive the car with his bottom, but the video firmly informed viewers that this was not cool.

Chapter Ten

'And a Fucking Big Duck'

Money problems were further eased by The Weathercock Tour 1495, which kicked off in October 1995. It was a sign of the swift success of *Shooting Stars* that T-shirts with the slogans Eranu and Uvavu were doing brisk business. The highlight of the live show seemed to be the increasingly popular random violence element. The Morecambe and Wise comparisons seemed less appropriate than ever. The new Tom and Jerry appeared to be more apposite. The success of *Shooting Stars* shunted Jim and Bob back into the limelight. They were no longer simply music press darlings or cult celebrities, but all-round perform-ers admired by their peers and a whole new swathe of fans. These were the kind of fans who dubbed any passing bald person 'George Dawes' and who aped Jim's thigh-rubbing gestures whenever they saw an attractive woman. Whether they would ever appreciate the more arcane attractions of the duo's sketch shows remained to be seen, but a Christmas special at the end of 1995 was certainly a ringing endorsement for the programme's growing mass appeal.

The popularity meant that Jim and Bob were in greater demand than ever to make extra-curricular appearances. Some of these weren't without their mishaps. In November 1995 Bob was bitten on the finger by a skunk during the filming of a Smell-o-Vision section of their *Children in Need* show. The BBC's Natural History Unit had been filming them during a picnic scene at Stourhead in Wiltshire. Bob was playing the part of a tomato juice salesman because tomato juice is the only known antidote to skunk spray. Bob had a tetanus injection and said: 'At least now I have an interesting skunk-shaped scar.' Jim, not wanting to be left out, claimed to have been bitten by a leaf-cutter ant which had crawled inside his shirt.

The beginning of 1996 came round and, despite their mainstream crossover, Jim and Bob were still as popular as ever with the music press. The *New Musical Express* had launched their own Brat Awards as a contrast to the industry's annual Brit Awards. The nominees included Oasis, the Stone Roses, Black Grape, Bjork, Supergrass and Paul Weller, and Jim and Bob were hired to present the shindig. Their diary was rapidly filling up. In March Jim donned his bondage pants and appeared at a United Nations Children's Fund charity gig at London's Astoria Theatre. They weren't known for their charity work but they were always happy to help out for a good cause. Even back in 1987, Jim had compèred a benefit gig starring Kevin Day, Mark Thomas, Hattie Hayridge and Johnny Immaterial in Crystal Palace to raise money to pay for someone to join the VSO (Voluntary Service Overseas). Sometimes, however, they could not quite maintain the right tone for the occasion. Charlie Higson recalls them getting involved in an AIDS benefit alongside some of the biggest names in British comedy and British drama. 'They aren't the most politically correct people and they agreed to appear at this benefit, but they hadn't really prepared much. Instead they went onstage and started talking about "a fucking big duck" that was about to come on. This went on for a while and then they left the stage. At the end of the show Stephen Fry stepped forward to make a pompous speech and, as everyone gathered onstage, proceeded with a roll-call of all the famous people who had died of AIDS. As this list went on there was a pause and from the back of the stage a voice cried, "And a fucking big duck." Fry told Jim off in a headmasterly fashion.'

It was the kind of incident that reminded people that, however famous Jim and Bob were, they would always be outsiders. They weren't from Oxbridge – Jim didn't even have a degree; they hadn't worked their way up through the circuit; and they had – for television – strange northern accents. Higson sees their behaviour at events like this as a constant reminder of their unique position in popular entertainment: 'They think of themselves as outsiders because there aren't many people in this business from the north-east. And they still think of themselves as naughty boys, they don't play the corporate game.'

There were times, of course, when it was impossible for them to resist the corporate game. In April 1996 it was announced at the Montreux Television Festival, where the *Shooting Stars Christmas Special* was an entry, that they had signed a £500,000 deal to stay at the BBC. Whereas their Channel 4 contract had not been exclusive, this arrangement tied them to the BBC in a lucrative marriage known as Golden Handcuffs. The announcement coincided with stories that ITV had tried to tempt them away with a larger offer. They wouldn't reveal any details, but Bob said it was 'enough to start up a small haulage company'. The BBC's extravagant deal certainly seemed vindicated when *Shooting Stars* picked up a Silver Rose at the Festival. They were particularly surprised the programme did so well because it had been subtitled for the international jury and the translation hadn't really done justice to their sense of humour. When they said 'Fifties throwback Mark Lamarr', the caption, when translated back into English, said 'Mark Lamarr, who is here representing the 1950s period.'

But the business side didn't stop Bob making up stories. At the Montreux press conference Bob also revealed that he and Jim were writing a show for Ulrika Jonsson. The story appeared in the press but it came as a shock to the proposed star, who found out through a fellow telly blonde: 'I was shopping in a girly clothes shop in Bond Street and Gaby Roslin came up to me and said, "Congratulations. I see on the front page of *Broadcast* you've got your own show." They were bored at a press conference, so just announced they had written a show for me.'

As it happened, Jim probably did require the services of a small haulage company to help him out on his house in Aldington. The old house was proving to be something of a money pit. By now Jim preferred to work at home rather than go to the office in Ashford, a one-street town with a strangely cosmopolitan air following the opening of the International Eurostar Terminal. There were more distractions at home, but he and Bob tried to write something funny every day. It was a distinctive house, even before Jim imposed his own identity on it, which didn't need an address. Everyone in the village knows it. Arriving at its high gate, an intercom allows you in, and as you travel up the long drive, two stone Buddhas give you the beady eye. On one side of the house there is a fantastic view down to the coast of the Kent and the Dungeness power station.

Aldington is a quaint English village, but one would be hard pushed to call it picture-postcard. There isn't exactly a green, just a picnic area and a playing field where local soccer teams congregate on Sunday mornings. There is a decent pub, however. The Walnut Inn on the corner of Forge Hill was voted Pub of the Year and does an efficient roast lunch. It also had a weekly quiz on Tuesday nights and Jim became a regular competitor, revelling in the chance to show off his grasp of trivia. Architecturally the village is a mixture of new detached constructions and large old buildings. Many were farms. More recently however, they have become retreats for the wealthy. A princess used to live in the village, but the most famous resident was Noël Coward, who retreated to his house, called Goldenhurst, in the 1920s. Apart from the few remaining farmers there is the distinct sense that no one in Aldington actually works there. They either commute or have reached a time and position in their life when they don't need to work at all.

It all seemed very different from Darlington, but on closer inspection it was probably more like the north-east than London. While the locals were friendly, there was also something guarded about them. Perhaps it was to do with a hangover of the wartime anxiety; during the First World War you could hear the artillery in France from here, and during the Battle of Britain dogfights happened directly overhead. There were stories of spies parachuting in under the cover of darkness, and road signs were removed to make invasion more tricky. These days the road signs are back, punctuated by signs encouraging people to eat British meat. One could easily imagine people around here closing ranks against an interloper, but Jim appeared to have settled in. As ever he threw himself into things whole-heartedly. Neighbours were protective about their local celebrity. If you wanted to find his house, the pub would give you directions – if they felt you were the kind of person they thought Jim would want to see. Noël Coward had his own way of keeping unwanted visitors at bay, instructing his staff that 'if God rings I'm not in'.

The southern half of Kent was also an attractive place to bring up children. The seaside resorts of Dymchurch and Hythe were near by.

Dymchurch was particularly tacky, but it did have some history which appealed to Jim — a Martello Tower on the seafront, complete with cannon on top, and a small, local working steam railway. It was all typically English, but as with the duo's best work, there seemed to be darker undercurrents too. As attractive as Aldington was, you couldn't help noticing that there was also a prison there.

This tension manifested itself in Jim's art. There was one picture hanging in the house which dated back to his pre-comedy days, and evoked all sorts of contradictory ideas. Perhaps inspired by Francis Bacon's 'Screaming Popes' cycle, it was a self-portrait of the artist, seated and sporting papal regalia, complete with mitre. He is reading a headline on something half-way between a scroll and a broadsheet newspaper. In Latin it says '*Res Ipsa* [sic] *Loquitor*', which loosely translates as 'The thing speaks for itself'. So maybe there isn't anything underneath the gags after all. Maybe all this talk of latterday surrealists, comedy Gilbert and Georges, is a smokescreen for a couple of northern blokes having a laugh. Then again, they never professed to be anything more than a couple of clowns, so maybe the joke was on all the intellectuals who attempted to deconstruct them over the years.

But there was no escaping the fact that Jim still maintained an interest in modern art. There was a time when Jim and Bob would go to the opening of an envelope. Now they were more choosy, but Jim was even pictured at a private view in the pages of *Vanity Fair*. Whether he courts them or not, the Bryan Ferry comparisons persist. When Ferry became the epitome of metropolitan style he had invested in rural property and reinvented himself as a country squire. It was hard to resist the connections. Ferry made a packet from the album *Country Life*; Jim's protégé Matt Lucas appeared in the video for Blur's hit single 'Country House', which was directed by artist Damien Hirst, a graduate of Goldsmiths' College who had a fondness for using dead farm animals and rotting meat in his conceptual art and had cited Vic Reeves as an influence.

Like Jim, Hirst and Blur were *habitués* of the Groucho Club (in fact Lucas had been cast in the video when Jim introduced him to Damien Hirst in the club), but it was a social scene from which Jim was trying to withdraw. He had his dream home, his family and his work to keep him amused and occupied. He would still come up to London for a drink, but it would be more like an SAS-style lightning strike than a leisurely pursuit. In 1927, at the height of his fame, Noël Coward had moved to Aldington to escape from the hullaballoo of London, and Jim seemed to be emulating him. It wasn't a reason he had moved there, but maybe fate seemed to be intervening. His unconscious connection with Coward stretched back to the name of his early band with Tom Fawcett, Design for Living. Seated at nightfall in Goldenhurst's gardens, Coward and his friends would watch the eerie dusk that regularly fell over Romney Marsh, treat themselves to a drink and tell stories of smugglers. The areas had changed little and yet lots in seventy years. The playwright didn't have Dungeness's nuclear reactor to consider in the distance; in his day there was only the lighthouse and, in the distance on clearer days, the French coast. But that part of Kent had always been a strange area, and one which attracted English eccentrics. In the Eighties film-maker Derek Jarman made his home in a glorified beach-hut in the shadow of the power station a short drive from Aldington.

In the edition of *Cosmopolitan* that came out in September Adrian Deevoy interviewed Jim at home in Aldington. He painted a rosy picture of a man at one with the world. Jim talked about his past and about his present. He explained how he loved to get up at seven in the morning and prepare Alice's lunch box. Deevoy concluded by saying, 'You'd be hard-pushed to find a man more content with his lot than Jim Moir.' If this was a true reflection of Jim when Deevoy met him, the impending events were about to shatter that calm.

On 29 September the *Sunday Mirror* ran an exclusive story that Jim's wife Sarah had left him for thirty-year-old builder Keith Burke, who had been working on their home. They had apparently begun an affair, and she had moved into Burke's Blackheath flat.

The story was quickly picked up by other papers, its presence on the front pages proving that thanks to the dislocated comedy of *Shooting Stars* Jim was now a major celebrity. Every aspect of their private life now became public.

While Jim was going through the most traumatic period of his life, Bob found out that he was going to become a father. His girlfriend Lisa was expecting a baby, which had finally motivated him to pass his driving test at Ashford Test Centre. He had always wanted to drive – 'because it's difficult lighting a cigarette on a motorbike' – and now he had the right incentive. He couldn't really imagine taking Lisa to the hospital in labour on the back of his saddle.

The tabloids continued to cover Jim's story throughout October. The main staple of the coverage was a thin gruel of rumour and unattributed gossip, with suggestions that the split was caused by anything from Jim's obsession with Ulrika Jonsson to his obsession with Eric Morecambe. The *Mirror* claimed that Sarah was driven to distraction by his endless Eric Morecambe impressions around the house.

Unfortunately Jim and Bob were not able to lie low at a time when they wanted to avoid attention. They had a couple of videos to promote and were due to start a thirty-four date national *Shooting Stars* tour at the beginning of November. For all concerned, Jim's domestic distress had to be addressed. Minimal light relief was provided by their *Top Tips* video in association with *Viz* magazine, which was released on 21 October. Despite *Viz* having started out in Newcastle, Jim and Bob had never worked with its founder Chris Donald, though their senses of humour did occasionally overlap, as Jim recalls: 'We were once going to do Blur Puppets, and the week of the show the new issue of *Viz* did a cut out version of Blur. We used to do consumer tests, biscuit trials for instance, and then saw *Viz* did it and we had to stop.'

The *Top Tips* video, based on the Top Tips page in the magazine, found Jim and Bob acting out various pieces of unwanted advice. To stop one's bread drying up, for instance, viewers were told to store it in a bucket of water. To save money, Jim suggested jogging to work behind a bus – or to save even more, jog behind a taxi.

With the *Shooting Stars* tour on the road, Jim tried to push his problems to the back of his mind, but it wasn't easy. Sometimes he rose to the occasion, at other times he was not so keen on the limelight. The press were following him everywhere, but he tried not to change his lifestyle for their benefit. He went to Old Trafford with Ulrika and saw Chelsea beat Manchester United 2–1; not a great football fan, he somehow got excited enough to break the arm of his chair. In Liverpool he went clubbing at Cream. The press would use any opportunity to speculate on Jim and Ulrika's relationship, finding it hard to believe it was platonic, recalls Jonsson: 'When the press saw us both wearing black leather trousers they thought, of course, we must be having an affair.'

It was a tense tour all round, with all sorts of personality clashes. To make the evening feel like a full show, the Legends of Rock lookalikes band had been booked as a support act. From the middle of the auditorium this resembled three podgy middle-aged men in various different wigs and outfits singing songs by Rod Stewart, Freddie Mercury and Elton John. It wasn't quite clear whether the gesture was a kind of so-bad-they're-good statement or a sincere wish to entertain with something middle-of-the-road, harking back to Jim's desire for the *Big Night Out* to recall the singer-comic-meal ethic of the northern club. The result was that to provide value for money the *Shooting Stars* show ran for seventy-five minutes when it should not really have gone on for more than an hour. There was general incredulity backstage when the team appeared before a crowd of over five thousand in Birmingham one night. This tiny afterthought of a game-show send-up seemed to be getting out of hand.

Mark Lamarr also felt that the format was being pushed to the limit: 'I think maybe there is only thirty minutes in that show.' His experiences of filming the TV show reinforced the idea of Jim and Bob being in a world of their own: 'Me and Ulrika aren't allowed in until 5 p.m. unless we had to rehearse a special bit. Generally they want to fuck us up as much as they want to fuck everybody else up. It wasn't that we weren't invited, we weren't allowed – if we got there early they wouldn't let us in. No one is part of Vic and Bob, no one is in on it, and there are a lot of in-jokes.' Lamarr has also seen examples of Jim's unbreakable self-belief. 'I smile when they do something that's bad, but Jim never admits something was shit, whereas Bob will. One of the best nights out I've ever had with Bob was when we went through all the shit bits in the series. Bob and I were laughing our heads off, but Jim would always say, "That bit was brilliant" – he just doesn't think along those lines. One joke Jim is proud of but Bob goes on about is when Vic asks Belinda Carlisle if she has ever been to Texas – "because", he says, "I prefer Do-It-All myself". And I swear it got the biggest laugh of the show. And Bob is wondering is this what people want? They've done some really brilliant jokes that have died, and that just brought the house down.'

There was, however, one exhilarating moment on tour which made the evening worth the haul. When Jim and Bob were having one of their regular fights, Bob put a silver fire bucket on Jim's head and started to hit it. When Jim lifted the bucket off, his head had turned into the same shape as the bucket. It was a pure Tom and Jerry-inspired visual gag which they pulled off with immaculate skill. They seemed as comfortable with physical humour as they were with verbal gags, parodying the classic Abbott and Costello 'Who's on first?' routine with a question about three dogs who were different colours, concluding with '*What* was the name of their mother?'. Bob delivered the lines, and much to Jim's bemusement the answer was 'What' (in the original burlesque sketch, Who, What and I Don't Know were the names of three baseball players – almost as unlikely as finding a dog called What).

While all of this was going on there was also a second series of *Shooting Stars*, which ran on BBC2 from late September to the end of the year. This was the best series, still inspired and fresh yet not too self-congratulatory. The fact that it had been filmed under immense press scrutiny didn't seem to damage it either. Both Matt Lucas and Bob recall one occasion when the press were hanging around outside the BBC gates and Jim gave his best performance of all. It was no surprise that when the tour ended in December they announced that there would not be another series: 'We all got on,' says Lucas, 'but we did feel a bit jinxed by it.'

Lucas recalls that in some ways things were easier the second time around. The first series had been difficult to film because the studio audience had not seen it before and did not really know what to expect. 'We had to be really concentrated. We did eight shows six months before it went out, and no one had any idea who I was.' By series two people knew what to expect and Lucas had developed his character into something darker and more threatening. Not so much a big baby now, sometimes he would sound like a luvvie, sometimes like an East End gangster. It was a rough approximation of his eccentric stand-up character Sir Bernard Chumley, but even more unpredictable. The line-up of guests gave Jim and Bob a chance to meet up with old friends. Stephen Fry showed that he bore them no malice after the Fucking Big Duck incident, while John Thomson (who had appeared in *The Weekenders* and *The Smell*) and Mark Williams from *The Fast Show* (and Slade) also chipped in. Mark Lamarr never smiled, Ulrika Jonsson pouted and argued with everyone about the scoring arrangements, and the ratings went higher than ever, maybe in some small part due to the recent tabloid coverage.

As well as the studio segments there were more sketches which broadened the quiz format. Jim and Bob played Mick Johnson and Jimmy Corkhill from *Brookside* (Bob particularly brilliant as Mick), Ulrika played Carol Vorderman and Lee Remick in a spoof of *The Omen*, and all the regular players joined in for a *Riverdance* send-up. There was a very strong sense that the show was becoming more popular than ever, with guests approaching them to appear on it rather than Channel X having to ask around for volunteers. This marked a significant change in status for Jim and Bob. Whereas on *Big Night Out* they had joked about forthcoming stars – and prompted Matt Lucas to complain to the duty log – now they really could offer their audience genuine famous faces.

The fact that *Shooting Stars* seemed to go from strength to strength appeared to be a strange contradiction, an example of the way that one cannot ever really be subversive on television. At one and the same time it was a critique of the cult of celebrity and a celebration of the very nature of being famous. The guests, such as Carol Smillie or Vanessa Feltz, were often only really famous for being on television. In Tamara Beckwith's case, it was a strange kind of famous-for-being-famous fame. Vic and Bob's antics helped to draw the viewers' attention to this. In this respect the show seemed to owe a debt to the Theatre of the Absurd of Beckett and Pinter. Martin Esslin's remarks in his book, *Theatre of the Absurd*, could equally apply to *Shooting Stars*: 'The Theatre of the Absurd forms part of the unceasing endeavour of the true artists of our time to breach this dead wall of complacency and automatism and to re-establish an awareness of man's situation when confronted with the ultimate reality of his condition.'

Esslin goes on to discuss Albert Camus's essay *The Myth of Sisyphus*, in which Camus writes about life as a 'senseless pantomime'. The original myth told the story of a man who was condemned to spend his life rolling a boulder to the top of a hill. It would then roll down again and he would endlessly have to repeat the task. There is a ring of familiarity here when one thinks of some of the futile tasks guests had to perform at the end of each show for trivial amounts of cash. Stephen Fry had to collect tomatoes for a children's party while propelling himself on an office chair. In an echo of Bob's schoolboy joke, Mark

Williams had to climb on top of a locker and avoid being rocked off. Ulrika Jonsson had to clean a car windscreen with her bottom and Mark Lamarr had to fend off stuffed animals with a small plastic shield. There was even a moment when a huge boulder swung on to the stage and knocked Vic and Bob off their seats. There was also a deeply existential motif when a Kafkaesque beetle crawled across the desks – in the end Vanessa Feltz squashed it with her bare hand. Despite outward appearances there was more to *Shooting Stars* than met the eye. In this respect at least, *Shooting Stars* has been the dumbest and most incisive programme on British television in the 1990s.

Out of the public eye, there had been developments on the domestic front. Sarah split with Keith Burke, and by the end of the month there had been a reconciliation with Jim. While Jim and Sarah were back together, Jim and Bob chose to work apart. They had always done things separately in the past: Bob had worked with Sean Hughes and had been a guest manager on *Fantasy Football League*, and had even appeared on *Top of the Pops* drumming for Hull band The Beautiful South, but this seemed like a concerted move to establish separate identities outside the double act. At the end of the year Bob shocked onlookers in a Blackpool fish and chip shop and at a Manchester taxi rank by trying to jump the queue by claiming he was the King of Brazil and the Prince of Darkness. It was all in the name of art, though. Mortimer was being paid a reported £100,000 to front the new campaign for telephone bank First Direct. A hidden camera in his thick black glasses meant that even if people realized who Bob was they didn't realize they were being filmed. They probably thought Bob always behaved like this off-camera.

In the spring of 1997 Jim also did a spot of promotional work, filming a Mercury One-2-One advertisement in a park in Slough. He was kitted out in tennis gear and following in the footsteps by saying who he would most like to have a one-to-one with. Surprisingly it wasn't Eric Morecambe but his childhood hero Terry-Thomas – he wanted to know if he really was a cad and, with the aid of computer technology, ended up flying through the gap in the actor's front teeth. Jim seemed in pretty good form. He told the *Independent on Sunday* that the previous night he had jumped into the Thames for a £40 bet: 'It had started at £150 but I got them down to £40.' Despite rumours that his relationship with Bob had been strained of late, he stood by his partner, up to a point: 'I wouldn't live with Bob, but would protect him if he was attacked by a bear.'

Things seemed pretty good for Bob. His beloved Middlesbrough had made it to two cup finals, and on 20 March 1997 Lisa gave birth to their son, Harry. Middlesbrough promptly let him down; they lost both cup finals and were relegated from the Premier League too. Not even Bob's contribution to their cup final single, local lad Chris Rea's reworking of his hit 'Let's Dance', could spur them on.

Jim did his best to suggest that it was business as usual. He turned up at the BAFTA awards in a blue-and-white striped double-breasted jacket, matching flared trousers, bow-tie and an odd moustache. He spoke about riding his pigs and talking to them about the meaning of life, and went shopping at the Tesco's hypermarket in Ashford once a week. Normal for Jim was never quite the same as it is for the rest of us. In June he was spotted carrying a handbag in Bond Street. In July his portraits of pop stars such as Oasis, Ginger Spice and Michael Jackson were used on Channel 5's new pop quiz, *Name That Tune*, presented by Jools Holland. For some reason best known to Jim, Liam Gallagher was featured thinking about an egg.

Maybe fertility was on Jim's mind too. In July the newspapers announced that Sarah had given birth to a baby boy at home, whom they named Louie. Jim was in no mood for press intrusion and dealt with it in typical style. On 13 August the *Sun* reported that photographer Stephen Petters had allegedly been attacked with a can of rice pudding. Jim had apparently confronted Petters, who had been parked outside Jim's house, and Ambrosia was indeed thrown, though the alleged injury was an accident and no malice was intended. The police looked into it, but there were no charges. If Jim had been having a traumatic time, at least he still had a sense of humour. One wondered what Judge Nutmeg would have made of it.

Chapter Eleven

Poldark on Mopeds

Over the years Jim and Bob had developed an intricate understanding of each other's sense of humour. They had a way of finishing each other's sentences and making ordinary spontaneous conversations seem like well-oiled routines. Their style of comedy had become second nature when they were together. At times they almost seemed like comedy Siamese twins, two men sharing the same brain. As a doubles pair they could win a game of verbal tennis in straight sets.

But what they had never really done so far was to create comedy for others. Admittedly on *Vic Reeves Big Night Out* and *The Smell of Reeves and Mortimer* they scripted, structured and storyboarded the entire show, putting words into the supporting cast's mouths, but everyone else had been extras, supporting players turning up, doing their lines and then disappearing until they were needed again. The duo always remained at the heart of their work. The success of *Shooting Stars*, however, put Reeves and Mortimer in the forefront of Michael Jackson's plans for the BBC. The young, media-friendly programmer was so smitten with the duo that time and time again he had asked them to do more television for him. *Shooting Stars* itself had been a fortuitous spin-off of that single episode made for *At Home with Vic and Bob*, when the duo had been given an evening's worth of air-time to indulge themselves and come up with their own fantasy schedule. Now Jackson was about to ask them to supply something different.

A further indication of the duo's considerable standing in Jackson's

170

eyes was their corporate advert for the BBC itself. As the portentous narration rather smugly informed us, the BBC was the place where talent could grow and develop. Where else could one get the chance to make *Poldark on Mopeds*? There may have been some truth in this, but Reeves and Mortimer were hardly an appropriate example of this spirit. Alan Yentob may have wanted to sign them up back in the Eighties, but it had been Channel 4 who had taken the real risk and had been instrumental in nurturing their talent. By the time the BBC became involved they had a proven track record. They were a cult act then, and without *Shooting Stars* they would have remained a cult act on BBC2. It was tantamount to signing up a Premier League footballer and claiming all the credit when he was chosen for the national team.

Reeves and Mortimer were now central to the BBC's future. They could attract a younger audience and hook them for life, and if they didn't do anything too silly they would not scare away older viewers. The theory was that as the duo sailed inexorably towards the mainstream, the fans that had followed them on BBC2 would stick with them as well.

And Reeves and Mortimer had another asset apart from being instinctively brilliant visual and verbal performers. Unlike, say, Tony Hancock or Morecambe and Wise, who had been the subjects of bidding battles between the BBC and ITV two decades earlier, they wrote their own TV scripts. There was an old Hollywood joke that the definition of a dumb actress was one who sleeps with the writer, but times had changed. In the world of broadcasting, the performers who could also write were the definitive dream team. Hancock thrived when he ditched his supporting cast and went solo, but his days were numbered when he decided that he didn't need writers Galton and Simpson. They went on to create *Steptoe and Son*; Hancock committed suicide.

This is what made Eighties stars such as Ben Elton, Rik Mayall and Ade Edmondson such attractive packages. Once the performers were on board you had everything you needed for a hit show, whether it was a sketch/stand-up show like Elton's *The Man from Auntie*, or a fallabout sitcom like Mayall and Edmondson's *Bottom*. While some new-wave comedians who had started out writing their own material had a tendency to use other writers when television began to eat up their material – and when they could afford to subcontract – Jim and Bob always generated their own material. The only exceptions were Dorian Crook's one-liners and Ian Coyle, who came up with questions for *Shooting Stars*, and even there Jim and Bob would add their own contributions when the show was recorded. They worked intensely but also seemed able to come up with new ideas at a frightening rate. Michael Jackson saw this as another way of harnessing their talents.

Shooting Stars had been a huge success not just for Jim and Bob, but also for Lamarr, Lucas and Jonsson. Lamarr and Lucas had carved out names for themselves in comedy circles already, but the series seemed to add a whole new layer to Jonsson's career. The only thing she had in common with Lamarr, for instance, was the fact that both of them had come to television prominence in breakfast broadcasting, Jonsson as a weathergirl on TV-am, all Alice band and Lucy Clayton enunciation, Lamarr as a rather more surly wake-up call on Channel 4's *The Big Breakfast*. Jonsson had gradually moved up the mainstream ranks, but until she appeared on *Shooting Stars* the viewing public had not seen a scintilla of a sense of humour. Even when she landed the job of co-hosting ITV's Saturday evening cartoon sports game show *Gladiators* – a concept which no one in their right minds would take seriously – she had presented it with all the wit of a Michael Howard parliamentary oration.

Yet Jonsson on *Shooting Stars* had been a revelation. While it seemed that other blonde female guests were often there to be drooled over, Jonsson had a real personality, which had gradually emerged. She was clearly a good sport, prepared to throw herself whole-heartedly into their finales, and – always a plus in Jim and Bob's circles – she could also drink a pint of beer in under ten seconds. Here was a woman who had a sense of humour and could take her drink. There was, however, a question mark over whether she actually grasped the fundamental absurdity of *Shooting Stars* as a parody of a game show. In 1996 Mark Lamarr said that Ulrika had argued vociferously for a point, before finally realizing that he and Jim and Bob were not taking it quite as seriously.

Bob had playfully announced that they were writing a show for Ulrika at the Montreux Festival in 1996, but Michael Jackson had taken their joke seriously. He asked them to write a variety show for her. In theory this was a fine idea. In practice, though, it was probably the first thing Jim and Bob did that was not an artistic success. While *Shooting*

Stars played to Ulrika Jonsson's strengths, her one-off BBC2 variety show, *It's Ulrika*, would reveal her weaknesses and do the writers no favours either.

The tone of *It's Ulrika* was out of kilter from the very start. For the show to succeed in absolute terms, to take things further into the mainstream than *Shooting Stars*, it should have been transmitted on BBC1 at 8.30 p.m. on a wintry Saturday night. Instead it went out on BBC2 at 10.15 p.m. on August Bank Holiday Monday – a period when ratings potential was notoriously low, since anyone with any sense would be out making the most of the final long weekend of the summer. According to Bob, the initial intention had been for the show to be transmitted on the more populist channel. 'It was always meant to be a light entertainment BBC1 show, but it got a post-10 p.m. slot, I don't know why. It got to the point where it hadn't been written, but she wanted to do it so she said she would take that slot.'

The format of the programme was loosely in keeping with classic variety shows fronted by women over twenty years earlier. One could imagine Michael Jackson hoping that in Ulrika he would have another Lulu or Cilla Black on his hands, a solo embodiment of Abba at their most exultant and Britt Ekland at her sexiest. An all-round entertainer with added droplets of pop credibility. The show included songs as well as sketches, but it all felt very uncomfortable to watch. The audience in the studio reportedly felt the same way. The filming of television comedies is a tortuous process at the best of times. Unless something is filmed 'as live' (as Channel 4's original *Big Night Out* was), even the best laid puns of mice and men can begin to wear thin by the second take. Scene changes and pauses for costume changes don't help either.

If the intention was to skew the variety genre in the same way that *Shooting Stars* had twisted the game show, the opening at least was promising. In a huge white studio with her name spelt out in large letters, Ulrika appeared in a patterned gold dress, stepping out of the 'U' (a parody of Vic and Bob's entrances through the R&M on their show?). As the camera panned back, her name had become her *Shooting Stars* catchphrase, Ulrikakakaka. The opening medley revealed the first flaw in the masterplan. Jonsson essayed 'Music Was My First Love', the sub-'Bohemian Rhapsody' Seventies rock ballad by John Miles. Her voice was reedy and unimpressive, her dancing dubious. Whereas when

Vic Reeves opened *Big Night Out* with a tune, the audience knew it was a send-up, here the intention was fudged. As a middle-of-the-road chanteuse Jonsson made an excellent weathergirl. This show-stopper then segued into a series of pop tributes: Dusty Springfield doing 'I Only Wanna Be With You', Cher, and finally Phil Collins gurning 'In the Air Tonight'.

Slowly, however, the Vic and Bob touches began to emerge. Springfield could have been a no-frills Tracey Ullman turn, but Cher had an RNLI tattoo on her shoulder and a large bug on her cheek. Collins turned out to be playing the piano keys with pigs' trotters and the pedals with webbed feet. Things went utterly surreal with an impersonation of Europop singer Gina G dressed as a blue Smurf. The press took great delight in reporting that Jonsson's commitment to getting the character right meant that there was still blue dye on the backs of her thighs even after twelve exfoliations. The Abba sign-off, 'Thank You for the Music', in which computer trickery meant that each of her creations could be onstage together, was a simple, unimaginative nod to Jonsson's Scandinavian roots, shorn of any real ironic, humorous content.

At least there was a semblance of an attempt at humour in this routine. Jonsson's version of 'Brass in Pocket' was a virtual note-perfect rendition of the old Pretenders song. If Jonsson had been a distinctive singer it would have sufficed as a musical digression. Instead it was more like an opportunity to put the kettle on. The sketches that punctuated the programme, which was later released on a BBC video with an additional nineteen minutes of material but few additional laughs, were a very strange mix indeed. Some were almost chillingly dark. In one fly-on-the-wall send-up, a mother and father continually brutalized their bespectacled son Danson, whacking him around the head for not living up to their vulgar, macho, Essex family expectations. The only comic relief came from the sight of Jonsson's enlarged posterior squeezed into padded white leggings. (Just as they were about to start filming, Rhys Thomas, who played the father, said 'Aren't you going to pad up, Ulrika?')

There were also the obligatory spoofs of popular television programmes. *Public Bathwatch* featured the star as a lifeguard at a municipal swimming pool who had to come to the rescue of an old man on crutches, who had dropped his shopping out of his string bag and into the water. A pair of inflatable breasts provided the comedy, but there was also a wry sidebar reference to Jim's recent run-in with photographer Stephen Petters. A tin of Ambrosia Creamed Rice could clearly be seen floating on the surface of the pool.

The best moments were actually Jonsson's impersonations which owed little to the scripts. Her *Watchdog* send-up ('Tonight – gargoyles on Westminster Abbey that could scare children and have no warning') took in an excellent bent-lipped Anne Robinson alongside a less convincing Alice Beer.

The one moment that really stood out was the breakfast television parody which gave Jonsson the chance to do Anthea Turner (alongside comedian Steve Brody), all dizzy blonde and gushing vacuity in a constant feud with her co-host (Brody). There had been a story in the press that Jonsson had been offered £500,000 to take over from Turner on GMTV and had declined. The impact of even this inspired spot of bitchery was lessened by Jonsson as Irish television cook Mary O'Connor, an ignorant fan of 'fillums' who only seemed capable of cooking pies. At best it looked like an out-take from Reeves and Mortimer's sublime *Masterchef* sketch; at worst it could have set back Anglo-Irish relations a hundred years.

Things brightened up when Jim and Bob actually appeared on the programme. A big production number featured Jonsson as a performer in a burlesque club. Jim introduced her, and a bewigged Bob was in the audience, his face twisted out of recognition by the blowtorch intensity of her gyrations. The finale was more like an out-take from *The Smell of Reeves and Mortimer*, featuring Jim and Bob as two of the Jimmy Hill Chin Singers, a quartet of sports pundit lookalikes with huge chins mounted on tiny wheels. (Comedian David Walliams was cast in the sketch and the day before filming he was run over and broke his toe. He was so eager to meet his heroes he performed in agony.) Ulrika attempted to sing 'Both Sides Now' at the front of the stage, but was mercilessly upstaged by her cohorts.

Too often, however, the programme seemed to be skidding down a path between easy parody and something more interestingly off-beam without ever hitting the mark. Even Jonsson's now familiar trademark, the downing of a pint in under ten seconds, seemed flat. Admittedly it was an impressive feat – particularly given that, according to Bob in *Time Out*, she had to do two takes – but many viewers would have already seen her do it on *Shooting Stars*. *It's Ulrika* was the kind of programme that would have made a very good trailer. Snippets seemed fine, but together the hit rate was minimal. Even director John Birkin, who had excelled on *The Smell of Reeves and Mortimer* and *Mr Bean*, was unable to turn Ulrika Jonsson into a consummate physical comic.

In *Time Out* Bob attempted to justify the showcase, but ended up revealing why material that might have been funny if they had performed it didn't work for a female performer: 'People think who the hell does she think she is, but she's proved herself. On *Shooting Stars* we were stunned by how good she was. This is the first time we have written a whole show for someone else, but we're not being grand and saying we can write from a woman's point of view. We've done what we usually do and put in what we think is funny.'

With hindsight, Bob still rates *It's Ulrika*. 'I stand by it, I think it was great, a couple of bits were. The dancing was great. I thought her Anne Robinson was very good and her Anthea Turner was very good.' Jim uncharacteristically accepts that something he was involved in was not perfect: 'The only place she fell down was doing the stand-up; she is a very good actress and singer but she couldn't get her head round jokes. All due respect to her, she will always have a crack at something.' The real trouble was that even the weaker material would have stood more of a fighting chance if Jim and Bob had been performing it. Throughout the programme one could imagine the lines coming out of them. It was written with the rhythm of their delivery in mind rather than hers.

While Jim and Bob stood by *It's Ulrika*, even its star was prepared to concede that it was not perfect: 'I'm good at something, but I'm not that sure what it is. I can be funny but I still have a lot to learn. It was very much written by them and it's very difficult for somebody else to wear their clothes.'

Other colleagues were less convinced. Charlie Higson agrees that the material wasn't the problem, it was the person delivering it. 'They were really convinced that they were making a big mainstream ITV-style light entertainment show and it was just a wank. There were various reasons why it didn't work, one of which was that they were trying to do something that they shouldn't have been trying to do.'

Higson feels that they should have done material themselves: 'I've known that from the start, it is definitely best when they do it themselves. The difference between them doing stuff and even Paul

Whitehouse doing it is huge. It is always best when it is them doing it. They know how to do it best. You can't write stuff for them, it is impossible to write in a Reeves style and perform in a Reeves style. The best thing is to try and do it straight and let them get the laughs. Ulrika is perfect for that if you keep her there. I think in retrospect it was a shame that the amount of work they put into it was the amount of work they should have put into their own projects.'

Matt Lucas, who took part in *It's Ulrika*, feels that something positive has come out of it: 'I don't think the show was a complete failure. It was very inventive and fast-paced; not all the ideas work, but there is some good stuff in there. The original intention was to write something with its own identity, and I would agree with you that the scripts in the end had Reeves and Mortimer stamped all over them and if it showed anything it was that anybody else doing Reeves and Mortimer doesn't work.' But he also believes that the press was planning to attack Ulrika before the programme had even been completed: 'People are scared of the idea that you can do something other than what you are well known for and I think many critics still saw Ulrika as a weathergirl.'

Had the show been a huge success, Jim and Bob might have been able to consider branching out further. Maybe they could have franchised out their sense of humour, writing scripts for other stars. Instead the palpable failings of *It's Ulrika* meant they would have to be content to consolidate their own performing career. The question was whether *It's Ulrika* was a blip or a portent of imminent decline.

Michael Jackson, who had championed them at BBC2, was now the head of BBC1, but despite his patronage it still came as a surprise when it was announced that the duo would be the subjects of a forthcoming profile on the BBC1 arts flagship, *Omnibus*. Not many performers could boast of being the stars of a variety show and the subjects of an arts show. Part of Jackson's motive must have been to test out Reeves and Mortimer on BBC1, but another motive was clearly to increase the ratings of his arts series. *Omnibus* had often been accused of being too élitist. Over at London Weekend Television, presenter/editor Melvyn Bragg had long ago bitten the bullet and made the *South Bank Show* into a curatorial appraiser of the pop arts. Morrissey and George Michael had been two of its more unlikely subjects. But with Reeves and Mortimer on *Omnibus*, there was something incestuous about an arts programme promoting artistes who worked predominantly for the same corporation. In fact a new series of *Shooting Stars* was due to commence five days after their *Omnibus*. It was redolent of the way that *This Is Your Life* had started out as a celebration of high achievers, but had latterly had a habit of looking like little more than another place to promote BBC presenters.

On the eve of the programme's transmission, *Time Out* honoured the duo with the rare accolade of alternative covers. The reader could purchase Bob Mortimer in profile or Vic in glasses. Or they could just browse in the shop and leave the magazine there.

Writer Steve Grant was the latest visitor to Jim's farm, travelling by train to Ashford and then by cab to Aldington on a blisteringly hot summer's day. He found the duo not exactly in rude health. Bob was hungover and wearing shorts, Jim was sporting blonde hair and a rifle. Grant had to go through the same quasi-Masonic ritual that many journalists have undertaken over the years. He asked a question, they wondered what flavour their ice lollies were.

Fortunately Jim, Bob and Grant found a meeting ground when discussing the recent Ambrosia incident with Stephen Petters. Bob wondered about the after-effects: 'I bet it lingers, though. Ambrosia. I bet it's difficult to shift its memory entirely. You should do it with custard next time. That would stink.'

The *Omnibus* was not your usual chronological rattle through a life in the arts, interspersed with the obligatory archive clips. Their old friend Paul Morley and Kevin Hewitt's film mixed biographical detail with thoughts on Jim's artistic side, comparing the Living Carpets to the work of Joseph Beuys, the artist with a penchant for covering things in felt, and showing Jim burying his Austin Somerset in his field, accompanied by Bob and the Sex Pistols' 'Anarchy in the UK'. The documentary wouldn't have been complete, of course, without glowing testimonials from the likes of Jonathan Ross, Michael Grade, Terry Jones, Ulrika Jonsson, Matt Lucas, Mark Lamarr, Jim Davidson and Sting, who provided the narration. Morley himself came closest to capturing the essence of the duo: 'Two very different minds that connect so beautifully. It's a match and a mismatch made in heaven.' As the commentary says, the duo have 'created a comedy out of all the comedy that has gone before and out of nowhere'.

The following Friday the third series of *Shooting Stars* appeared on BBC2 at 9.30 p.m., despite stories that they had wanted to quit after two runs. It opened in pretty spectacular fashion. One of the guests was Seventies singer Leo Sayer, and Jim memorably looked at his follicles and in a hilarious close-up viewers could see a pig rooting around down there. Weathergirl-socialite Tania Bryer, presumably hoping for some of Ulrika's credibility to rub off on her, instead found Jim rubbing his legs in front of her. Jim, now blond, played the fool and seemed to have an answer for everyone. Hirsute cook Anthony Worral Thompson soon got a Reeves tongue-lashing: 'Me mam used to be a chef but she never wore her beard in the kitchen.'

The formula was pretty well established by now, but they tried to give it a stronger feel of a sketch show with more pre-recorded segments than ever before. In one notable round, the panel had to identify a pop song that was being acted out on video by Vic and Bob, sometimes with the help of Ulrika, Mark and Matt Lucas. The effect was rather like a comic version of Dave Lee Travis's old BBC series that created promos specially for pre-video era hits which always looked as if they had been filmed on a budget of half a shoestring. It was a chance for Jim to revisit some of his heroes. In the Christmas special the Human League's 'Don't You Want Me Baby' was reinterpreted, and in the series Rod Stewart's 'Maggie May' had another outing.

Although the format was established, the third series did not run as smoothly as its predecessors. Jim and Bob had a very distinctive way of creating the show, which the regular production team on the first two runs understood. Charlie Higson recalls that scripts had become shorter and shorter as those involved developed a better understanding of what was expected of them. 'As *Shooting Stars* has gone on their scripts have got less and they usually just write a few odd bits on scraps of paper. They've got so busy now they haven't got the time to write things in as much detail as they used to.'

If in doubt, Jim and Bob resorted to hitting each other. Their Tom and Jerry violence was now an integral part of the act, reflecting the antagonistic nature of their onscreen relationship. In the past catchphrases had been largely verbal, now they were also physical. Jim's knee-rubbing was the new 'You wouldn't let it lie', while belting each other was as blunt as 'Look at the size of that sausage'. It seemed to sum up their onscreen relationship pretty well. As Bob told *The Independent* in 1997, 'People like to be voyeuristic and look at others bickering. That's part of any double act, from Laurel and Hardy onwards. We're inseparable but irritated by each other's presence.'

Post-modern cultural guru Jean Baudrillard recently wrote about the death of originality in a world saturated by media. He said that reality became more questionable as everything came to us through a 'hyper-reality'. Likewise, *Shooting Stars*, having started out as a hyper-real comment on celebrity game shows, was in danger of simply becoming a celebrity game show. Mark Lamarr put the predicament more succinctly. Speaking to me between the second and third series of *Shooting Stars*, he seemed unsettled by its success: 'The pilot which I wasn't on was a piss-take of a game show, and it's just completely become a fucking game show in its own right, with its own catchphrases and its own style of … shit.' Which didn't, of course, mean that he didn't enjoy doing it or banking his cheques. It was more a reflection on the way that one cannot be involved in showbusiness without becoming a part of it. It seemed to echo the predicament of Jim and Bob. They were moving towards the mainstream whether they liked it or not. The question was how they handled it and how it affected their work and their ability to stand apart from the machinery of mass entertainment. Their comedy had always depended on their differences – northern accents, non-Oxbridge, post-punk non-conformity – and they had to retain that vision to remain funny.

This time round the regular production team was working on *The Fast Show* and a new director, David G. Croft, came in, slowing down the process and the spontaneity. Things were redeemed by the pre-recorded sketches, usually slipped in to cue up pointless observation questions. One of Ulrika's favourites was a marvellous take-off of the American sleuthing show *Hart to Hart*: 'Jim was Max – "it was moider" – the butler with raw new potatoes connected with wires on his face. I was supposed to be Stephanie Beacham when it was originally Stephanie Powers. And Bob said do it in an Irish accent. It was very interesting to see the way they advise each other. They tell each other in front of everybody when they think something is shit – they don't care.'

The new production team wasn't quite on their wavelength, and Bob felt it missed some of the subtlety of the show: 'Sometimes the most important thing was to make sure there was a camera on Jim's face, although the actual joke can be irrelevant, and we got caught out on the third series of *Shooting Stars* because everyone was working on *The Fast Show*.'

Charlie Higson was also tied up with *The Fast Show* when the third series was filmed and feels that it caused some problems: 'They have the skill to busk *Shooting Stars*, but they had a bit of a shock on the third series because they had developed a shorthand with the old team and suddenly they were sitting there on the day of filming the show and things weren't happening as they were used to them happening. David G. Croft is a good director (he went on to direct *Top of the Pops*), but he was new to *Shooting Stars*.'

The audience figures crept up, but some cynicism crept in. Some critics even had the nerve to suggest that, like other quizzes on television at the time, the panel was told the questions in advance. Mark Lamarr dismissed the idea. 'People watch the show to be entertained. I don't think they give a shit who wins.' He did admit that there was a certain amount of fiddling, though. 'It is fixed so that we both win some games, but Ulrika gets so fucking excited when she wins and I'm thinking, "Ulrika, it's not as if you've got anything *right*."' Mark Lamarr probably had the right idea. Perhaps the show had just become a laugh and a pay cheque rather than a treatise on light entertainment and mass communications at the end of the twentieth century.

By the end of the third series the show was attracting over five million viewers. In other words, it was taking about a quarter of the time to make that *The Smell of Reeves and Mortimer* took and was attracting over twice as many viewers. It seemed as if Jim and Bob were the only two people not surprised by the success. As Bob observed, though, this level of success had not happened overnight. Instead the show had gradually built up viewers each series. Jim sees that as a reflection of their career as a whole: 'I don't think you can ever get surprised, because it has never happened overnight that we have suddenly become popular.'

They even felt that the concept of *Shooting Stars* was consistent with their work ever since they had started out. 'There were always quizzes in our work,' says Bob. 'The centrepiece of Goldsmiths was a quiz. We have quizzes on our own – if we have a night out we are constantly having quizzes, it's just what we like doing,' says Jim, whose TV début had been presenting the quiz *Square Celebrities*. Most appositely of all,

Bob observes that it is the format that has helped to increase their audience: 'It was an obvious structure. People would know where they are, which is quite reassuring.' Jonathan Ross, who also encouraged Jim and Bob to get involved with quizzes when he got them to do Knock Down Ginger on his show, thinks this is why the quiz format has worked better for them over the years: 'A panel show has a structure, in a comedy show they impose a structure on themselves.' *Shooting Stars* may have signified a dumbing down after *The Smell*, but they had been so far ahead of the game that it was necessary to allow the viewing public to catch up with them.

Chapter Twelve

Don't Gum up Darlington

By 1998 Reeves and Mortimer had managed to establish themselves at the pinnacle of the British comedy scene. This was particularly refreshing to them because the British comedy scene was not the moribund, depressed and worthy excuse for homegrown light entertainment it had been when they first emerged in 1990. In 1998 British comedy was stronger than it had been for three decades. The hegemony of the first wave of alternative comedians had been well and truly blown apart. Vic and Bob had opened the floodgates and now there was a deluge. Apart from Vic and Bob there was *The Fast Show*, which had been the modest brainchild of Paul Whitehouse and Charlie Higson, but which had now spawned countless characters and catchphrases which seemed to unite the nation. Caroline Aherne had been an original member of the *Fast Show* ensemble (and had had bit parts in *The Smell*), but her success as Mrs Merton meant that she had latterly taken a smaller role in the recent series.

And then there was Steve Coogan (another bit-parter in *The Smell*) who, in *I'm Alan Partridge*, in the autumn of 1997, had come up with the best sitcom since *Fawlty Towers*. Coogan had worked with John Thomson and Aherne at Granada Television and had also worked with Armando Iannucci, Dave Schneider and Peter Baynham on *The Day Today*. They were now dragging satire into the Nineties with *The Friday Night Armistice*, having earlier worked with Chris Morris, the maverick loose cannon behind Channel 4's controversial *Brass Eye*.

Another act who had been influenced by Vic and Bob was Harry Hill, the former south London doctor who had seen them at the Albany. Hill's C4 series wasn't a poor substitute for *Big Night Out*, it was actually a very good substitute, but he would never have broken through without Vic and Bob paving the way for his surreal non-sexist, non-racist brand of humour. Even Eddie Izzard, who had evolved at the same time as Jim and Bob, owed a debt to them in the way he felt he he could free-associate onstage.

All of these performers and series seemed to owe a debt to Vic and Bob, who had shunted comedy away from the alternative, Thatcher-bashing Eighties and on to a more intricate, complex, artistic level. In the clubs Johnny Vegas and Lenny Beige were creating their own worlds as Vic and Bob used to. Comedy was no longer about moaning about the sock monster that would always cause you to leave one sock at the laundry. It was about something even more fundamental: the human condition. Reeves and Mortimer had a dislocated sense of humour which seemed to mainline into our dislocated sense of identity at the end of the millenniuim. They had also grown up watching too much pulp television. Suddenly these two disparate influences seemed to have gelled to form a cohesive comedy unit. And, as Mark Mylod points out, these could be only the beginning. 'We haven't yet seen their influence come to fruition. They are just being themselves, but it happens to take in vaudeville, slapstick, that kind of stuff. I think if anything they have opened the way for a more eclectic kind of comedy, going away from the straight sketch show or the sitcom.'

Mark Lamarr, on the other hand, thinks they are strictly a one-off and we will never see their like again: 'There will never be another Vic and Bob. It feels as if there is no room for another Vic and Bob now.' Maybe the comedy world is too business-like for mavericks like them to break through. 'Channel 4 were very brave to sign them up,' adds Lamarr. 'Jim and Bob didn't do the circuit, they went off and made their own circuit.'

For Jim and Bob, everything seemed to be slotting neatly into place. On 7 January 1998 they were guests on *The Des O'Connor Show*. This was prime-time ITV mainstream television and somebody else's show. Their entire television career had been marked by a conflict between their unqualified success on their own shows and their rather ungainly appearances as others' celebrity guests. They had invariably divided the viewers into believers and non-believers. There were no half measures, as their Comic Relief début had proved. Outside their own universe their humour had a habit of losing something in the translation. It didn't travel well. This time, though, it seemed as if everybody else had caught them up. It was a brief appearance but a resounding success, and a great way to start the new year. They had actually been recorded before Christmas, but Des had a habit of wearing the same suit for each recording so that different interviews could be seamlessly rearranged to balance each show. The other guests included the actors who play Vera and Jack Duckworth in *Coronation Street*, Lee Evans (another physical comic who had made a bee-line for the mainstream ever since winning his Perrier Award in the early Nineties) and Janet Jackson, who sang a song and brought a glow to Des's dimpled cheeks by talking about her body piercing.

The idea of joining Des O'Connor had a kind of synchronicity about it. Ever since Vic and Bob had been getting reviews they had been compared to Morecambe and Wise. Now they were appearing with the crooner who had been the butt of Eric and Ernie's jokes throughout their career. If there was an element of irony to their appearance, a knowing in-joke, it was lost on Des, whose interviews tended to take the form of the host providing the guests with cues for their prepared ancedotes. Vic, for instance, turned up in a shamelessly fake beard, but refused to admit that it was false even when the edges started to curl up under the studio lights.

As they sat next to each other on the large beige sofa they looked uncomfortable, but eager to please. Des tried, in vain, to get them to describe *Shooting Stars*. The best explanation they could come up with was the old '*Blankety Blank* without the pens' line, which seemed reasonable. There was a lot of enforced jollity as they told their bemused host about some of the highlights: how Sue Cook from *Crimewatch* had had a young boy lowered on to her, for instance. Vic did Matchstalk Men and Matchstalk Cats and Dogs in the club singer style, while the resident band struck up a percussive beat. Vic tried to play his trumpet, but when he pulled it out it was squashed because someone had been sitting on it.

Eventually Bob agreed to sing a duet with Des and they moved over to a couple of stools where they perched and broke into 'Love is in the Air'. Bob and Des seemed to get quite a long way before mayhem ensued. Vic, feeling left out, hit Bob from behind with an enormous frying pan, knocking him off the stool and taking over himself. Bob then turned up with a fire extinguisher and did the same to Vic. Things quickly went from bad to surreal as Vic retaliated with a huge wind machine, normally used to clear leaves from parks. Bob responded with a six-foot cheese grater. There was only one thing for it. Vic produced an iron and promptly singed Bob's cheek, before chucking the iron at him. Des looked on and laughed heartily. He had a habit of laughing heartily at almost anything, but there was a real feeling here that he had enjoyed seeing something which harked back to his own early days. Des wasn't old enough to have been a real vaudevillian veteran, but with his cheesy grin and perky all-round entertainer demeanour he had the sensibility of that era. In their latest incarnation as true knockabout clowns Vic and Bob seemed to make that connection too and Des seemed to approve. It was also a nod to Eric and Ernie, and to their own past, when Vic came onstage and disrupted Bob when he was trying to be Rick Astley. They didn't have to impersonate other stars now, though, because they were stars in their own right.

It might not have been pushing back the comedy envelope as far as they might have once hoped, but Jim and Bob were now huge entertainers. Their giant-size props seemed to echo their growing appeal. What they now needed was a suitably huge platform for their talents.

Paul Whitehouse says that the Hammersmith Apollo shows were Bob's brainchild. There had been talk of a joint tour, but Bob came up with the idea of a long run in one venue because so many of them had families now and it was difficult getting together. There was also the thought that one show alone might not be enough of a draw, but that two shows together would definitely guarantee a full house. White-house also says that it was Bob's idea that *Shooting Stars* should go on first. So that they could get to the bar first? 'I wouldn't dismiss that thought.'

The Hammersmith Apollo is a vast auditorium for a comedy show. The west London theatre, better known for its rock extravaganzas, can hold an audience of 3,854 people. A veritable aircraft hangar of a venue. Not quite in the same league as when David Baddiel and Rob Newman appeared at Wembley Arena in 1993, but the latter duo appeared just once. The *Shooting Stars/Fast Show* package was announced in autumn 1997, and as the tickets sold out, the run was continually extended. In the end the two acts were booked to do thirty-two dates. They had already broken the box-office record for a comedy show, overtaking Billy Connolly in 1997, and they talked about adding another two weeks of shows, but some members of the ensemble had other commitments. A quick calculation: 32 multiplied by 3,854, at around £30 a head. Plenty. And certainly not bad for what Mark Lamarr calls 'a six-hour working week'. Plus, of course, a wide range of T-shirts, from Uvavu to Eranu and back again. Not so much a comedy concert, more a comedy event. *Shooting Stars* was really only the support act in the sense that someone had to go on first. This was rather like comedy's equivalent of U2 supporting the Beatles. For Matt Lucas, having *The Fast Show* there was a good way of preventing complacency: 'We were aware that we couldn't just go on and show our faces and expect the world to applaud. It was a good motivator having them on too.'

Despite the size of the operation it didn't feel that different to the old days at the Goldsmiths Tavern. There were fewer fights, certainly, but there was the same piquant aroma of expectation in the air. The soundtrack that played before the show seemed to have been devised by the duo. It could almost have come from a home-made tape entitled 'I Remember Punk Rock'. The Rich Kids. Stiff Little Fingers. The Clash. And 'Life's a Gamble' by Penetration, the north-east's answer to Siouxsie and the Banshees, led by elfin vocalist Pauline Murray. She was kohl-eyed, while the boys around her looked more like coal miners. Twenty years on from those wayward punk days, there was a sense that things had come full circle. Just over two decades ago, Jim had turned up at a venue just like this in Newcastle as a member of the audience, dressed in his car coat and 'looking like Sid James', as Jack Dent recalled. Jim had always cherished dreams of being a rock star and now he was back at the home of rock.

Shooting Stars opened the proceedings and had the makings of a sublime variety show. Vic was in boots, bow-tie and tuxedo, Bob was in his trademark jacket/white trousers/suede boots combination. But the opening musical routine, expanded but almost identical to the one they had toured the country with in 1996, seemed slightly shopsoiled.

Ulrika Jonsson came down on a throne and flashed a pair of false breasts before she and Lamarr joined the medley. Jonsson did 'I Am a Cider Drinker', and Mark Lamarr did 'Wannabe', a very late entry into the canon of Spice Girl parodies that undercut his image of studied cool but was hardly a comedy breakthrough. The guests weren't quite of the same calibre as on the TV show. Emma Harrison from *Neighbours* played the rentabimbo, while Linda Nolan joined Jonsson's team. Portly stand-up comedian Phill Jupitus seemed to be reprising his turn on BBC2's *Never Mind the Buzzcocks*, while the only treat was Ben Elton.

It was a show that certainly had some very funny moments, but it was more of a greatest hits selection than an airing of new material. Given the patchy acoustics, it probably worked in their favour that their best material was visual. Vic and Bob played their parts to perfection. This was more Abbott and Costello than Morecambe and Wise, and there were few complaints. Many people had turned-up to see their favourite moments, and the duo had delivered them. The crowd had seen their heroes in the flesh beating hell out of each other with foam stools and were suitably delighted.

But who were their fans now? It seemed unlikely that many of the original Goldsmiths Tavern followers were still faithful enough to cross London to see them. In fact even the fans who saw them on their first tours and first TV shows seemed to have moved on. There was proof of this in a sketch that *The Fast Show* did. Paul Whitehouse was doing his Indecisive Mate who kept changing his opinion depending on what his mates said. After a preamble about Vic and Bob being 'two silly northern cunts in dodgy suits' (an irony which the audience didn't pick up on) the punchline was 'Les was always the funny one'. There was barely a ripple of laughter in the auditorium, suggesting that this crowd did not even know who Les was. The sketch was eventually dropped from the run in recognition that it was too subtle for current fans. Matt Lucas agrees that *Shooting Stars* has drawn in a whole new audience: 'I don't think the current audience of *Shooting Stars* even knows who Charlie Chuck is.'

John Irvine was disappointed by the new audience, who seemed less demanding: 'It's a totally different set of people. They are not interested in that early anarchic stuff, and more interested in coming to see celebrities onstage, which closes things down. Things Jim and Bob would have done four years ago would now fall flat. It's a cross between a family audience going to see a celebrity show and a laddish element there to shout at Ulrika.'

The press response to the *Shooting Stars/Fast Show* live shows was mixed. Vic and Bob had always divided the critics, but this was different. The press now seemed to want to play up the rivalry between the two shows and create a Blur versus Oasis stand-off. Many reviews even cited the 'silly northern cunts' line as evidence that the *Fast Show* team thought it was superior to *Shooting Stars*. Talking in the dressing-room towards the end of the run, Jim didn't appreciate the press's attitude: 'Reviews have either said they like us and not them or vice versa. The press set it up as a sort of competition, but that's the Nineties for you, everything has to be a battle to see who is the best, but we don't see it like that.'

They were attacked from various sides, which in itself was an indication of their success. Some critics felt uncomfortable about the crossover from screen to stage, others felt uncomfortable about the amount of merchandising on sale (*Shooting Stars* mugs – a comment on the audience paying nearly thirty pounds for a ticket?). Others felt that the sponsors Carlsberg Ice were mentioned too many times during the show. Everyone but Bob – who had his ever-present can – seemed to be drinking from a bottle, but this was just as much down to thirst as product placement. Of course, Carlsberg didn't mind the criticism. Every attack got them another mention.

Overall, though, Vic and Bob came in for the most flak. *The Fast Show* had become the new press darlings. As *Shooting Stars* had been championed on television first, it made sense that it would be the first to be on the receiving end of a backlash. Admittedly the *Shooting Stars* tour of 1996 had been better received in many places, but there was no denying that the audience had a huge amount of affection for the team. From the moment Ulrika Jonsson was lowered on to the stage the laughter didn't really let up. Maybe the critics felt let down because the show lasted less than an hour, but that seemed rather churlish since they had never complained that the TV version lasted only half an hour.

Some of the best moments were those that were unplanned and unexpected. One night Mark Lamarr was indisposed and the Fifties throwback was played by John Thomson from *The Fast Show* in an Elvis wig. Towards the end of the extended run, Thomson himself was unavailable, owing to other acting commitments, and Bob stood in for his whispering jazz man Louis Balfour in matching copper pudding-bowl wig. Ironically, Matt Lucas, whom Jim and Bob had originally recommended to Whitehouse and Higson, ended up in *The Fast Show* for a week during the run, doing John Thomson's northern comic Seymour Clearly in a sketch with Whitehouse's Max Miller-esque Arthur Atkinson.

There were some marvellous set-pieces in *Shooting Stars*. During one of the duo's inevitable fights which broke out after Vic tricked Bob into wiping dog dirt all over his face, Bob whacked Vic so hard with a pan that he fell beneath the desk; when he rose up again Bob pummelled his head completely out of shape. It took a few moments for the audience to realize that Vic had been replaced by an inflatable dummy dressed in a similar spectacles, black tuxedo and bow-tie.

Everything had to be done in one take, and this meant that while some moments were lacklustre, others had an added sparkle. Onstage Vic and Bob could indulge in the kind of physical humour that required a lot of space. During their magician's double act, they came to the front of the stage and Bob somehow managed to place his short, stumpy leg through a long thin tube. At the other end Vic tickled the foot while Bob laughed. It was obviously a false foot, but that didn't stop it from being funny. It was one of the few moments that really recalled the magic of the Goldsmiths Tavern and the hackneyed hypnotism of Dr Heinz Mindpeeler.

In the *Observer* Sam Taylor felt he was 'trapped in a New Lad panto'. He seemed intent on rubbishing the show, and he had a pertinent point when he asked whether *Shooting Stars* was misogynous or ironic. Vic and Bob didn't hate women, but maybe they were becoming more sexist than they had ever been before. The show had come to rely on a resident dollybird for Vic to rub his thighs in front of, and while this could be construed as comic lechery in the tradition of Chaucer, he did have a habit of over-egging the pudding. At one point he asked singer Linda Nolan to touch his bottom, but when she was about to do it he shouted 'Get off!' as if he was about to land her with a sexual harrassment lawsuit. Jim had been a vulgarian back in the days of part-checking as an apprentice, and no amount of bespoke suits could conceal the tendency. You can take Jim out of the shop-floor but you can't take the shop-floor out of Jim.

It did seem one-sided to champion *The Fast Show* over *Shooting Stars*.

Without Reeves and Mortimer one could argue that *The Fast Show* would never have taken off. Most of the *Fast Show* team had worked with Jim and Bob, and Jim even claims to have come up with their title: 'When we were working on *The Smell* I was talking to Paul and I said it's got to be a really fast show, with sketches and quick things.' The humour of Vic and Bob had also paved the way for *The Fast Show* by reinventing the catchphrase. The overlap was even closer than newcomers might have realized. Charlie Higson's would-be-worldly second-hand car salesman Swiss Toni had made his television début in 1995 on the second series of *The Smell of Reeves and Mortimer*, attempting to sell a sports car to the Bra Men: 'I can picture you now driving along in the summer with your top down.'

There is no doubt that Reeves and Mortimer have changed the face of comedy. And maybe they've helped to change the face of Britain. Take Friday 13 February 1998. BBC News announced the resignation of Mr Justice Harman, known as 'the kicking judge' because he once attempted to boot a cabbie who he thought was a member of the press. Harman had also been criticized for taking nearly two years to reach a judgement over a farmer, Rex Goose. Somehow the spirit of Judge Nutmeg and his twisted court seemed to live on.

Or take another nugget of news on the same day concerning the very city that Jim grew up in. Darlington Borough Council announced that it was launching a campaign to curb chewing-gum deposits on the pavement by mounting up to thirty gum signs on lamp-posts around the recently revamped Market Square. The red, bullseye-based circular targets even bore a striking if unwitting resemblance to the backdrop of *Shooting Stars*. Pedestrians were invited to dispose of their gum with slogans such as 'Park Your Gum Here' and 'Don't Gum Up Darlington'. It was a novel solution to a sticky problem which could have been conceived by Councillors Cox and Evans. No doubt the concept would be incorporated into one of their service posts in the future, along with the comb, shoehorn, can-opener and packet of Handie Andies.

There is another side to the story, however. Over the years a number of people have been left behind as Jim and Bob have moved on. Tom Fawcett enjoyed his time in bands with Jim and might have been a part of the *Big Night Out* if only he had had Jim's phone number. Alan King was marginalized when television beckoned. It was clearly a difficult, transitional period, when what had become a laugh suddenly had to be taken much more seriously.

Of all of their former colleagues Fred Aylward is probably the most bitter. If Jim Moir is comedy's Bryan Ferry, Fred the bald-headed boffin lookalike was clearly his Brian Eno. In 1993 he told *Time Out* that Jim had passed him a note, just when he was about to go onstage, saying, 'I just want to work with Bob.' And after that tour they didn't work again. Fred made a short series, *Les Lives*, for BBC2, before fading from the picture. Seamus Cassidy recalls Fred's unhappiness: 'I remember Fred being very bitter and twisted that he wasn't considered to be part of a comedy threesome when *Big Night Out* took off. There was a bit of unpleasantness. He was more than just a bit part, but he wasn't the show.'

It is a difficult conundrum which seems to have two sides to it. You only have to look at the video of the live 1991 tour to see that Les had a significant following of his own. People at the filming of *Big Night Out* claim that some of the bits Les did to fill in during pauses in shooting were some of the funniest moments.

Jim and Bob's association with others will always be different now, because post-Les it is very much their world which others are invited into. Charlie Chuck has undoubtedly benefited from their patronage. After twenty years of working men's clubs and holiday camps, he is now a cult figure (and a lucky one – all he needs to do is flatten his frizzy hair and he can travel anonymously) of some notoriety. He has made a pilot for a series of his own for Granada Television and has recently starred in an advert for bras, screened on French television.

When tackled on the issue of sloughing off colleagues, Bob tried to put the matter into perspective: 'Charlie and Les are not left behind – you couldn't gather a load of people and take them along for ever. You rent people, like you do if you are making a film; you have people playing parts and you do it for every film you make. But they're written by us – they're just other characters that have a limited life really.'

Matt Lucas seems like a different case. His role in their work has grown, but he has also developed his own separate career simultaneously and has a number of television projects in the pipeline. He is an interesting pointer, though, because he is the first comic Jim and Bob have worked with who was actually inspired by watching them on television while still at school. 'They gave me the confidence to create Sir Bernard Chumley, a character who said whatever came into his head. They made me realize it's not about getting a good gag, it's about getting the audience liking you as a person.'

Although he is immensely talented himself, Lucas is the first to acknowledge that without their help his career might not have taken off so quickly. 'When I went to meet them in the Groucho they said they would only work with me for a couple of years and then get someone else in. This seems to be the best and fairest approach – so that no one feels they have a job for life or an easy meal ticket.'

Some critics might draw comparison with Tony Hancock, who gradually dropped his colleagues when he felt that he didn't need them any more. The difference with Jim and Bob, however, is that although they drop people, they constantly pick others up. In the last year they have also worked with newcomer Rhys Thomas, who apeared in *It's Ulrika* and has contributed to *Shooting Stars*. Bob is always on the lookout for new talent, and has championed up-and-coming comedian MacKenzie Crook too.

And, of course, there seems to be little likelihood of Jim and Bob splitting up. They may have had their rocky periods, particularly during the first *Shooting Stars* tour, but they both know that they work too well together. Their perspective on their career is complex, however. While Jim seems to be the fidgety one, it is Bob who tends to do the moonlighting. Bob worked with Sean Hughes on *Sean's Shorts*; Bob has been a guest on *Never Mind the Buzzcocks*; Bob appeared in some spoof sitcoms with Matt Lucas when Channel 4 had a themed sitcom weekend in 1997. Jim, on the other hand, doesn't do a great deal of television without Bob, although just before *Never Mind the Buzzcocks* started, Jim helped out his friends Mark Robson and Graham Smith and appeared as a panellist on a rival ITV pop quiz pilot called *Music for Pleasure*. He didn't need the work, and he didn't need the money, and he was snowed in in Kent at the time, but they recall him fighting his way to the studios on London's South Bank to help them out. In return he got the chance to sing 'Alright Now' by his beloved Free and do some sketches to illustrate pop songs while the other panellists guessed what the songs were.

There is no doubt that Jim and Bob see their work differently and have different goals. One colleague suggests that Bob is probably more driven by money: 'I remember having a conversation with Bob. It was after they had done their first big tours which had a lot of extras, a lot of stunts – very successful but very expensive to put on – and he was going on about all the stand-ups like Jack Dee and Eddie Izzard who just went out with a mike and made a fortune from touring. Bob was very very envious of this and said that next time he wanted it to be him and Jim in the back of a van doing gags and making a fortune.'

By contrast, Graham Smith doesn't think Jim has the same motivations: 'I've never really found Jim to be that ambitious. Since he married and moved out of London and had a family, I think he needs to be wound up to work. I don't think he is the sort of man that is eager to get into the next thing, which is why the BBC deal suits them. It is an exclusive deal and it pays very well.' It seems that Bob wants to make money, while Jim wants to spend it. In the end, though, they both have to be creative to achieve their respective aims – Jim can't spend his money unless he makes it.

Success has brought the added attraction of advertising, which the exclusivity deals allows. Over the years Jim and Bob have been able to supplement their incomes substantially with their commercial work, which probably makes their BBC wage – rumoured to be around £500,000 a year each – seem like a pittance. Their advertising work may look like a compromise, but others don't see it that way. Jonathan Ross compares it (and *Shooting Stars*) to the way the great painters of the past would paint pictures of rich old ladies for lots of money to subsidize their true art. Jack Dent doesn't think it is a compromise, because it is no different from what Jim was doing nearly twenty years ago: 'I saw him doing the voice-over on a Fanta ad the other night and it was just like these fake film trailers he used to make back in Brixton in 1980. He would sit in his room and come out with his deep voice, announcing the forthcoming movie, "The Big Fucker and the Bear".'

While most performers might have taken a month off after a month's stint at the Hammersmith Apollo, Jim and Bob barely paused for breath before flying to Provence to film the latest Renault Clio ad. It was clearly a lucrative deal, but just as importantly, it gave them major mainstream exposure: the much-trailed ad made its début on May 29 during *Coronation Street* and was screened extensively during the World Cup.

If the intention of the screening was to let everyone see Jim and Bob, this was in sharp contrast to the veil of secrecy over the filming of the ad. During the four-day shoot, there was only one brief period when Jim and Bob and the regular stars, Estelle Skornik and Max Douchin, were together. To keep the project under wraps, a selection of unmarked cars ferried the cast separately to and from the location, recreating the mood of a real French farce on set. At one point it was rumoured that Hugh Grant was to star, but after his in-car appearance with Divine Brown maybe the ad agency, Publicis, thought better of it.

Jim and Bob didn't write the copy for the ad – which was basically a spoof of the wedding finale in *The Graduate*, with Bob in the Dustin Hoffman role – but they weren't completely new to the Renault campaign: they had spoofed it themselves in a Les Petomanes sketch in *The Smell of Reeves and Mortimer*. As their characters broke wind, they too had exclaimed the names of 'Papa' and 'Nicole'.

If there was a sense of closure about the ad reworking their own send-up, there was a further example of things coming full circle for Jim that month when he was invited to attend LWT's *An Audience With Rod Stewart*. As a lifelong Stewart fan, who had modelled his microphone technique on Stewart and didn't need much prompting to break into a chorus of 'Maggie May', this was a real treat. He even got to speak to Rod. He asked the singer what he would do if he inadvertently lost 20p under the fridge – would he have the fridge removed or would he retrieve it with his walking stick? Stewart replied that he had a specially trained cat for tasks like that.

Chapter Thirteen

Smells to Come

If fame is measured by mentions on quiz shows, then Reeves and Mortimer are very famous indeed. They claim to have been on *Fifteen-to-One*, when a contestant had to say how Vic and Bob met; they've been on *Crosswits*, where the question was which duo's three favourite sketches were anvil-throwing, pan-fighting and three-men-in-a-bath; and they've been on *Family Fortunes*. 'They had to name seven things associated with *Shooting Stars*,' says Bob. 'I came very low.'

Their reputation seems to go before them. When they were on *The Mrs Merton Show* she drew attention to the fact that their comedy isn't about gags by asking them to tell her a joke. They didn't say much. In fact she was behind the times. In recent years the sense of humour of Reeves and Mortimer has been very much about conventional joke telling – except they do it in such a distinctive style it would be hard to replicate it outside their own exotic world.

The question Mrs Merton should have asked is what do Jim and Bob do next? They appear to have reached the traditional career crossroads and they seem spoiled for choice. There is talk of selling the format of *Shooting Stars* to America, which perhaps reflects Mark Lamarr's feelings that it has ceased to be ironic – would the USA, a country that worships TV almost as much as it worships money, really buy a quiz that sent up TV quizzes? Then again, even if it was made there, it is unlikely that they would be involved any further.

In fact Bob in particular is keen on the idea of coming up with lots of ideas for other people to do. When they originally devised their own game show featuring members of the public, *Families at War*, they were hoping that someone else could present it. Alan Marke thought it would be a good vehicle for Shane Richie and Ulrika Jonsson and felt that Jim and Bob would prefer to do something else. 'Jim and Bob were not sure if that's the sort of thing they wanted to be doing, but the BBC want their take on it so that it isn't just another version of *The Generation Game*.' The BBC was keen for Ulrika to be involved in it, but, eager to establish her own comic identity, she was less keen when she heard that they also wanted Jim and Bob to present it: 'I didn't want it to turn into Reeves, Mortimer and Jonsson.' In the end Jim and Bob filmed a one-off with *Big Breakfast* presenter Denise Van Outen. Then they decided that they would co-present it themselves, joined by *Watchdog* presenter Alice Beer and BBC1 scheduled a series for March 1999. The BBC clearly feels that Jim and Bob are ready to negotiate the choppy prime-time waters. 'It's the nature of the beast that they want us to front it,' muses Bob, 'but we never have enough time.'

Despite giving an outward impression of louche, alcohol-fuelled decadence, the duo are always coming up with ideas. There is another idea for a hidden cameras series which they are keen to market. And Jim and Bob both have a soft spot for Councillors Cox and Evans. They still think the characters have sitcom potential in their own right, and don't think they have done them justice yet: 'We would really love to do that with a proper budget.' The main problem, however, isn't so much raising the money as finding the time to write some scripts.

Director Mark Mylod is 'a bit dubious about it, but they are really fond of the characters. But at the moment the plan is for them to be a regular segment in the new series but not beyond that. For them *The Smell* is pure Vic and Bob – Cox and Evans would be the distilled version – and *Shooting Stars* is pure energy. *The Smell* is where they concentrate their comedy, they are well up for that kind of writing process. They do really get into that, it is the complete opposite in style from *Shooting Stars*. It is very honed rather than that rolling thing with *Shooting Stars*.'

And then there is *Randall and Hopkirk (Deceased)*. When they heard in late 1997 that the production company Working Title had bought the rights to the old Sixties detective variant they were quickly in touch, suggesting themselves for the title roles. There was a pleasing symmetry to the idea, too. In the early TV days Vic was extremely proud of his own white suit, which was cut very much in the style of dead private detective Marty Hopkirk's outfit. ITV head David Liddiment recalls them talking to him about remaking the show about five years ago. There was also a Nöel Coward connection: the detective show was loosely inspired by his play *Blithe Spirit*. If *Randall and Hopkirk (Deceased)* is made, it will mark a significant departure for Jim and Bob. Charlie Higson is currently writing the fifty-minute scripts, and it will be the first major thing Jim and Bob have done that they haven't written themselves apart from the Renault ad. Charlie is, however, writing it in such a way that 'there will still be room for them to put their bits in'. Annalisa Barreto, the Head of TV development at Working Title had originally been thinking of remaking *Randall and Hopkirk (Deceased)* in a straighter paranormal vein, more in keeping with *The X Files*: 'But when Jim and Bob came on board it clicked not as a drama or a comedy but in completely new territory. They can take the drama seriously but bring a wonderful silliness to it.'

They seem to have more career opportunities than they ever dreamed of. But Jonathan Ross wonders sometimes if they are happy with their position: 'I don't think they necessarily want to be any bigger. *Vic Reeves Big Night Out* was like their first novel, the one they were burning to get out. But how do they perpetuate it? Jim more than Bob has that punk ethos. I got the feeling they were somewhat disappointed that their biggest hit was a take on a panel show, which is ludicrous. It is so consistently funny I thought they would be proud of it.' Charlie Higson also wonders if Jim now has what he wants. 'In some ways he might have been happy to be a pop star. What he wanted was to be famous, but the comedy side took over.'

There is no doubt that success makes them happy, but unlike 'serious' artists they don't seem to crave respect, they just want to be funny. As they once said: 'We don't want people to applaud, we want people to laugh.' On those terms *Shooting Stars* is undoubtedly their biggest triumph to date. But there is also this feeling that they need to return to their 'day job', a series in the vein of *The Smell*. They spent the summer of 1998 working on this show, though it probably won't be called *The Smell*: 'Until *Shooting Stars* we always did things in twos, so we will call it something else – *The Wits of Reeves and Mortimer* was one alternative suggestion. We hope it is going to be as different to *The*

Smell as *The Smell* was to *Big Night Out*, but it'll be interesting to see how many of the six million who watch *Shooting Stars* stay on board.'

A lot of people will be watching to see if the millions start to drop away if they go all dark and difficult again. Jim was certainly planning something less accessible than *Shooting Stars*: 'I'd like all the characters to have nothing to do with reality at all.' He will certainly be keen to get away from the cult of *Shooting Stars*: 'It's been surprising how long we've been doing it really. Kids on the street used to shout "You wouldn't let it lie", now they shout "Ulrikakakaka".' Then again, Matt Lucas is equally keen to point out that they have not categorically said they will not do another series.

Graham Smith is one of their many friends in television eager to see what they come up with next: 'Jim does what he thinks is funny, and others laughing is a bonus. The next thing they do is going to be interesting, because whether they like it or not, there is going to be an enormous amount of attention focused on them. It is like a band following a platinum album – do you redo that album or do you go off and do something else?'

Such was their popularity that a 1997 report suggested that the BBC should get them to read the news if they wanted more people to be interested in world events. It is more likely that they will eventually go to the opposition. ITV has talked to them but nothing as yet has come to fruition. In the long run, however, a move to ITV doesn't seem out of the question. David Liddiment was always a champion of Reeves and Mortimer, and in 1997 he succeeded Marcus Plantin as head of the ITV network. Liddiment has publicly declared that his mission is to reinvigorate the station, and who could do it better than Reeves and Mortimer? Liddiment would probably jump at the chance to put them into a prime-time spot, but it is up to them to decide whether they want to do that just yet. Mark Robson feels it is a case of later rather than sooner: 'The impression I have is that they are happy doing what they are doing. *Shooting Stars* has been a huge success, they can do a sell-out tour on the back of it. Slowly they can fulfil ambitions, shoot documentaries and do things like that, and not necessarily just comedy.'

An anonymous ex-colleague isn't so sure that ITV would be a good move for them: 'Everybody would be foolish to enter into that. ITV isn't good enough for them. ITV knows it has to find a young audience for comedy but doesn't understand how to do that. They would need eight million viewers or they would be off the air. Look how ITV gave away *Men Behaving Badly*. It is a very broad and downmarket channel and actually quite old – they would be mad to go there.'

Graham Smith, who has always been a huge fan, concurs, suggesting that it would make much more sense for them to go to BBC1: 'The move from BBC2 to BBC1 seems more natural. *Absolutely Fabulous* did it, Harry Enfield did it. BBC1 can protect new performers with a terrible media term, 'hammocking' the show between others, but on ITV it is a cold world. The new-wave comics who have made that leap on ITV – Jack Dee, Lee Evans – ITV tried them on Saturday nights, and when they didn't work ITV didn't want to know.' Perhaps, if they were ever able to make it, Cox and Evans could be their *Absolutely Fabulous*, the series to propel them on to a higher levels of acceptance. But their most loyal supporters seem to disagree.

Charlie Higson is not so sure that they can ever sit comfortably on a mainstream channel. There will always be a tension between Jim, who is wayward, and Bob, the sanity anchor: 'They would be happy to be on BBC1, but their idea of what is mainstream and commercial is not the same as others.' Bob always has this problem that he'll be talking about a film – "it's about these two guys and they are on an adventure" – and then Jim will say "and they are all dwarves and they live in a giant cesspit and the main character is a horse brass", so there is this constant struggle.'

Graham Smith cannot see how they can move to prime-time and be 'true to their comedy', based on their past work: 'Go back to the *Big Night Out*; a lot of it is obscure and very, very odd, but there was enough of an audience to make it work. *The Smell* was sometimes incredibly obscure and it got about two million. It was only when they used the most traditional television format that there is, the celebrity quiz, and put their interpretation on it, that suddenly their humour became much more accessible to a wider audience. Whether they are prepared to compromise to make the leap from five million on BBC2 to ten million on BBC1 – I'm not sure that they can do that. It would mean just selecting the most accessible, simplistic elements of what they do and I'm not sure how interested they are in doing that.'

Another colleague believes that Jim and Bob themselves fluctuate between craving prime-time success and shying away from it: 'As pop fans they know that however talented they are they might not last for ever. Look what happened to Bad Company and Jim's other heavy rock heroes when punk came along.' 'Bob has always said "I've got fifteen years in this business",' says a friend. 'They are very aware of their place in showbiz. They know that people like Ben Elton were comedy gods once and to a certain extent they do go out of favour, at least with the youth audience. And Jim and Bob, like Paul Whitehouse and Charlie Higson, are in their prime now, and it is difficult to stay there because things move on.'

Some critics might say that they have compromised and done one series of *Shooting Stars* too many, but Jim and Bob must also know that a greater compromise could bring greater financial rewards. Mark Mylod sees it as a real dilemma for them: 'But once you've done that there is no way back; your cult, core audience can be very unforgiving. They can go either of two ways – stick on BBC2 and stay culty, or think "fuck that, I'll do just what I want to with whatever ideas I come up with". I would suspect Jim and Bob will do the latter. I shouldn't imagine it bothers them very much. I imagine they are very circumspect about their longevity in the industry anyway. I would love to see them do a film. I hassle them regularly to write a film script, but they want to do another TV series first.' Mylod thinks that if they did this even cracking America might not be beyond them: '*Monty Python* did it, *The Full Monty* did it. The most bizarre kind of English culture can travel, and a film would work because it would still be them in their own world.' If you look at the career of, say, Jim Carrey, it is clear that Hollywood is open to the idea of physical humour these days. The secret is, as Rhys Thomas says, 'They haven't gone mainstream, the mainstream has come to them.'

Matt Lucas started off as a fan watching Jim and Bob at home and is more of a fan than ever, having worked with them: 'They have reinvented the comedy song. In *The Smell of Reeves and Mortimer* they were the highlights for me. Songs such as 'Hello We're a Couple of Girls' and 'Oh How I Wish I Was Middle Class'. It's the music that marks them out. I think that's where the Morecambe and Wise comparison comes from.' Peter Baikie from the *Absolutely* team deserves some credit for his contributions to the music too. Lucas has ambivalent feelings about a move to BBC1: 'BBC1 could be the making of them and the breaking of them.' He too worries a little that they might get distracted by more *Shooting Stars* and succumb to a further series: 'I love *Shooting Stars* and I love Vic and Bob, and I hope for those two reasons there isn't another series. I'm a purist.'

Paul Whitehouse, another purist dating back to the Albany days, is equally passionate about them, able to look back nostalgically at their pre-television days but also confident that they will come up with even bigger, better ideas. 'I can bore people silly about them being the future of British comedy. They were just a joy to behold, they created this little world every week and a lot of thought had gone into it; there were so many areas – music, language, costume and make-up ... it was like seeing the Sex Pistols at the 100 Club. I thought they would destroy the purity of this thing by cutting it down to go on television, but half an hour was absolutely right.' There is one area which Whitehouse thinks they have really gone out on a limb on: 'The underlying thing with Jim which I take my hat off to is making Seventies rock cool. Sometimes you think they are having a laugh at other people's expense, but they have so much gusto they pull it off.'

While their humour has stayed broadly the same during the Nineties, they have evolved in other respects. Matt Lucas points to the gradual evolution of the character of Vic Reeves. There has always been the vexing question of where Vic Reeves ends and Jim Moir begins (even a problem when attributing quotes in this book). Now it is more complex than ever: 'Vic Reeves then and Vic now are very different things. At first he was an evil character who would kidnap The Man with the Stick's children, then it became a persona in *The Smell* ...' Now it seems as if in *Shooting Stars* Vic and Jim have merged into one monstrous celebrity, fused together in one body. There is no doubt that Reeves, who was initially a parody of a light entertainer, is becoming a light entertainer. Alan Marke suggests that even Jim doesn't know who Jim is any more.

Writer Andy Darling says that 'if there was a Venn diagram with Jim in one circle and Vic in the other, the shaded area would be quite big.' A lot of the confusion is to do with the very nature of celebrity and I am reminded of the episode of the old BBC series *Colditz* where the prisoner got himself sent back to England by pretending he was mad. Except that he pretended for so long, by the time he was sent home he *was* mad. Jim seems to have assumed Vic's larger-than-life character 'off-duty' as well as at work. One story suggests that he was convinced the AA used to salute his driving and members of the Equestrian Society used to compliment him on his horsemanship when he trotted past them. For anyone who lives in the spotlight, there is a risk of them forgetting they are not in it all of the time, and Jim is no different. Then again, Jim and Bob's life has always involved a bizarre succession of fantasies. This was simply how they used to get through the daily grind. A friend recalls that long before they were household names Bob used to claim that he had blacked up his face with burnt cork and taken part in the Brixton riots. This was the kind of storytelling that later turned into the Living Carpets act and produced the 'I started that rumour' catchphrase. Sometimes it seemed as if life among their peer group was just an ongoing competition to come up with the biggest fiction.

But Jim Moir, who was once starstruck by celebrity, is now a celebrity himself. He is fighting it, though. The tabloid intrusion of 1996 hurt and he has become more withdrawn. Seeing his picture in the papers has not been quite such a thrill since then. And yet he has never been a performer prone to the dark moods of a Hancock or the depression of a Milligan. This has been one of the benefits of being a double act. Travelling alone and writing alone can be unsettling, but they have always had each other's company. They keep each other relatively sane. *Shooting Stars* may have defined their roles for now, but Lucas hopes that they can change again: 'Jim does the funny stuff while Bob drives the quiz along, and they do that well, but I hope they swap around again.' If they don't *Shooting Stars* will begin to seem more like a millstone and less like a golden egg.

Jonathan Ross certainly still believes that they have a golden future: 'I don't think they are particularly happy with *Shooting Stars*, though they have stayed true to their vision, which is hard to pin down. Bald people now get called George Dawes — it seems to be working on a different level for some of the audience, like when footballers copy Jim's leg-rubbing when they score a goal. But they do now have a greater genuine mass viewership than, say, Spike Milligan has ever had.' An experienced programme-maker as well as a cult personality who has attempted to cross over into the mainstream himself, Ross doesn't think prime-time would suit them: 'I don't think the dynamic of a double act lends itself to that.' Ross tries hard not to be nostalgic or élitist, but does think that some of the magic went when he himself got Jim and Bob on to television. In the same way that some say *Shooting Stars* emasculated them, Ross believes that that process started with *Vic Reeves Big Night Out*. Like Paul Whitehouse, he too draws a comparison with punk: 'They were at their very best at the outset, like the Sex Pistols. You needed them to have two-and-a-half hours to do what the fuck they wanted to do. When it was structured it maybe lost some of its personality. The props were prepared in advance, they rehearsed ... it was a real joy to see Bob come out with his stick with a bottle of cough medicine on the end that they had bought on the way there.'

As someone who also saw them in the early days, I am inclined to agree with Jonathan Ross. But only up to a point. The early live shows had an anarchic energy, but they could also be a shambles. Television has enabled them to do things that they could never have done onstage. *The Weekenders*, for instance. Or the *Masterchef* sketch. In some respects *Shooting Stars* is more like the live shows than the other series because it also retains a nervous, febrile energy. Although you know it has been edited and tidied up, there is still a sense that Jim and Bob are flying by the seat of their pants.

Maybe their influence will always be greater than their ratings. In the same way that Scorsese may never make a box-office blockbuster, maybe Reeves and Mortimer will never top the television ratings. But in the same way that Scorsese is a huge influence, so Reeves and Mortimer will continue to inspire. Just as they themselves were dubbed the post-modern Morecambe and Wise, so their name has become a showbusiness shorthand: children's TV comics Trevor and Simon are the Junior Reeves and Mortimer; Channel 4's Mel and Sue are the Female Reeves and Mortimer. As Lucas says, 'They've influenced the aesthetic of television visually and verbally.' The advertising industry should give them an award for the ads that they haven't been in as a thank-you for using their ideas.

Besides, if their television career falters, there is always pop recognition again. Following Jim's distinctive cover version of Noël Coward's 'Don't Put Your Daughter on the Stage, Mrs Worthington' for the Red Hot AIDS charity album, *Twentieth Century Blues*, which had come about when Neil Tennant rang him up at home (and had nothing to do with his old band Design for Living or the Aldington–Coward connection), his interest in music seemed to have been rekindled. One of their other plans was to make a documentary about novelty records. They were recently talking about making one themselves, with sixteen celebrities singing the theme from *The Great Escape*, but the duo miming in the studio. There are even rumours that Jim might make a progressive rock concept album. He is still playing Free, Hendrix and really obscure Kraut rock at home in Kent, and it does not look like he will ever stop.

Bob, meanwhile, seems to be becoming the unspoken business manager of the partnership. The sharp brain he put to use in the courts is now applied as much to expansion plans for a Reeves and Mortimer franchise (which has more than a shade of the old Reeves and Mortimer Products ring to it) as it is to comic ideas.

Yet he is a strange kind of entrepreneur. As his friend Keith Bridgewood says, he is 'not a wallet man'. Someone who works with them says that he is not even organized enough to run a bank account. His house has papers scattered everywhere, and if he feels like it he can let a phone continue to ring and not bother to answer it. He also finds it awkward to take advantage of his position. He can always get tickets for Middlesbrough now, but found it uncomfortable ringing up for tickets when they were in the Coca Cola Cup Final.

And yet it was Bob's idea to do the lucrative Hammermsmith shows with *The Fast Show*, though now he is fairly self-effacing about them: 'I think we worked well as a support act, by the end of the night people feel they've seen a complete show.' It seems as if he is able to compartmentalize his mind to concentrate on the things in hand that matter. He and Jim don't keep diaries and yet they never miss an engagement. Underneath that scatterbrained exterior there is the brain of a northern realist doing overtime.

Ever since Bob was in Bill Whittingham's politics class at school in Middlesbrough he has been known as a quick learner, and now he seems wonderfully clued up about the business of television. He has clearly realized through working in television that the people who make the programmes often drive bigger cars and live in bigger houses than the people who star in them. It is as if the roles on *Shooting Stars* have bled into their real-life job descriptions. As Paul Whitehouse says: 'Bob does seem to have taken on the role of doing all the serious hard work. He does the planning and organizing, Jim just does the more bonkers stuff.' Ever since they first met they have worked well together. There is a psychological bond between Jim and Bob. At first Jim was very much the senior member of the firm, but he always needed approval and Bob gave it to him. There were never ego battles and Bob would always pass praise on to Jim.

There is no doubt that Bob Mortimer is crucial to Jim's success. That's why he didn't ever make it in any of the bands he was in. That's why he didn't make it as a solo stand-up comedian. In the same way that *Shooting Stars* made their double act more accessible, so Bob paved the way by making Vic's solo act more accessible. Despite his huge talents, without Bob Jim might still be doing strange, artistic things in south London. As Malcolm Hardee says, 'Bob pulled it all together.' Jonathan Ross agrees. 'I don't know what Jim would have done without Bob. He has some strange ideas.'

Paul Whitehouse pays tribute to Bob, but is sure Jim would have been a star eventually anyway: 'Bob is crucial. They complement each other: Jim's character Vic is the star and Bob undermines him, Bob is the human face to Vic's showbiz monster. Jim would have always got somewhere because he was very ambitious and ruthless and focused, but at the same time I think Bob has been an enormous help to him. Most other people Jim couldn't work with in an equal partnership, they were more at arm's length. When Bob came along he thought here was someone he could work with properly.

'They obviously have a similar sense of humour, which is why they got on so well. Jim definitely does more of what people think of as Reeves humour – people living inside giant walnuts – and Bob has taken on the role of question-master/organizer in *Shooting Stars*, and that has sort of filtered into the way they work in general, but when they are actually writing they have a fairly equal input.'

Reeves and Mortimer are probably less than half-way into their career, but one issue keeps coming up. And it is a question that Morecambe and Wise never had to answer. Is it art? Partly because of the strong visual element, partly because of the cultural references, there has always been a temptation to compare their comedy to art. At first it was surrealism, then Dada. Paul Morley suggested that the Living Carpets were cousins of conceptualist Joseph Beuys. More recently, Damien Hirst's pickled animals seem to owe a debt to Jim's meat fixation.

Jim has always shied away from these suggestions, but there is definitely a desire to be seen as an aesthete, even if he denies it. He just says he does artistic things because they amuse him, and if people want to make them into statements, that is up to them. In 1997, for instance, he buried his old Austin Somerset in his field in Aldington. It certainly looked like a modern piece of art. In fact there is an artist in America who has created a kind of motorized Stonehenge by burying a circle of automobiles standing up door-high in the ground. But Alan King claims this is just an extension of a standard childhood prank of vandalizing cars.

Mark Robson has thought about the same proposition and has concluded that Jim cannot be put into such conventional categories: 'I think he is quite unique. I don't think he cares whether he is funny or not. He just sees things in one way, which is totally different to anybody else. Jim grew up watching Jack Hargreaves in *Out of Town* on television and finds something funny about it. Whether it is art or comedy I don't know. Time might tell you that.'

Robson has no doubt that Jim is an intensely creative person and that this seems to have created a two-way traffic between comedy and art: 'A lot of what he does is driven by wanting to express himself artistically. He is desperately fond of painting and drawing. He has this special talent that what he does is naturally interesting, and he also is genuinely keen to show it to other people. When you visit him he always wants to show you his things – a chair he has made for his daughter, or how he has painted a bedroom. Or he wants you to come and look at a pig and he wants to tell you about it. It is the same with his professional life. He has these great ideas and he is desperately keen to share them with other people. It has proved to be a wonderful combination. If he wants to do something he has this tendency just to go and do it, and as he has got more and more famous it has got easier for him to do it. Like when he had an idea to record Deep Purple's 'Black Night' with Phil Oakey – he just went and did it.'

Dorian Crook, who was at art school with Jim, doesn't think art has a great part to play in their craft: 'The fact that Jim has an artistic eye helps. The details made it more special than it would have otherwise been, but as for this surrealism thing, that's taking it a bit too seriously really. It is all having a laugh, but it is quite bright, quite clever. I think punk might have been more important in opening his eyes to doing something new. It might have showed him an attitude, that he could come down to London and stop work for a while and make his own way.'

Mark Mylod, on the other hand, thinks that in TV terms at least, what they have done on *The Smell of Reeves and Mortimer* may be art: 'I'm not saying it is art, but it gets close at times. That kind of purist work is really a closer expression of themselves. That is why it is never going to be as popular as a very accessible variety or game show.'

Whatever Jim and Bob are plotting, their real secret is they have remained true to their adolescent innocence. Jack Dent has known Jim for over twenty years and he does not think he has changed that much. 'Ninety-five per cent of him hasn't changed. He is well off, but still daft. He is the same whether he has a pound in his pocket or a thousand pounds, the difference is just scale.' It is almost as if Jim is, after all, playing the notion of celebrity just as much as he was when nobody knew him and he called himself 'Britain's Top Light Entertainer'.

The trouble with celebrity is that it is hard to control once you have it and it comes with a lot of baggage. Anything he does for fun can be blown out of proportion and become a statement. He recently heard about a friend of one of his workmen who played the bagpipes, and he invited him down to Aldington. Stories started to appear that Jim was disturbing the neighbours by playing the bagpipes himself every morning. When he put two stone Buddhas on his front gate, the press tried to suggest that his wacky antics had enraged the village. In fact they were not particularly bothered by it. Aldington is small, and everyone knows and likes Jim; he has brought some life to a place that has not seen much excitement since Nöel Coward left in the 1950s. More recently he has become interested in the symbolism of witchcraft; no doubt the press will have a field day with that too.

After over ten years together, Jim and Bob's professional partnership has lasted longer than a lot of marriages. Each offers the other something that they will always need. Bob keeps Jim rooted in something like reality; Jim keeps Bob from being bogged down in the angst of adult life. In the words of one colleague, Jim is the 'self-acclaimed genius' who always has total confidence in his ideas, while Bob can be a bag of neuroses, expecting things to go wrong at any time. For years Bob has suffered from bad indigestion and rarely goes out without a packet of Rennies, but Reeves and Mortimer saved him from a life in law and even greater stress. The duo are inextricably bound together, more than any double act in recent years. Comedy is the outlet that keeps Bob sane. At school his attitude used to be 'What can we do for a laugh?' and thanks to Jim he has managed to retain that undeniably healthy attitude. While Jim is the one invariably perceived as the artist, he could never have done it without Bob's guiding hand and support for his wilder fantasies.

The importance of Bob Mortimer cannot be overstated. Without him Jim might have found his voice, but he might not have turned it into a marketable one without betraying his essential lunacy. And, of course, Bob is a brilliant performer in his own right. This was why his arrival marked the prompt change from Jim and his mates larking about into Vic and Bob and some others filling in the gaps. His Matthew Kelly and Noel Edmonds impressions on *The Smell* are conclusive proof that Bob can hit the mark in the most original and cruellest ways imaginable. If there is going to be tension between the duo in the future it may well be because Bob will have more offers to work with others. While Jim is a pure one-off, Bob has the enviable chameleon-like ability to dovetail comfortably into other people's projects while retaining his own character.

Maybe the conclusion to this whole conundrum is that Jim Moir's work is not his art. Vic Reeves is his art. He inhabits the same world as ex-Goldsmiths' student Damien Hirst and Jarvis Cocker, where celebrity and the cerebral collide. In the same way that Gilbert and George used to try to be pieces of living sculpture themselves, so Jim Moir has been making an exhibition of himself for twenty-five years, as a schoolboy Rod Stewart, Sid James at the Ramones concert, as a country squire in New Cross Road. From Rod to Jim to Vic. In the Seventies, artist Bruce Maclean once pretended to be a glam rock band called Nice Style – 'the World's First Pose Band'. Jim Moir has taken the idea much, much further. Vic Reeves is a comic creation, but also one that is funny enough to have an enduring career in comedy. Jim has always been a painter, but one should never mistake him for a Ron Wood type who does a bit of brushwork between tours. He is more like Captain Beefheart, an artist for whom entertainment sometimes got in the way. Jim Moir's career as an artist may have been thwarted when his father scoffed at his art school ambitions, but that didn't seem to hold him back. Vic Reeves is his greatest masterpiece.

Index

Index